William Windsor

Loma

A Citizen of Venus

William Windsor

Loma
A Citizen of Venus

ISBN/EAN: 9783743326996

Manufactured in Europe, USA, Canada, Australia, Japa

Cover: Foto ©ninafisch / pixelio.de

Manufactured and distributed by brebook publishing software (www.brebook.com)

William Windsor

Loma

Sincerely your friend,

William Windsor

LOMA

A CITIZEN OF VENUS

BY

WILLIAM WINDSOR, LL. B., Ph. D.

AUTHOR OF

"*The Science of Creation,*" "*Phrenology, Choice of Professions, Matrimony,*" "*Great Secrets of Happiness,*" "*Health, Wealth and Sunshine,*" *Etc.*

ST. PAUL, MINN.
THE WINDSOR & LEWIS PUBLISHING CO.
1897

To the Beautiful, True, and Good

Women

Who have appreciated my devotion to their sex,
and who have cheered me with their smiles, encouraged me with their applause,
delighted me with their companionship, and sustained me with their love,

 Lona

The child of my brain, consecrated to the emancipation of woman
from the enthrallment of Sex Slavery,

Presents an Affectionate Greeting.

Preface.

Twenty years of active professional experience in occupations bringing me into intimate touch with human needs and a comprehension of the difficulties of supplying those needs under existing social conditions, combined with a nature yearning with infinite love for humanity, and especially that part of it which is represented in womanhood, have produced within my brain the thoughts which are herein expressed. Eight of these years were passed at the bar, in an active practice defending criminals, where I learned something of the causes and results of crime, and, most of all, the monstrous injustice of the criminal code of the entire civilized world. The last twelve years have been occupied in visiting every state of the Union, in the capacity of a lecturer, teacher and adviser, disseminating the truth as I have comprehended it, and listening with ears awakened by love and controlled by conscience, to the cry of the distressed in every department of life.

The more I have studied and observed, the more I have loved. With the growth of love, came the comprehension of the evil conditions under which my beloved brothers and sisters in the race are laboring. To comprehend the conditions was to discover the cause. When the discovery of the cause of crime, degradation and poverty, disease and deformity was made and I began to realize that I held the key to a higher and better order of things in my grasp, I had no choice but to speak and to write. Had I restrained my voice or my typewriter, I would have sacrificed my manhood.

I may offend many. So did Jesus and every philosopher who has dared to speak the truth against existing institutions, since the world began. With him, I will turn to the scriptures and read to the multitude as follows:

"The Spirit of the Lord is upon me, because he hath anointed me to preach the Gospel to the poor; he hath sent me to heal the broken-hearted, to preach deliverance to the captives, and recovering of sight to the blind, to set at liberty them that are bruised, to preach the acceptable year of the Lord."

This book is not "orthodox." It gives interpretations of passages of scripture that will set the doctors of divinity by the ears. The aforesaid doctors will probably take satisfaction in abusing the author, instead of answering the interpretations. I care very little what they do in the premises, but I have one word to say to my Christian friends who may feel shocked at the liberties I have taken with the old romance of the life of Jesus. It is more reasonable to believe that he was scientifically translated to Venus, a place known to exist, and within reach of our physical senses, than it is to believe that he was miraculously translated to an unknown region, by unknown causes. To those who may feel offended because I regard him as a man, and not as a monster, as the highest type of a philosopher, and not as a low type of a god, I will urge the serious consideration of the fact, that by teaching the mothers and fathers of this generation how to produce offspring which shall be like him, I have rendered to him the most sincere worship, and the only kind which he himself would accept.

The central idea in the work, is, that womanhood, wherever found, whether degraded to satisfy the brutal passions of ignorant man, or condemned by orthodox philosophy to social ostracism for a single mistake, is worthy of uplifting help—help which comes with healing in its hands, with the caress of compassion on its lip, with the love of humanity in its brain. I despise that kind of philanthropy which holds out a crumb to an erring woman, upon an icy finger, at the same time crying, "I am holier than thou!" When a woman errs she does so through misdirected love. It is only by love, correctly directed and expressed, that she can be saved.

I sincerely believe that this work contains the crude announcement of principles by which a true civilization can be reached. The four great articles of the code of Gallheim are submitted as a statement of these principles, and I anxiously await their analysis by competent critics. If what I have written may be the means of making one human life happier, if it may give a single impetus to the advancing wave of civilization, if it may solve one problem in the direction of relieving aching hearts and throbbing brains, the joy of the author will be complete.

Sincerely your friend,

WILIAM WINDSOR.

An Acknowledgment.

The work contained in the following pages, together with the philosophy expressed therein, is original with the author, with the following exception.

The extraordinary doctrines in relation to astronomy, and the fundamental principles of electricity and magnetism, gravitation and electrical receptivity which are declared by Loma, were originally discovered and published by Mr. Samuel T. Fowler of Philadelphia, Pa., in a remarkable little work entitled "Genetics," and a small pamphlet entitled, "The Reconstructionist," both of which were published by him about the year 1885. In these works the doctrines concerning these subjects which I have elaborated and put into the mouth of Loma, were expressed in such a condensed form that nearly everybody who has attempted their study has given it up in disgust and regarded the work as the idle attempts of a lunatic to express something of which he knew nothing. These works were produced by Mr. Fowler, after incredible labor, and printed by him, with a small printing press, he himself setting the type. It is a sad commentary on the industrial system of this age, that the brilliant and scholarly attainments of this prince of philosophers should have been almost lost to the world through lack of appreciation. Much of his work has perished and he himself languished and died in poverty, regarded by relatives who possessed more wealth of property and less of intelligence as an inferior member of the family. The truth is that he possessed a mind so deep in its philosophical faculties, and went so far beyond the confines of human knowledge, that few persons have the ability to understand his writings at all. I confess that I have pondered over some of his sentences a whole week before I fully comprehended their tremendous significance. Only a glimpse of his sublime philosophy is given in this work, but enough is said to prove the true philosophy of genesis, to show the untenableness of the commonly accepted theories of the origin of planets and stars, together with the mistake which exists in the Newtonian theory of gravitation and the absurdities of the commonly accepted theories of astronomers in relation to the origin of light and heat.

In this connection I desire also to express my obligation to my personal friend, Mr. Joseph P. Steiner of Washington, D. C., who enjoyed the friendship of Mr. Fowler, for his persistent efforts in getting me to study the above mentioned works, and for material help in unraveling some of the hardest problems.

It is my intention to develop this philosophy to the fullest extent of my own capabilities, and to this end I have enlisted the aid of many bright intelligences in discussion and criticism of my presentation of it. I shall be pleased to welcome any adverse criticism of any proposition embraced in the present work or those which may follow it.

Sincerely your friend,
WILLIAM WINDSOR.

Proem.

The Coming Day.

There is coming a bright to-morrow,
  And the time is hastening on,
When the burdens of those who sorrow
  Shall fall and a glad new song
Shall fill the sad world with music,
  And the listening air shall ring
With the pæan of love triumphant
  And the end of unholy things.

No more shall the usurer strangle
  The hope of the toiler brave,
No more shall the haughty nabob
  Exult o'er his cringing slave;
No more shall women and children
  In hovels and rags be found,
But Equal Rights shall extend to all,
  And virtue and peace abound.

No more shall the tongue be silenced
  Which would speak for human weal;
No longer shall men be licensed
  To murder and rob and steal,
To murder the hapless victim
  Of the thirst for poisoned rum,
And steal from his wife and children
  Their birthright to their home.

No more in the streets of the city
  Shall children be crying for bread,
And never shall erring brothers
  To dungeons and shackles be led,
And never a gallows or prison
  Be reared to insult the free air,
To tell of the cruel unreason,
  Which we of the present must bear.

Oh, never in that bright to-morrow,
   When the sunlight of love shall be known,
Shall woman in travail and sorrow,
   Maternity bear with a groan;
But reason and knowledge combining,
   With science to bless and preserve,
Shall crown her a queen in her gladness,
   And love as her vassal shall serve.

And never in that fair morning
   Shall virtue's trust be betrayed,
And never the world's deep scorning
   Toward helplessness be displayed;
But with help for the erring sister,
   And love for the fallen man,
The reign of justice will soon reveal
   A better and wiser plan.
WILLIAM WINDSOR.

Contents.

			Page.
CHAP.	I.	The Rescue,	1
CHAP.	II.	A Remarkable Guest,	13
CHAP.	III.	The Comforter,	23
CHAP.	IV.	The Citizen of Venus,	35
CHAP.	V.	The Mission of Loma,	55
CHAP.	VI.	The Annunciation,	69
CHAP.	VII.	Myrtle's First Lesson,	83
CHAP.	VIII.	New Light on the Bible,	99
CHAP.	IX.	An Unexpected Meeting,	115
CHAP.	X.	The Philosophy of Love,	131
CHAP.	XI.	A Lesson in Ethics,	149
CHAP.	XII.	Reconciliation,	161
CHAP.	XIII.	The Code of Gallheim,	177
CHAP.	XIV.	The Labor Problem,	189
CHAP.	XV.	The New Education,	205
CHAP.	XVI.	Social and Sexual Ethics,	223
CHAP.	XVII.	Commerce and Wealth,	245
CHAP.	XVIII.	Immoralities of Christianity,	265
CHAP.	XIX.	The Religion of Love,	285
CHAP.	XX.	The Reign of Justice,	311
CHAP.	XXI.	Four Great Mistakes Corrected,	331
CHAP.	XXII.	The Nativity,	359
CHAP.	XXIII.	Marriage under the New Civilization,	363
CHAP.	XXIV.	The Ascension,	391
SCIENTIFIC PHRENOLOGY,			401

LOMA,
A CITIZEN OF VENUS.

CHAPTER I.

THE RESCUE.

"One more unfortunate!
Weary of breath,
Rashly importunate—"

"O God, forgive me!"

A wail of unutterable sorrow, a cry, a sob, two white hands convulsively clasped above a head of classical outline, from which a wealth of disheveled hair streamed back and glistened in the moonlight, showing a golden sheen more beautiful than the rays which for a moment caressed it,—a quick movement of a lithe, sinuous figure, and then the heavy splash of a body falling into the dark waters of the lake, which seemed to ripple with demoniac laughter in exultation over its prey.

At the foot of Van Buren street in the city of Chicago a long pier extends out into the body of Lake Michigan, which is the popular landing of excursion steamers. On the night of the third of September, 1895, Dr.

Edward Bell, physician and scientist, had strolled out on this pier for two reasons: first, because he enjoyed a walk in solitude with the accompanying pleasures of moonlight and a lake breeze; and, secondly, because on this particular night, at 11 o'clock, an eclipse of the moon took place, and the doctor, being an enthusiastic amateur astronomer, wished to have the privilege of contemplating the phenomena in a place which was sure to be free from interruption at that hour. In one hand he carried a small tripod, and over his shoulders was suspended a case, which contained a three-inch refracting telescope. The doctor himself was enveloped in a long mackintosh which might serve as a protection against too cool a breeze, which in the latitude of Chicago is not uncommon, and the possibility of a shower which certain dark clouds on the western horizon indicated as a possible termination of his astronomical observations.

Doctor Bell had reached the extreme outer edge of the pier on the eastern side and was contemplating the splendid orb of the earth's satellite, when his attention was arrested by the exclamation above noted, and turning quickly to the other side of the pier he was just in time to see the figure of a woman poise for a moment on the edge, and then take the fatal plunge. The doctor was a man of quick perception, and in the moment which elapsed between the exclamation and the splash, which told that the woman had accomplished her purpose, his quick professional judgment had comprehended the situation. Being accustomed to act promptly in emergencies, his action in this case was superb. An athlete and swimmer by education, and a lover of mankind in general and womankind in particular, by nature, it was impossible that he should hesitate. It was the work of one movement of his left arm to disengage himself from his mackintosh and telescope, which fell on the pier unheeded, and, while his powerful and graceful limbs carried him in two bounds to the spot where the woman stood a moment before, his coat and vest fell from his person, and he poised himself upon the edge of the pier waiting for the reappearance of the woman upon the surface, when he could make sure of her rescue.

As he stood in the attitude of a diver, waiting for the opportune moment, an exclamation of astonishment escaped him, followed by another of intense interest. As he gazed into the water of the lake, at that point in the shadow of the pier, he saw that it was illuminated by a glow as if a powerful arc light were burning beneath the surface of the water. In this glow he plainly distinguished the figure of the woman, rising and struggling in the water, but just as he was about to dive after her, another actor appeared upon the scene. This was the perfectly nude figure of a man, darting through the water with the rapidity and accuracy of a fish. Indeed, his actions were so rapid that for a moment Doctor Bell believed that the woman had been attacked by some species of shark. But when the stranger clasped her in his arms and rose to the surface, turning toward the pier on which he stood, with the appreciation which true manhood always gives to the brave action of another, the doctor forgot everything in his enthusiasm over the rescue. In a moment he was down on the pier at full length, stretching his arms toward the rescuer and his quarry at the edge.

"Bravo! Bravo! Bring her along! Steady. Brace yourself against that post and I'll pull her up. That's good. Excuse me a moment, ma'am, until I lend a hand to our friend here. Now, sir! Ah, here we are, safe and sound. Now for the patient!"

The reactions of the human mind are a curious study in themselves. As Doctor Bell bent over the prostrate form of the half-strangled woman, who a moment before had courted death at her own volition, she threw her arms around his neck in the desperation of fear and cried out, "Oh, save me! save me! Don't let me drown!"

"Bless you, my dear girl, we have no such intention. But I am afraid if it had not been for our worthy friend here, you might have succeeded better—or worse."

Having satisfied himself that his patient was uninjured except by fright, which promised nothing worse than hysterical demonstrations, the doctor rose to his feet, resumed his coat and vest and extended his hand in congratulation to the rescuer, who had remained in dignified contemplation of the situation. As his hand met that of the stranger, the physician became conscious of a thrill which pervaded his entire being. A delicious sense of warmth and an indefinable magnetism was conveyed in the touch of the stranger's hand, which for a moment bewildered the senses of the astute and learned scientist. It was an experience which left a never-to-be-forgotten impression, and for years afterward Doctor Bell found it a profitable study to analyze his feelings of that moment. It seemed to him as though the contact of the hand conveyed to him a flash of light in which were blended the colors of the rainbow, and at the same time he became distinctly conscious of a delicious sensation of taste, and an exquisite odor which seemed to emanate from the body of the stranger. We have already remarked that the doctor was a man of quick perception. His naturally acute faculties had been trained by a long course of professional observation, and the peculiarities of this man, who had so miraculously appeared in the bosom of Lake Michigan, impressed him profoundly. Even in the uncertain light of the shaded pier, on which they were standing, the doctor did not fail to note that the stranger possessed a figure of faultless proportions, above the medium height, surmounted by a massive head, made still more imposing by a crown of long, curly hair which seemed to glow with a peculiar luminosity which to some extent pervaded the entire body of the man.

"By George, sir, that was well done! It was lucky for our misguided young friend here that you were just where you were, and so well prepared for the emergency. You are the most magnificent swimmer I ever saw. But I do not understand what you were doing with that electric light under the water. Are you a professional diver?"

And the doctor stepped to the edge of the pier and looked into the water from which the two persons had just emerged. It was dark and no trace of the luminous glow was visible. Realizing, however, that he still had duties to perform, the doctor lost no time in speculation, but again addressed himself to his patient who was sitting upon the floor of the pier sobbing convulsively.

"Come, my dear girl, cheer up," he said, with that finely modulated tone of sympathetic encouragement which long practice in dealing with unfortunates of every description had made a part of his professional equipment. "You must let me take you away from here, and, after you have had proper attention, we will take you to your friends."

"I have no friends," sobbed the girl, as she buried her face in the folds of her dress, which was still dripping with the water of the lake.

"Tut! tut! that's another one of your mistakes. You have two good friends, right here on this pier, one of whom has risked his life for you within the last five minutes, and thereby prevented the other from doing the same thing. You let me manage this business for you, for the present, and I'll warrant that to-morrow will be one of the brightest days of your life. But you, sir," said the doctor, turning to the stranger, "I would like to have you accompany me to my residence with this young lady, and when we have disposed of her in a comfortable manner, I should like to cultivate your acquaintance further."

Up to this point the stranger had not spoken. He had watched the rapid and professional actions of the physician with dignified and active interest, but had not moved from the position he had taken when he had first stepped upon the pier. Now, in answer to this direct and courteous address, he made an exceedingly graceful movement with both hands, a gesture which expressed complaisance, kindness and respect, inclined his head slightly forward, and said:

"I am at your service."

The effect of his voice upon the physician was as startling as his touch had been a moment before. The tone was deep, rich and musical, and could only be compared to the notes of perfectly attuned bells. The doctor, in addition to his other accomplishments, was a critical musician, and the quality of the stranger's voice impressed him as deeply as his other peculiarities had already. He delighted in adventure, and the fact that he was dealing with an extraordinary person and an unfortunate woman, under very peculiar circumstances, gave him unusual zest in the problems of the moment. One thing which now impressed him was the fact that this remarkable man was standing in the presence of a female, in a state of perfect nudity, and yet he had made no effort to conceal his person or to procure his clothing. On the contrary, he could not have been more self-possessed and dignified if he had been arrayed in kingly robes in the highest court of royalty. In fact the superb dignity of the man was his most noticeable characteristic. The physician had noticed this, but he was too well versed in dealing with people of peculiar habits to allow it to influence his conduct. Turning to the stranger, he said:

"We must take this girl to my house at once, where she can have attention. If you will get into your clothing as quickly as possible, we will go to the end of the pier where we can get a cab."

"I have no clothing," said the stranger quietly, but in a tone which carried the conviction that he meant what he said.

Doctor Bell regarded the man fixedly for a moment and then muttered, "The deuce you haven't! Well, this is no time to ask questions. Here, you can wear my mackintosh, and when we have gotten to my house it will be time enough to arrange matters. By George! I have broken my telescope, but I guess I won't be likely to be interested in any eclipse to-night. There, put this mackintosh on and nobody will know or care, at this time of night, whether you are dressed or not. Now, my dear, we will take you to better quarters, and I will introduce you to the best woman on earth, in the person of my mother, who will see that you are comfortable in both mind and body, in short order."

Slipping his telescope case once more over his shoulder, with a rattle which told of broken glass in the interior, and taking the tripod in one hand, the doctor supported the light figure of the girl with one arm, while the stranger supported her on the other side. As for the girl herself, she allowed the two men to carry her unresistingly, and barely supported herself on her feet. The extreme tension of her nervous system had given way, and was succeeded by a collapse which almost amounted to stupor.

Arriving at the end of the pier, the doctor hailed a cab, and placing his guests within spoke to the driver:

"Drive quickly to No. ——, Michigan avenue."

The man bowed and closed the door of the cab after the doctor, who had stepped lightly inside as he gave the order. In a moment they were rattling over the pavement, and in a few minutes the cab stopped before one of the elegant residences which line the popular thoroughfare which the doctor had mentioned.

Handing the driver his fee, the doctor carried his patient up the broad flight of stone steps which led to the front entrance. Touching a button, the call was instantly answered by a young maid servant, whose face expressed no surprise as she admitted the doctor and his companions.

"Has your mistress retired?" asked the doctor, in a low tone.

"Yes, sir; she has been asleep about an hour."

"Call her quietly, and tell her that an emergency case requires her attention, and then attend me in the east bedroom."

Turning to the stranger, the doctor said, with easy courtesy:

"My dear sir, if you will enter this room on the left, you will find every provision for your temporary comfort, and in the meantime you will excuse me, while I attend to the wants of the one in which we have a common interest. As soon as she is provided for, I will join you."

The stranger bowed and entered the apartment indicated. The doctor closed the door, and picking up the figure of the girl as though she were an infant, bore her up a broad stairway into a spacious apartment on the second floor, where he was joined by the maid, who reported that her mistress would attend at once. The doctor deposited his patient upon a divan, and said:

"Undress this lady and place her in bed. Give her a sponge bath and one ounce of this cordial, and leave the rest to my mother."

Having thus disposed of the case, the physician turned and left the room. At the threshold he encountered a sweet-faced, elderly lady, in a lace cap and satin wrapper, who greeted him with a peculiar smile.

"I thought you went out to view the eclipse, Edward," she said.

"So I did, mother dear, but there are eclipses and eclipses. Sometimes it is the moon, and sometimes a human life which is eclipsed. Let us hope that in the present cases both are only temporary. Come away a moment and let me tell you."

In a few brief words the doctor acquainted his mother with the facts which are already known to the reader. At the conclusion of his statement, his mother took his face in her hands and imprinted a kiss upon his bearded lips.

"This adventure is very characteristic of my boy," she said, with motherly pride. "I will see that the dear girl is comforted, while you attend to the courtesies that are due to your extraordinary guest in the mackintosh." Then a mutual smile was exchanged between the mother and son, a smile suggestive of everything that is good, benevolent, helpful and sympathetic. A keen observer would have noticed that there was a remarkable similarity in the expression of the two faces, and that the son had inherited all of the mental and physical peculiarities of the mother. And as the good lady proceeded to the guest chamber, the doctor returned to the library, where the stranger awaited him, conscious that his patient would receive every ministration which human sympathy could devise, when prompted by the purest and best of motives.

CHAPTER II.

A REMARKABLE GUEST.

"Be not forgetful to entertain strangers; for thereby some have entertained angels unawares."

When Doctor Bell returned to the library, into which he had ushered his strange guest, he found that gentleman still arrayed in his mackintosh, reclining in one of the easy chairs, and intently regarding a handsome oil painting which was suspended above the mantel. On the entrance of the doctor, however, he arose and made one of his characteristic gestures, which, being executed with inimitable grace and dignity, expressed so much of genuine sincerity, friendship and graciousness that it carried a conviction of the excellent breeding of the man and inspired a confidence which was irresistible. Doctor Bell was in the best sense of the word, a man of the world, and prided himself on his knowledge of human nature, and his professional experience had sharpened his natural perception to an acute degree. He realized that he was dealing with an extraordinary character, and yet it was with the utmost confidence in the integrity of his guest that he addressed him.

"After the remarkable occurrence of this evening, sir, in which we have both played a part, it may not be presumptuous if I express the fact that I am very much interested in you. In the excitement of the adventure, we have neglected to introduce ourselves. I am Dr. Edward Bell, and the house which you honor with your presence is my residence."

The stranger, in acknowledgment, extended both hands to the doctor, who clasped them in his own. Again that wonderful thrill of magnetic effect passed through the doctor's frame, and the sensations of exquisite odor and taste assailed his senses. At the same time he was distinctly conscious of the luminous glow which had attracted his attention on the pier and which he was now certain was an emanation from the remarkable person of his guest.

"Your name is very familiar to me, doctor, although this is the first time I have had the privilege of a personal meeting. But I have looked forward to this moment with great happiness for many years. My name is Loma."

"Of Chicago?"

"No, sir," said Loma, with a smile of exquisite diplomacy, "of quite another country. You will excuse me, doctor, if I postpone naming my residence to you to-night. I am exhausted with the fatigue of a long journey, but to-morrow, after a good night's sleep and the enjoyment of your hospitality, I shall be able to give you a better account of myself. In the meantime let me ask, is there any reason why I should retain the use of this garment?"

"Certainly not," replied the doctor; " in this room we will not be disturbed, and I beg that you will make yourself perfectly at home. This bedroom is at your disposal," he continued, opening the door of a sumptuously furnished chamber adjoining the library, "and here you will find a bathroom and all of the conveniences you require. In the morning I will place my valet and my wardrobe at your disposal, for temporary purposes, and after that your requirements in the matter of clothing will be attended to. To-night you may wear this robe," taking an elegantly embroidered garment of the finest silk from a closet, "and while you are bathing, permit me to order some refreshments. What would you like to eat?"

"If it is convenient, doctor, a bunch of grapes and a glass of cold water will be all I require to-night."

"I will get them myself, so that our privacy will not be disturbed," said the doctor; and leaving the room he immediately returned, bearing a large silver basket filled with the choicest Concord grapes and a pitcher of water.

"These grapes," said the doctor, with the pride of a horticulturist, "were raised on my farm, near Elgin, in this state, and this water is shipped to me daily from the famous Waukesha springs in Wisconsin. I hope you will find both as refreshing as the one is luscious and the other is pure."

Placing the fruit and water upon a table in the center of the room he had just assigned to his guest, the doctor returned to the library, where Loma, who had divested himself of the mackintosh, was reclining at his ease upon one of the luxurious divans which adorned the room. For the first time the doctor had an opportunity of critically inspecting the personality of the remarkable man he was entertaining.

Loma, reclining in an easy attitude upon the divan, presented a picture of classic beauty. We have already noted that his figure was of faultless proportions, but in the electric light of the library the doctor, who was an enthusiastic student of physical culture, noted his splendid development with admiration he could not conceal. Loma noticed it, and said with a smile:

"I know you consider me something of a curiosity, doctor, and I will not consider it an impertinence if you subject me to as much scrutiny as your professional curiosity may dictate. To-morrow, after I have rested, I will also aid you with as much information as I myself possess."

Loma was indeed a magnificent specimen of manhood. He was evidently about thirty-five years of age, and no trace of decay or breaking down of the tissues was perceptible in any part of his person. His height was within a fraction of an inch of six feet, and his weight about one hundred and ninety pounds. His build was athletic, and the rounded perfection of every muscle gave evidence of systematic and intelligent culture. His head, however, was the most remarkable part of his person, and while the general result of his appearance was that of a graceful and powerful man, yet it was his head which impressed the observer with his kingly dignity. The features of the face were harmonious and classic, the mouth, which was only partially concealed by a full beard, especially possessing curves which gave it a remarkable sweetness and versatility of expression. The lips were full and red, the nose straight and Grecian in outline; the eyes were large, blue in color and wide apart, and above these rose a broad, high forehead, across which the skin was tightly and smoothly drawn, and the doctor noticed that it shone like polished ivory. The rest of his head was crowned with a wealth of dark brown, curly hair, which hung down to his shoulders and gave him a peculiar graciousness of appearance, and the doctor noticed that this particular feature was never without some traces of the magnetic glow which was one of the remarkable peculiarities of the man. The head was wide at the base of the brain, and the whole expression of the personality was that of great force and courage, held under complete control. Being an ardent devotee of Phrenology, the doctor's curiosity was not satisfied until he had taken the measurements of Loma's head with a tape measure which he took from his vest pocket. Adjusting the tape to the base of the brain, he noted that it measured twenty-four inches in basilar circumference, and a measurement across the crown registered sixteen inches. But what most impressed him was the fact that the head was complete. Passing his hand from the altitudinous crown to the massive occiput, and comparing the frontal developments with the remainder, the doctor was obliged to confess to himself that he could not say that any part of the head was deficient in development.

Loma submitted to this critical inspection with smiling complaisance. At its conclusion, the doctor said:

"You are the most perfect specimen of manhood it has been my good fortune to meet. But you are tired and need rest, so I will give you my conclusions, at length, at another time. Good night, sir, and may your sleep be as pleasant and restful as the events of this night have been exciting. When you awake in the morning, and are ready to communicate with me, touch the bell button in your room, and I will have the servant summon me."

Loma had stepped into the bedroom and now stood facing the door looking into the library. The doctor, looking toward him, saw him make another of his impressive gestures, saw the room illuminated for a second with the warm light of the magnetic glow, heard him pronounce the words "Good night," in his peculiar, rich, bell-like voice, and then the door was softly closed and he was alone.

Left to himself, the doctor placed himself in one of the easy chairs and became absorbed in deep meditation. The events of the evening had all been of such an extraordinary character that he was somewhat bewildered. The attempted suicide and his benevolent attentions to an unfortunate woman, he would have treated as very ordinary occurrences, for Doctor Bell was a philanthropist of the highest type, and hundreds of unfortunate men and women in the great city in

which he resided spoke his name with reverence and
gratitude. But the exciting circumstances of the rescue and the remarkable character of the rescuer impressed him profoundly. Had he been a believer in
supernatural agencies, he might well have considered
his guest in the light of an angel. But Doctor Bell was
a philosopher and a reasoner, and long training in
scientific habits of thought had enabled him to look
for a natural cause for every phenomenon, no matter
how surprising its manifestations might be. He had
inherited his scientific proclivities through several ancestors. His mother was a physician and the daughter
of a celebrated surgeon. His father had amassed a
handsome fortune in the practice of law in Chicago,
and had died just as his son had obtained his diploma.
Under the wise direction and assistance of his mother,
Doctor Bell had, in a few short years, reached the goal
of his ambition, and found himself in the possession of
one of the most lucrative practices in the metropolis
of the West. The rise in Chicago real estate had more
than quadrupled the fortune left by his father, and at
the time of our narrative begins the young physician, at
thirty years of age, found himself in possession of
ample means to gratify all of his ambitious desires, as
far as money, property and social position could aid
him. Unlike most rich, young and ambitious men, his
prosperity had not spoiled him. In early youth his
mother had instilled into his mind the broadest principles of humanitarianism, justice and philanthropy, and
she had lived to see these principles bear the sweet

fruits of a multitude of noble deeds. She had, also, from the moment of his conception, impressed him with a love for knowledge. In this, also, she was not disappointed. He had distinguished himself in college, was the valedictorian of his class at the University of Michigan, and received first honors at Rush Medical College, Chicago, in which he was now an honored member of the faculty. He had distinguished himself in the medical societies of the state, and was regarded as one of the highest authorities in all departments of medical jurisprudence, to which he had devoted special attention. He was well versed in the intricacies of Latin and Greek, and spoke English, French and German with equal facility.

In personal appearance, Doctor Bell was universally considered a handsome man. In height he was slightly above the medium; his shoulders were broad, his body compact, and indicative of excellent vitality and endurance. His head was large and well poised upon a strong, thick neck. A careful observer would have seen that it was unusually wide between the ears and in the region back of the ears. His forehead was smooth and symmetrical in outline and wide at the top. His hair was cut short and was of a rich chestnut brown, and his full and well-trimmed beard was nearly of the same color, but somewhat more tinged with red. His eyes were brown, and were shaded by very large and prominent eyebrows, and when he looked at a person there was a peculiar steadiness and penetration in his gaze, which was sometimes uncomfortably impressive, unless the person was well able to stand the scrutiny. His voice was pleasant, sympathetic and mellow, but it possessed a quality which conveyed the impression that it could be harsh if occasion demanded. Altogether, Doctor Bell was a very complete specimen of the highest type of American, nineteenth century civilization.

He remained in meditation about a quarter of an hour, when having reviewed all of the circumstances of the evening's adventure, and not being able to satisfactorily account for all of the peculiarities of his guest, like the philosopher that he was, he dismissed the matter from his mind, for the time being, and seeking his bedroom was soon lost in the delicious slumber which comes to the innocent, virtuous and just man, who reposes in the consciousness of having performed his whole duty for that day.

CHAPTER III.

THE COMFORTER.

"For I was a stranger and ye took me in. * * * Verily I say unto you, inasmuch as ye did it unto one of the least of these, my brethren, ye did it unto me."

When Mrs. Bell entered the room into which her son had carried his patient, she found the well-trained maid servant had undressed the young woman and was engaged in administering the sponge bath which the doctor had prescribed. The patient lay upon the luxuriously furnished bed with her eyes closed, and evidently submitted to the kind ministrations of the attendant in a condition of extreme collapse of all will power. When the maid had finished the bath and had administered the cordial, which the woman received without opening her eyes, she discreetly and noiselessly withdrew and left Mrs. Bell by the bedside.

Fifty years of experience in human affairs, and a complete medical education, had made Mrs. Bell fully equal to any occasion where combined skill and sympathy were required. In an eminent degree she blended the qualities of an educated and practical philanthropist with those of an affectionate mother and sincere friend. The unfortunate and the oppressed found in her a ready assistant, but she was seldom imposed upon by those who appealed to her from unworthy motives. Her eyes were large, brown, and handsome in expression, with a peculiar questioning look in them at times, which seemed to compel a truthful answer. Wavy brown hair, slightly tinged with gray, was combed back from a forehead which was very high for its breadth. In fact, her forehead would have been called narrow by a superficial observer, but the remarkable altitude was largely responsible for this impression. Her face was open, frank and sincere, but there were traces of suffering in the lines of the mouth, as there was ample evidence of fortitude to bear it and resolution to conquer difficulties.

Such was the face which the unfortunate woman beheld when she opened her eyes, after a cool hand had been laid upon her forehead and a sweet and sympathetic voice had spoken:

"My dear child, how do you feel now?"

For an answer, the eyes closed again, and a tear fell from each upon the pillow. The sensitive lips quivered and sobs shook the slight frame under the rich folds of the elegant embroidered counterpane. Mrs. Bell, looking into the face of her charge, saw that she was young and beautiful. The face was oval and harmonious in its outline, and the pillow was covered with a wealth of golden hair which formed an exquisite frame for the lovely picture. A hand which would have inspired a sculptor lay motionless outside the cover. It was small, and the fingers were tapering, and the skin was as fine grained as silk. Yearning with infinite compassion toward the unhappy girl, the philanthropist took the hand and, holding it tenderly, bent over and impressed a motherly kiss upon the feverish brow of her charge. Again the young girl sobbed convulsively.

"There, my dear child, do not grieve so. You have had trouble, and it has been hard to bear, but it will all come right, if you will be brave and hopeful. You are with friends now who will help you out of all difficulties, and I want you to realize it and compose yourself."

"Oh, madam, you have all been so kind to me. May God bless you all for your goodness; but I must go away; I cannot stay here."

"My poor child, you are hysterical. You must compose yourself and let me help you out of all your troubles." And again the good woman pressed a kiss upon the brow of the sobbing girl.

"Oh, madam, do not kiss me. You do not know what I am or you would not touch me with your lips. You would turn away from me if you knew, as they all did. Oh, why did I not die in the lake. Oh, let me go away and die. It is the only place for such as I. Oh, I want to go to my mother. But she is in heaven, and they will not let me come there, either. Oh, God! why was I born?"

The experienced perception of Mrs. Bell did not need any more elaborate explanation of the case before her. But as the unhappy and desperate girl buried her face in the pillow and sobbed out her grief, an observer would have been interested in the expressions which played over the face of the philanthropist. First, her eyes filled with tears, and for a moment her hand passed caressingly and soothingly over the head of the girl, while she softly murmured, "Poor, innocent, misguided, persecuted darling." Suddenly she clasped her hands and rose from her seat and for a few moments walked the room rapidly, while an expression of fierce, energetic resolution pervaded her entire manner. Then she paused, and raising her eyes to the ceiling, stretched out her hands and in a low but intense tone uttered the words, "How long, oh eternal Truth, will you be disregarded! How long must the good and the beautiful be trampled upon by selfish prejudice!"

Soon, however, she had composed herself and approached the bedside. For a moment she paused and gazed upon the fair young form before her, with an expression of infinite tenderness and love. All traces of her recent emotion had disappeared when she again began to caress the golden head. Gently inserting one hand between the pillow and the face of her charge, she turned and raised the girl's head until the blue eyes opened and met her own.

Something in the look of unutterable love with which the philanthropist regarded her penetrated the confused perception of the girl, for she caught the hand which pressed her cheek in her own and covered it with kisses.

"Oh, you look like my mother. She would not turn away from me if she were here, and you do not, although I have told you I am bad. Oh, I did not mean to be bad! I did not know. They never told me. Oh, do not drive me away from you! I will do anything you say. I will be your slave if you will only show me how to be good!"

"My poor, little, persecuted darling," said Mrs. Bell, as she continued to caress her charge, "who told you that you were bad?"

"They did, my aunt and uncle, with whom I lived. They found it out last Sunday, and they told me that I was a bad woman and that they would never speak to me again, and they made me leave their house. My aunt said I had disgraced them, and my uncle said I was only fit for hell, and the quicker I went there the better. Oh, it was awful! I went to my Aunt Mary's, but my uncle came there and said if she gave me a home he would never speak to her again, and as he supports her, I had to leave there too. Then I tried to get work, but I never did anything of that kind, and people would ask for references, and I could not give any, and I was so excited and crying that they would not help me."

"My poor girl!"

"I slept in a doorway Sunday night, and in the morning the man came and ordered me out and said he would get a policeman to take me to the station house. I walked the streets all day Monday, and last night I did not sleep at all, but I stayed in the doorway part of the night. This morning, as I was walking down State street, I saw a man's name on a sign, that I knew I had met at my uncle's Bible class in Sunday-school. I went into his office and asked for him, and told him my uncle had turned me away, and asked him if there was any place I could go where Christian people helped a girl in such cases. He said there was, but that I need not go to such a place, but that I could stay with him. I asked him what he meant, and he took hold of me and tried to kiss me, and do something else which I felt was wrong, and I ran out of the office. When I left my uncle's house, I only had a dollar in my pocket, and I spent that for something to eat, and it was all gone this morning, and I was so tired and hungry, and everybody was against me, and I could not stand it to stay on the streets another night, and I went out on the pier and tried to end it all. I jumped into the lake, and then somebody pulled me out, and the gentlemen brought me here. Oh, you are so good and kind."

More than one tear had fallen during this recital, from the overflowing eyes of good, motherly Mrs. Bell. Now she bent over the pillow and covered the face of the girl with kisses, while her tears flowed freely. The girl threw her arms around her neck and kissed her in response, saying, "Oh, you are so good, so kind; you are just like my mother."

"Was your mother a Christian?"

"I do not know. She died when I was ten years old, before I knew much about such things. But I remember my uncle quarreled with her once, because she said that she believed more in doing good than in talking so much about it."

"Your uncle is a Christian?"

"Oh, yes; he is a member of the Presbyterian Church, and teaches a large class in the Sunday-school. My aunt is also a teacher in the Sunday-school and is president of the missionary society. That was one thing my aunt said, that I had disgraced them, and unless I was driven out none of their fashionable acquaintances would call, and she could not be reëlected president of the missionary society."

Mrs. Bell's lip curled for a moment, and again the expression of a fierce resolution gleamed in her eyes. But it gave way in a moment to her habitual expression of tender compassion, as she spoke to the girl.

"Listen, my dear. If I tell you that I am your friend, that I love you as I would my own daughter, and that I will help you in every way, will you believe me and trust me, and do as I tell you in all things?"

"Oh, madam, will you? I will do anything you say. I could trust you as I would my mother," and the girl placed her hand in Mrs. Bell's and looked appealingly into her face.

"That's a dear, sensible, good girl. Now listen. First of all, you must realize that you are not bad. That is a horrible, ignorant mistake. Your uncle is blinded by a false philosophy, and will live to regret his course toward you with bitter remorse. So will your aunt. You shall stay with me and be my daughter, and I will help you out of all your trouble. I am a physician, and my son who brought you here is a physician and one of the best in the world. Now, put your arms around my neck and kiss me, and then go to sleep, unless you feel that you would like to have some nourishment."

"I could not eat anything now," said the girl, as she disengaged her arms from the neck of her benefactor, while a heavenly smile illumined her features. "I am too happy. This seems like heaven. I will believe it is and go to sleep and dream of you and my mother."

Slowly the fringed curtains drooped over the blue eyes, and the lips parted in a smile of sweet rest from pain and sorrow. Mrs. Bell sat by the bedside until the regular breathing of her patient told that her slumber was complete. Then she arose and stood for a moment by the bedside with her eyes upraised and her hands extended as if in prayer. Her lips moved, but no sound disturbed the sleeper. For a moment she stood in an attitude of invocation, then she turned toward the sleeping girl and extended her hands over her in an attitude of benediction. Stooping to press a kiss lightly upon the brow of the sleeping girl, she noted with satisfaction that it was cool and moist. The girl's lips moved and smiled, and Mrs. Bell caught the whispered word, "Mother."

The philanthropist moved noiselessly to the door of the apartment. As she passed out into the hall she met the maid.

"Nora, you may lower the light in that room and take your position just outside the door. I do not think the patient will need any attention to-night, but if she awakes and makes any demonstrations, attend to her wants. If anything occurs that you cannot manage, call me at once. I shall now retire."

The maid did as she was told, but not without pausing to cast an admiring glance in the direction of her mistress. She took her place at the door of the apartment, saying softly to herself, in a rich Irish brogue:

"Yis, you'll retire, afther you have taken all the tears away from the blissid young lady and lift her sleepin' as if it was in her own mither's arms she was, an' she a two-year-old baby, with niver a sin or a throuble on her white soul, at all, at all! An' sure, if the loikes of you don't go to heaven, its mesilf that's wonderin' whether there'll be any dacint people there, afther all. And Father McGinnis says you're a haytheist, an' that yer goin' straight to the divil. Ochone!"

Entirely oblivious of these reflections on the part of her faithful servant, and conscious only of having performed a duty toward a suffering sister, Mrs. Bell reached her apartment, and laying aside her wrapper and donning a robe of snowy whiteness which was not more pure than her own good motives, she disposed herself upon her bed and was soon enjoying the peaceful slumber which was the portion of all her household, except the faithful Nora, who remained at her post.

Sleep! Gentle, restful, healing, peaceful sleep! It fell upon the great city like the brooding wings of a benevolent angel, and everywhere it carried a blessing and a benediction. The clanging bells of the cable cars and the shrieking whistles of the locomotives, the buzz of ten thousand wheels and the smiting of a thousand anvils were hushed, and tired men laid down the weapons of toil and temporarily forgot their sorrows. A cool breeze, fresh from the bosom of the lake, fluttered over the tops of the houses, wound its way through the narrow and stifling streets, swept them of millions of disease-breeding germs, and deposited its burden on the green prairies of the South, where they became harmless fertilizers to the teeming fields. And Sleep said to the breeze, "I will be your companion," and together they wandered over the great city. They visited the tenements of the poor and kissed the cheeks of half-starved children and the pinched faces of the parents, and gave them the first sensation of comfort they had felt in forty-eight hours. They penetrated the stables, and the tired horses yielded to their influence, and rested. They entered the homes of the men of business, and strong men blessed them and sank to the negative recuperation of their energies. Tired clerks inhaled the breeze, with a sense of relief, and embraced Sleep with a sigh of satisfaction. They rushed through the saloons, and weary debauchees drank the breeze, and Sleep gave them brief respite from remorse. In the brothels, weary, jaded women paused from cursing, to bless the breeze, and Sleep kissed into temporary oblivion, even the most depraved.

But the breeze said to Sleep, "Let us make one more visit," and they entered the mansion of a millionaire on Prairie avenue. And the breeze bore on its wings a grain of conscientiousness, and it fell into the brain of the millionaire and disturbed him. And Sleep said, "I will depart, until this man learns the way of righteousness." And it came to pass, that the millionaire did not sleep, and he was tortured with remorse and he said, "Woe is me, for I have not considered the case of the unfortunate, neither have I listened to the cry of distress."

And while he was yet meditating upon the evil of his ways, the sun arose and Sleep departed from the city, but the breeze remained to comfort the inhabitants thereof.

CHAPTER IV.

THE CITIZEN OF VENUS.

"There are more things in heaven and earth, Horatio, than are dreampt of in your philosophy."

When Doctor Bell arose on the morning following the events recorded in the preceding chapters, his first thoughts naturally reverted to the guests who were in such a remarkable manner placed within the courtesies of his hospitality. He arose and dressed himself at once, and, as he did so, resolved that he would follow the adventure to its finale, regardless of expense or personal inconvenience. He was very sure that his mother would give to the unfortunate young woman every needed attention, so he did not concern himself about her as much as he pondered about the extraordinary character of Loma. He had just completed his toilet, when a servant appeared at his door and announced:

"The gentleman in the library bedroom has just rung his bell, sir, and you left word that you were to be called."

"Quite right, Thomas; I will attend to his wants myself."

The doctor proceeded at once to the library and knocked gently on the door of the bedroom to which he had conducted Loma the night before. Loma opened it, and seeing the doctor, his face was at once illumined with one of his peculiar and affectionate expressions. He extended both hands to the doctor, who grasped them cordially and exclaimed:

"Good morning, my dear sir. I am delighted to see you looking so well. I hope you found your quarters agreeable, and that you are fully recovered from the fatigue of your journey."

"Delightful, my dear doctor. No one could fail to be refreshed in the enjoyment of such hospitality as yours. Those grapes were delicious, and I have enjoyed the bath and other conveniences to the fullest extent."

"That reminds me, sir, that I came to provide for your breakfast, after which we will consider such other matters as may be necessary for your comfort. Is there anything you would specially prefer? I will have my steward provide the breakfast for both of us in the library, and then withdraw, and while we are discussing the viands, I will listen to any suggestions you have to offer, in regard to any matter in which I can be of service to you."

As he spoke, the doctor glanced curiously at Loma, who was standing in an easy attitude, in the state of perfect nudity, which he seemed to prefer, and at the covers of the bed, which were laid carefully over the footboard and had not been used, while the print of Loma's body was evident upon the sheet where he had rested. The elegant silk night robe had not been used, and was lying upon the chair where the doctor had placed it when he called Loma's attention to it.

Evidently his guest had considered his own comfort rather than fashion, and it was also evident that he preferred to be nude whenever he could be so with propriety. The doctor's quick eye also noticed, what had escaped him the night previous, that Loma's body was covered with soft, downy hair, of exquisite fineness of quality, but sufficiently copious to afford a very comfortable covering against ordinary exposure. The color of this hair was very much lighter than that which hung in such profusion from his head, and was in fact almost the same color as his skin, which accounted for the fact that the doctor had not noticed it before.

"Thank you, doctor," said Loma, "All I require for food is such fruits, vegetables and nuts as you may be able to supply without inconvenience. My only beverage is water, and that which you so kindly served last night is superb in quality. I am aware that you are accustomed to animal food and grains, and you will not offend my taste by ordering for yourself anything which you may prefer, if you propose to entertain me with your own good company."

"I will be with you in a moment," said the doctor, smiling; and quitting the room he gave his orders to an attendant, which were soon executed. In a few minutes, when the doctor again stepped to the door of Loma's apartment, he invited the latter to the library, where a delicious repast awaited them on the table, in the center of the room. A damask table-cloth had been laid, and a delicate service of silver and cut glass glittered upon the table. In baskets of solid silver were tastefully arranged apples, peaches, pears, plums and grapes. In the center of the table was a large glass urn filled with the choicest of nuts, while two smaller dishes were filled with large Florida navel oranges. Two handsomely engraved silver goblets flanked a silver water pitcher near the doctor's seat, and in a receptacle above the urn was arranged a choice bouquet of flowers. As Loma stepped into the library, the doctor placed a chair near the table and invited his guest to be seated, saying, in his usual gracious and courtly manner.

"Permit me, sir, to offer you the best my resources afford. The fruits, with the exception of the oranges, are from the farm near Elgin, which I mentioned to you last night. The oranges are from another farm which I am fortunate enough to possess in Florida. For nuts, I am compelled to depend upon the Chicago market, but I trust you will find these not altogether unpalatable."

"My dear doctor," said Loma, as he took his seat and began the repast, "your hospitality leaves nothing to be desired. These peaches are delicious," he continued, as he paused to inhale the aroma of a superb specimen before removing the skin. "Is it not strange that in the development of your civilization your people have not learned to apply the same principles to the development of humanity, that you have mastered so well in respect to horticulture?"

"That is one of the facts which have often struck me as singular," said the doctor, as he poured out a goblet of sparkling water for Loma, and then filled the remaining one for himself. "Yet, I have attributed it to this cause. In the evolution of intelligence, man must first become cognizant of his environment, and the facts which apply to it are more interesting than those which more nearly concern his own individuality. As he learns more of those objects which surround him, his curiosity in that direction becomes satisfied, and he then begins to contemplate himself. It must necessarily follow that he will give more attention, therefore, at first, to the improvement of his environment than to the improvement of his own personal condition. For that reason, in his present stage of development, man gives greater attention to the improvement of horticultural products, and even to his own domestic animals, than he does to the improvement of himself. There is another reason, and that is that these products are immediately marketable, and therefore as at present man is largely dominated by his acquisitiveness, he expends his energies in improving that which he can convert into money in a very short time. He entirely overlooks the fact that human intelligence and superiority are the final and most powerful factors in prosperity, but to comprehend this would require a depth of philosophical reasoning of which our people are, alas, sadly incapable. But the trend of our best minds is now in this direction, and many movements are on foot having for their ostensible end the improvement of the race. Of course these movements are chaotic and conflicting, but that is to be expected in the beginning of any great stage of evolution. I am confident that the close of the present century will witness a marked advance along this line of thought."

Loma had paused in his dissection of the peach, and had listened to the doctor with interest and admiration depicted upon his fine countenance. He now spoke with enthusiasm.

"Your remarks, my dear friend, have shown you to be the philosopher you are reputed to be in my country. I am delighted to be the guest of a man who is capable of viewing things as they are, and of solving, in a measure, the problems which stand in the way of advancement. When we have finished this delightful repast, and have gathered from it the strength we shall both require to comprehend the situation, I shall take pleasure in enlightening you concerning myself."

Loma continued his breakfast with the air of a man who has an important mission to perform in which he evidently took great delight. There was an air of suppressed excitement in his manner, which, nevertheless, detracted nothing from the superb dignity which he always maintained. Doctor Bell regarded him with respectful curiosity and great interest. He had never been in the presence of such a man before, and he was certain, as he considered all that had happened since their first meeting on the pier, that he was confronted with the most remarkable episode that had ever occurred in his experience. He had thoroughly resolved to be equal to any emergency, and he was prepared for any extraordinary phenomenon which might develop itself in the premises. But he could not suppress the feeling that something was about to occur which would transcend the usual line of events, and he awaited the conversation of his guest with intense interest.

Having finished his breakfast with evident relish and appreciation, Loma arose from his seat and stood before the doctor with folded arms. The latter regarded him with fixed attention. Loma's eyes blazed with a strange luster, and as he stood looking into the face of the physician, the expression of his countenance was animated, sincere and enthusiastic. Doctor Bell was impressed with the volume of intelligence which seemed to flash from the eyes of Loma, and his first impression was, that whatever the extraordinary man before him should say, would be true. In fact, the doctor had already noted as one of the peculiarities of the man his power of seeming to compel belief.

"Doctor Bell," said Loma, impressively, after a brief pause, "are you prepared to receive a most unusual declaration from me, and to receive it with the same degree of candor with which I deliver it?"

"I am," replied the physician, still regarding his guest with fixed attention. "The events which I have already observed have in a measure prepared me for the reception of still further surprising phenomena, and even if that were lacking, your own personal character is such that I would be compelled to treat with respectful consideration anything which you might feel disposed to communicate. I am deeply interested, even impatient, to see or hear anything which you may have to offer, and I have sufficient confidence in you to believe, that what you have to disclose, however surprising, will stand any test which I, as a scientific investigator, may be disposed to apply."

"Thank you, doctor. Your confidence is appreciated, and I will proceed upon the plane of perfect candor. I will now give you my residence, which I, for reasons which you will perfectly understand, withheld from you last night. Doctor Bell, I am LOMA, A CITIZEN OF VENUS.

"Of Venus?"

"Yes, sir, of Venus. The beautiful star which illumined the western heavens last evening, which you have studied through your telescope with the interest of an astronomer, was until last evening, a moment before we met, my home and abiding place. I arrived upon this planet at the precise moment that the young woman who is now enjoying your hospitality in another apartment touched the waters of Lake Michigan in the mad attempt to end her existence, which we both witnessed. Strange as it may appear to you, our meeting under such peculiar circumstances was not accidental, but in accordance with the plan of certain great events which have been arranged by forces entirely unknown to you and to her, but in which you are both destined to play important parts. My own position in this important drama is that of an humble agent of the aforesaid powers, but a position of which I am extremely proud. I am intrusted with a commission fraught with consequences of the greatest moment to the inhabitants of this planet, for the execution of which I am directed to rely upon your assistance. It may be a source of satisfaction and pride to you, sir, to know, that, from the moment of your conception in your mother's womb, you have been selected by the powers to which I refer as the person to aid me in this enterprise, as I was selected from an equally important moment for its prosecution. The credit for the selection, in each case, is due to our excellent mothers, who, by conforming to the most perfect conditions of gestation and subsequent education, endowed us each with the requisite powers for the successful consummation of the most important service ever rendered to mankind."

As Loma finished this declaration, he extended his hands and clasped those of the doctor, in a fervid and enthusiastic grasp. The doctor returned his grasp with enthusiasm, and while he thrilled under the magnetism of Loma, which for the moment seemed to be of more than its former intensity, he felt that he himself was glowing with a corresponding emanation, which the association of Loma seemed to have suddenly called out. He was conscious of the most delicious sensations and he surrendered himself to them without reserve. He could not help believing every word spoken by Loma, but the disclosure was so wonderful that he was confused and bewildered. Loma noticed this and said:

"Compose yourself, my dear friend, and let me give you the substance of my narrative, as you are able to receive it. In the meantime, if you will drink this goblet of water which I have charged with certain magnetic conditions not known to your therapeutics, you will be considerably strengthened."

As Loma spoke, he handed the doctor one of the goblets which he had filled, and which he had held for a moment under the palm of his hand. The doctor drank it, and as he did so noted that it had a strange aroma and flavor, and that it sparkled unusually. As he drank it he felt his excitement subside, his senses became perfectly collected, and he awaited the further disclosures of Loma with the cool interest of a scientist and philosopher.

"I am astonished at what you say," he said to Loma, as the latter resumed his seat; "but I am prepared to follow you through your entire statement, and to receive such arguments and proofs as you may desire to submit."

"That is what I have expected from a man of your caliber," said Loma, admiringly, "and I will proceed. Know, then, that it is a part of the economy of the Universe, that each planet shall, at certain intervals, not regular as to time, but determined by the progress of development, receive from that planet in the same solar system which precedes it in development, certain impulses, which are accomplished by the translation of germs from the preceding planet to the succeeding. These germs are translated by an electro-magnetic process, which I am not at liberty to disclose, for the reason that this planet has not yet reached that stage of development at which it would be practicable for men to use it. It is sufficient for me to say, that, when

it becomes necessary for a germ to be translated, a
proper vehicle is provided, and the germs are translated from the first planet to the second with the same
rapidity that a dispatch could be sent if a telegraph
line were established between them. It is in this way
that vegetation first appears upon any planet, and later
that the various forms of life are evolved. In each case
the parent germs are deposited upon the planet from
the planet preceding it in development. The planet
Venus, being the precedent of the earth, is the source of
supply for the germs of all the developments which you
have. The operation of this law has been known in
Venus for many centuries, and our scientists have
watched with great interest the outcome of the many
varieties of germs that have been, from time to time,
translated from our planet to yours. The law of translation not being recognized on this planet, you have remained in ignorance of it, and have not even known the
effect of the translations of vegetation which have been
made to Mars from the earth, which is the precedent of
Mars. These translations have been going on from remotest time, and you have long since received all of the
varieties of germs of vegetation which are known upon
our planet, but they have not reached an equal stage of
development. The same fact is true of the animal
germs and the germs of humanity. What remains to
be translated now are germs of thought, and of such I
am the honored custodian. In obedience to the great
law of development of which I have spoken, the time
has arrived when it has become necessary for the fur-

ther progress of your civilization, that certain germs of thought should be translated from our planet to yours, which, taking root here, will marvelously accelerate your advancement. In the accomplishment of this design I am the vehicle of certain thoughts which I am commissioned to deliver upon this planet. To enable them to take root and accomplish the purpose of the powers which sent me, it is necessary that they should be planted in fruitful soil and cultivated with the utmost solicitude and intelligence. The beautiful young female whom we caught from the bosom of Lake Michigan last night has been destined from the first moment of her existence to be the receptacle of the germs which I am commissioned to plant. Yourself, your honored mother, and such other persons as we shall hereafter take into our confidence, are the husbandmen who will cultivate and disseminate these germs of living truth."

"This is magnificent," exclaimed the doctor. "I think I understand the outline of the plan, but there are some questions I would like to ask."

"As many as you please."

"How does it happen that your planet Venus is the precedent of the earth? Our astronomers have discussed that question to a great extent, and they are generally agreed that Venus is a younger planet than the earth. In fact, one of the most eminent observers has recently declared that Mars is the planet which precedes ours in development, and that our advancement does in some measure depend upon the study of conditions upon its surface. An animated discussion has recently been carried on as to the possibility of communicating with the astronomers of Mars, and various plans have been suggested, but nothing as yet has seemed practical."

"There are no astronomers on Mars," said Loma, smiling, "and if your observers should succeed in divining the true condition of affairs on that planet they would get more information as to the condition of matters on this planet hundreds of centuries ago. Your astronomers are, as a rule, brilliant and astute men, but they have utterly failed to understand the true rule of progression, because they have ignored the primal laws of genesis, which govern the production of stars, as well as of planets, animals and human beings. Ignoring these laws, they have been led into fatal errors as to the origin and nature of the stars themselves, as well as the effects produced by one star upon another, hence their conceptions of the causes of solar heat and light are totally erroneous."

"It is commonly supposed," said the doctor, "that, Venus being at least twenty-five million miles closer to the blazing mass of the sun than we are, the increase in the amount of heat received would be sufficient to preclude the possibility of any form of life with which we are familiar existing upon its surface."

"Here, again, your astronomers are in error. The sun is not a blazing mass, nor does it radiate heat or light. The conditions upon Venus are so nearly like those upon this planet that in my sudden transition to this earth I have experienced no inconvenience whatever. If you could be as suddenly removed to the surface of Venus as I have been from Venus to earth, you would find yourself in a region in which the physical characteristics are so similar that you would be insensible to the change, did you not observe the radical difference in the inhabitants and their accomplishments. In these latter respects we are many centuries in advance of you in the development of humanity and all that that implies.

"I will now proceed to explain the cause. Stars and planets are the product of growth, as is every other object with which we are familiar. If the sun were a blazing mass, as you have supposed, and the planets simply cooled cinders, according to the popular hypothesis, the process of combustion would have entirely devitalized them, and being dead themselves, they would be incapable of sustaining life. On the contrary, the planets of each solar system are living organs, of which the central sun is the parent, and they are projected into space according to the operation of the same law which governs the gestation and projection of every other object. The grand principles of sex are the potencies which produce this result. You are familiar with the operations of the male and female principles, as expressed in plants and animals. The same principles are expressed in the operation of creation throughout the universe. Stars are generated continuously from a prime potential source in which the genitive factors are space, matter, omnipresence, limitation, persistency, consistency, continuance and divisibility. The first two of these factors, to-wit, space and matter, constitute the prime source, the male and female principles, from which all creation is derived. Space is negative, matter is positive. Space is female, matter is male. Space is omnipresent, persistent and continuous. Matter is limited, consistent and divisible. The eternal affinity which exists between these negative and positive principles produces worlds, stars and solar systems, as well as the most minute forms of growth of every organism which exists.

"Your astronomers and philosophers say that nature abhors a vacuum. The true statement of this principle is that matter loves space. Wherever unoccupied space exists, matter tries to fill it. The omnipresence of space and the limitation of matter makes this a never-ending struggle, which produces all the phenomena of growth. The constant mutations of matter are the result of its eternal effort to occupy space.

"By virtue of the genderic degree of state with which space, matter, omnipresence and limitation are endowed, like degrees of genitive passion are generated among them. The negative degree of this genitive passion is ever generated in unoccupied space, and we call it electricity. The positive degree is ever generated from all matter, and we call it magnetism. In other words, electricity is the love of space for matter and magnetism is the love or passion of matter for space. It is therefore evident that the entire creation is founded on love as its great creative principle, and that when man places himself in harmony with the universal law of love, his advancement is as rapid as growth is possible.

"It follows from the principles that I have announced that the stars and planets, being composed of matter, are all masculine. You are doubtless familiar with the fact, that all genesis proceeds by the successive steps of impregnation, incubation and parturition. The passion of the male produces a germ, which is deposited in the female, who nourishes it during the period of incubation, when final parturition endows it with a separate life.

"The sun may, therefore, be properly recognized as the male parent of all the planets within this solar system, as space is the female parent. The grand passion of the sun for the space which surrounds him, has caused him at various intervals to produce the germs of the planets, which, as they have matured within his substance, have been deposited by him, in the fervency of his love for space, within the broad womb of her maternal receptivity, where they have been nourished by her during their respective periods of incubation. This nourishment is derived from the immense quantity of matter which space constantly holds as a product of the disintegration which is continually resulting from the depletion and death of planets and stars. This product, orginally devitalized, is regenerated with her electricity after an inconceivable period of time, and being brought into contact with a germ from the sun which is glowing with magnetism, a mutual attraction results which causes them to unite. This beautiful phenomenon is visible to you every night of the year. A meteor, which is simply the fragment of a dead planet, long held in the embrace of Space, and by her reduced to a condition in which electricity preponderates over magnetism, but still retaining some magnetism, comes within the attraction of the center of electrical receptivity of the earth, which is simply one of the living germs still requiring nourishment. The receptivity of the earth attracts this meteor, and finding an affinity for its remnant of magnetism, it rushes to the embrace of the earth, and in doing so, encounters the resistance of the earth's magnetism and atmosphere, which fuses it and causes it to dissipate itself by the fervency of its own passion. It will become incorporated into the earth's substance and will remain until it is again thrown off by some other manifestation of the eternal energy of the passion of matter for space.

"Meteors and asteroids are the fragments of dead planets, held in solution by space. The asteroids and meteors which we encounter are the fragments of dead members of our solar system which have not entirely **disintegrated,** hence the fragments retain the original orbits in effect. Space holds an immense quantity of matter which is entirely dissolved, and is therefore absorbed without any phenomena which is visible to our senses, as the meteor is, after it has been entirely fused in our atmosphere. As the sun gives out his energy in new generations of planet germs and magnetism, he is constantly depleting himself, and will ultimately die, when a large portion of his substance will remain, to be disintegrated by decomposition in the form of a comet, as in the case with all dead bodies. Comets are simply the decomposing bodies of dead worlds, glowing with the phosphorescence which always accompanies decomposition. The planets will continue to grow until they have reached the full limit of their vitality, which is only measured by the quantity of nourishment which space holds in the regions in which they move, and their inherent absorbing power, which is an inheritance from their parents, space and matter, and which is decided by the conditions of space and matter under which they were generated, precisely as the vitality of any earthly child depends upon the conditions of his parents at the moment of conception.

"The moon is an example of a planet germ in the process of incubation, as are all the moons of the planets Jupiter, Saturn, etc. While a planet germ is in the period of incubation, it has no atmosphere and no diurnal motion. These limitations as to atmosphere and diurnal motion correspond to the limitations which you see imposed upon all germs during the process of incubation. The young chicken in the egg does not breathe, nor does it manifest the motions which after birth enable it to manifest life. Atmosphere is the breath of a planet. Diurnal motion is the regular manifestation of its functionality.

"Star and planet germs, like all others, have their vicissitudes. Some may be devitalized during the period of incubation; some are destroyed by the opposition of superior forces, and some live out the full period of their existence.

"From this brief statement of the nature and effect of genesis in the solar system, it follows, as you would readily infer from the observation of growth in other forms, that those products of gestation which lie nearest to the parent are the oldest. Some of the older children of our sun, which originally lay nearer to him than Mercury, have already died and have been decomposed into their original elements, and are now held in solution in the everlasting arms of space. Mercury is the oldest living member of our solar family, and from him, as from an older brother to younger members of the same family, there is a constant radiation of magnetism, containing germs of good will and progress, toward all the younger planets.

"Venus ranks next in order, and there is from him a constant emanation of these germs to other and younger planets. There is also a form of reciprocal affection, exercised from a younger planet toward an older one, but as it does not imply the transmission of progressive germs, it does not concern us to consider that at this time.

"It is in obedience to this great law of the translation of germs from an older planet to a younger one, that I have been sent to this planet, to deliver the thoughts which by careful impression and education have been implanted in my brain, and have reached the proper stage of growth to be transplanted to the brain of an inhabitant of this planet. How this shall be accomplished, I will now proceed to explain."

CHAPTER V.

THE MISSION OF LOMA.

"There is one glory of the sun, and another glory of the moon, and another glory of the stars; for one star differeth from another star in glory."

Loma had held the undivided attention of his listener during the foregoing narrative. In fact, Doctor Bell had never heard from human lips as brilliant and lucid an explanation of the phenomena which for years had possessed for him all the fascination of an absorbing study. In a few brief words, Loma had set before him a complete and reasonable solution of the greatest problems of astronomy, and many which he had considered as practically unknowable were now made perfectly clear. The philosophy itself would have charmed him if the ideas had been crudely expressed by an uninteresting person. But the faultless language of Loma, his superb manner and his magnetic and convincing delivery, combined with the absolute reasonableness of all he had uttered, raised the doctor to an ecstasy of enthusiasm.

"My dear Loma," he exclaimed as the latter paused in his narrative, "this is a transcendent experience. You convince me that all you say is true, and yet it contains a perfect demolition of all our cherished theories. But I am impatient to know how you, at a distance of twenty-five million miles, came to be acquainted with my existence, and also with the existence and destiny of the young female whom you say has been selected for the high office of receiving the germs of thought which you are to implant. Moreover, how does it happen that you, a citizen of a world many centuries in advance of this one, are so perfectly acquainted with the language which we speak on this planet."

"Nothing is easier," replied Loma. "You are doubtless familiar with the crude phenomena of clairvoyance, as practiced here. Well, in our world we have developed this power to such a degree that it is entirely possible for our adepts to see what is transpiring on another planet with far greater ease and much more satisfactory results than your best clairvoyants here can discern what is transpiring in another city. In that way we have not only learned at what time you are ripe for the reception of other germs, but the precise conditions and locality in which to plant them. Your conditions, as well as those of your excellent mother, and of the young female who is, at this moment, receiving her ministrations, have been carefully noted, and at the proper time our meeting has occurred. In the same way, knowing that it was my high destiny to be the bearer of the germs of thought to her and to you, it has been a part of my training to prepare myself thoroughly in your language and literature."

"In what way, may I ask, are you to impress her

with the thoughts which you are commissioned to deliver?"

"In order that you may properly understand my answer to that question, it will be necessary for you to know more of her history, which you will, of course, understand has been known to me for many years, and you may imagine with what affectionate interest I have followed all the details of its development. In brief, her history is as follows: She is the daughter of Charles Burnham, a teacher and writer of great ability, and a man of spotless integrity, who died in this city in 1878, when Myrtle was three years old. Her mother, a beautiful and supremely cultured woman, survived him seven years, when she also died, and little Myrtle was taken by her mother's brother, who became guardian for the small property which Myrtle inherited from her parents and which was exhausted in her education, which has been quite extensive. She is an accomplished linguist and musician, and has inherited all of the superb talents of her father as a teacher and writer. Her uncle and aunt, with whom she has resided until three days ago, are well meaning people, but the victims of the false philosophy of that form of Christianity which is expressed in the strictest form of Presbyterianism. It is one of the curiosities of the Christian religion, as it is practiced on this planet, that it condemns to social ostracism, starvation and contumely every female who imitates the example of the mother of the man they worship as God.

"About one year ago, Myrtle became acquainted with

a most excellent young man, by the name of Albert
Caldwell, who was a member of a literary society of
which she was secretary. They were complete complements of each other's natures, and the acquaintance
inevitably ripened into love. They were engaged to be
married, and the wedding was set for the twelfth of
June. As is customary, the young people were accustomed to spend much time in each other's society, and
they indulged freely in kisses and caresses, and other
demonstrations of affection. Myrtle is a superbly sexed
young woman, and the excitement of her lover's caresses brought on a degree of sexual passion which
neither of them could control. Believing that they were
perfectly safe, and having perfect confidence in each other, they participated several times in the act of coition.
It is hardly necessary for me to say, doctor, that this
was the result of forces which were entirely beyond
their control and a preparation for the events which
are to follow in connection with my mission. Albert
was entirely honorable in his intentions, and would
have killed himself before he would have permitted any
harm to come to his sweetheart through his rashness.
In one of these acts of coition, in which her sexual passion and her love for her betrothed found its most
complete and full expression, she conceived the son
with which she is now pregnant, and which is now in
the fourth month of incubation. On the eleventh day of
June Albert was killed in an accident on a cable car in
the La Salle street tunnel as he was on his way to visit
Myrtle. The girl bore this calamity bravely, although

her heart was almost broken. She had, however, owing to the buoyancy of her temperament, practically recovered from this grief when she began to discover the changes in her organization which are familiar to you as the first indications of pregnancy. It is only fair to remark, in this connection, that up to the present time she has had no instruction whatever in the mysteries of physiology, her aunt and uncle, and nearly all others of that faith, regarding such instruction as the height of indecency, and unfit for a virgin to even have mentioned in her presence. As a consequence, when Myrtle cohabited with her lover she was totally ignorant of the consequences, and in her innocence and ignorance, when she began to notice the changes which are the symptoms of pregnancy, she went to her aunt, to whom she naturally looked for advice and instruction, and asked her what it meant. Imagine her dismay, when her aunt had, by a few shrewd questions, discovered the truth, which Myrtle made no effort to conceal, when she was informed that she was an outcast from the comfortable home in which she had been reared, and that those to whom she had been accustomed to look for protection were now her most bitter enemies, following her with a mercilessness which even prevented her from being harbored by another relative who was more compassionate. Driven from shelter, hounded by those who should have been her protectors, insulted by a lecherous scoundrel and rebuffed by everybody with whom she came in contact, after two nights and three days of despair, she sought rest in the waters of Lake Michigan, and found it in the sympathizing bosom of your family."

"Thanks to your opportune appearance, and your superb rescue," interrupted the doctor.

"All of which was for a purpose," resumed Loma. "My appearance at that moment was in obedience to a natural law which I had no power to resist and in fulfillment of my destiny and yours.

"For the accomplishment of my mission in the translation of germs of thought, the following conditions are necessary: First, there must be a vehicle, sent from the precedent planet to the succeedent, as I have already explained. I am the vehicle, and the thoughts are in my possession.

"Second, there must be a young and impressionable female who is in a state of pregnancy, and advanced as far as the fourth month, at which time it is possible for her to impress her offspring with the germs of thought which she may receive from conversation with the person who bears the germs to her in that manner.

"Third, the offspring with which she is pregnant must be of such superior quality, and she herself must be such an impressionable medium of communication between her instructor and her offspring, that the best possible results may be obtained from the process.

"I am delighted to state that in the present case all of these requirements are met, and that the offspring with which Myrtle Burnham is pregnant is as perfect as it is possible for human beings at this stage of the world's progress to produce. Her boy will be a complete reproduction of all her own good qualities, resembling his mother in form and feature, reinforced by a superb vitality from his father, and such other and further excellencies as I shall be able to impress upon him with your assistance. Being conceived in the purest expression of love, at a time when both his parents were in the best possible condition, he will develop into a teacher and writer, the like of which has never been seen upon this earth, for he himself will be pregnant with great truths, the utterance of which will revolutionize society."

Doctor Bell could no longer contain himself. He embraced Loma with all the ardor of his affectionate nature, exclaiming, "It is grand! Magnificent! Sublime! My entire personal resources and services are at your disposal for the accomplishment of this noble purpose. But tell me, dear friend, why have I been honored by being selected to aid you in your grand mission?"

"You have furnished a practical answer to your own question, my dear brother," said Loma. "Your own superb character, inherited from the best of mothers, your advanced and liberal ideas, your magnificent generosity, and your ample fortune, which you eminently deserve, have all combined to make you the one man of all the world, capable and worthy to aid me in this, the grandest of all enterprises."

"I am yours to command, at any sacrifice," exclaimed the doctor. "But before we terminate this interesting conversation, I wish to ask you a few more questions.

You have stated that the sun does not radiate light or heat. I should infer, therefore, that the sun, like this earth, is a world, perhaps having substantially similar physical characteristics, and only differing from this earth in the fact of being older and larger by growth, as earthly parents are older and larger by growth than their infant progeny. Am I correct?"

"Precisely."

"How, then, do you account for the phenomena of light and heat which seem to be developed by the sun's rays as soon as he rises above the horizon?"

"You, of course, understand, from what I have already said, that the sun, being a living organ, composed of matter, is radiating constantly an emanation of magnetism, which, having a natural affinity for space, penetrates space as far as his influence is capable of making itself felt. Of course a certain amount of this magnetism strikes that side of the earth which is presented to the sun."

"Certainly."

"Now, coldness is the phenomenon of electricity and composure. Hotness is the phenomenon of magnetism and fervency. Darkness is the phenomenon of receptivity and gravity, while light is the phenomenon of radiation and vibration. To be more explicit, in the ratio in which electricity and composure dominate over magnetism and fervency, we have coldness as a result; hence it is colder on that side of the earth which is turned away from the sun, because there is no magnetism striking that side, and it is in a state of composure. On the other side, that is, the side next to the sun, the rays of magnetism are striking the atmosphere of the earth and penetrating to its surface, and we have magnetism dominating over electricity, and heat is produced, and it is more intense as the ray is more vertical or direct. The heat, therefore, which our consciousness ascribes to the sun is really generated in the atmosphere of the earth, by the magnetism of the sun striking a resisting medium. The proof of this is found in the fact that the higher we ascend into the atmosphere of the earth the colder it becomes, because as the atmosphere becomes more rare the sun ray is less restrained. Beyond the outer atmospheric limits, heat is impossible until another atmosphere is reached.

"Darkness is exhibited in the ratio that receptivity and gravity dominate over radiation and vibration. Conversely, light is exhibited in the ratio in which radiation and vibration dominate over receptivity and gravity. Consequently, on that side of the earth upon which we have the radiation of the sun's magnetism, and the vibrations of the atmosphere caused thereby, we have light. Beyond the outer limits of the atmosphere, light is as impossible as heat, until another atmosphere is reached.

"This explains why, as I have said, there is no reason for supposing that the sun is a blazing mass. This conception grows out of the impression produced upon the consciousness, which is a totally unreliable guide. It is just as absurd to believe that the earth is flat, yet, until science proved the contrary, such was the universal belief."

"Recent experiments have certainly shown, that the higher we go in balloon ascensions, and the closer we get to the outer limits of the atmosphere, the darker and colder it becomes," said the doctor.

"Certainly," said Loma. "Now, if the observer at high altitude had a mirror, if your commonly accepted hypothesis were correct, he should be able to reflect as bright an image of the sun as he can at the surface of the earth. We know this is not the case; and if he were beyond the outer limits of the atmosphere, he could not get any image at all, for under such conditions light and heat are both impossible."

"But," said the doctor musingly, "if such is the case, how does it happen that light is developed on the surface of the moon which has no atmosphere?"

"There is no light or heat from the sun, developed on the moon. The rays of the sun's magnetism which strike the surface of the moon are reflected to this earth, and passing into our atmosphere produce light, which enables us to form an image of the moon. But if an observer could be translated to the center of the apparently illuminated surface of the moon, he would find himself in total darkness and absolute cold, as far as the sun is concerned. All the heat which the moon has is internal heat generated by its own fervency of magnetic passion, which is very small comparatively until it passes from incubation to actual activity. Then it will form an atmosphere, and the magnetism of the earth, acting through the laws we have just discussed, will

give it light and heat, as the sun gives light and heat
to the earth. When the sun dies, there will be no perceptible diminution of heat and light on the moon, for
the earth will be the source of its supply.

"Our solar center, the sun, has heat and light on its
surface, developed by its parent, a super-solar center,
around which our sun revolves. This super-solar center is too remote for us to determine whether it has a
revolution around an extra-super-solar center or not.
It is probable that it has, but if our super-solar center
is the center of a complete stellar system, which is
true, if its more remote ancestors are dead, then this
super-solar center is enshrouded in perpetual and
almost total darkness and frigidity, for although radiating magnetism itself, it is receiving none, except from
very remote stars, which would, of course, afford the
same quantity of starlight we receive, but hardly an
appreciable degree of heat. When it has become depleted and has expired, then our sun and all his brother
suns who revolve around the same super-solar center
will become centers of complete stellar systems, and
will be perpetually shrouded in darkness and frigidity.
But they will continue to animate their children with
the radiation of their magnetisms until they in turn are
depleted. When this finally occurs, this earth will
have grown by accretion, as I have already described,
to the dimensions of its parent, our present sun, more
or less, according to the conditions of its existence, as
is exhibited in all other growths. In the light of this
philosophy, the destinies of your father, the earth, and

my father. Venus, are something glorious to contemplate."

"Why do you say 'father?'" inquired the doctor.

"Because each world is masculine, being composed of matter," replied Loma. "Space is the universal mother of us all"

"This is a sublime philosophy," exclaimed Doctor Bell. "My dear Loma, you have in one brief interview given me a better grasp of the mysteries of astronomy than I have been able to obtain in years of study. I will not press you with more questions at this time, but will take immediate measures to secure your personal comfort Now, what is your pleasure in regard to your clothing and the employment of your time?"

"I am not accustomed to the use of clothing of any kind," said Loma. "In Venus we have long since outgrown the barbarism of that practice. A very large per cent. of disease which afflicts the inhabitants of this planet is due to the habit of wearing the absurd costumes which are seen on your streets. Moreover, the outrageous belief that the exposure of the human form is indecent is responsible for most of the sexual crimes which afflict your civilization."

"I have long believed that to be true," said the doctor, "and my mother, who is one of the purest and best of women, from my infancy has inculcated the same doctrine. She, my father and myself, always enjoyed the luxury of a sunbath in the conservatory, which my father built for the purpose and which I shall be pleased to introduce you to. Here in my home, surrounded by my faithful servants, all of whom owe their lives to my professional services in some way or another, we are perfectly safe in the prosecution of any actions which we may deem conducive to health or morality, without consulting our neighbors. But if you expect to visit other localities, it will be necessary to conform, to some extent at least, to the customs of those who are not as far advanced as ourselves, in order to avoid unpleasant consequences."

"That is true, and in the immediate future we will give that subject proper consideration. If you will give me the freedom of the conservatory you mention, and the use of your library, I shall be perfectly comfortable. In the meantime, I desire to cultivate the acquaintance of your mother and Myrtle. I greatly prefer to meet them as I am, for it is intolerable to me that their first impressions of myself should be associated with the ridiculous effects which would be produced if I were attired in any of the fantastic costumes which have come to be regarded as a part of the personality of your citizens."

"My mother will be delighted to meet you," said the doctor, rising. "And now, if you will excuse me, I will attend for a few hours to other duties. I will join you again in time for lunch, and in the interim I will have arranged for your complete entertainment. With your permission, I will now conduct you to the conservatory, where you may entertain yourself until I can again avail myself of your delightful companionship."

So saying the doctor took Loma by the arm and conducted him to the second floor of his residence. At the top of a broad flight of steps he unlocked a large door, and a scene of surpassing beauty delighted the expectant eyes of the citizen of Venus.

CHAPTER VI.

THE ANNUNCIATION.

"Blessed art thou among women, and blessed is the fruit of thy womb!"

When Myrtle Burnham opened her eyes on the day following her attempted suicide, it was with an exquisite sense of rest, luxury and safety. The treatment she had received at the hands of Doctor Bell and his mother, the gracious sympathy of the latter, and above all the impression that she was now with friends upon whom she could rely, filled the mind of the girl with hope and thankfulness. The events of the three preceding days were too severe and momentous for her to understand, and she did not attempt it. She only knew, that, whereas, she had before felt like a hunted fawn, pursued by dogs and harassed by enemies, she now had a delicious sense of protection, comfort and congenial association. It is one of the curious facts of human constitution, that the most delightful sensations are those which immediately ensue upon the relief of pain. Myrtle was now experiencing one of these reactions. When she entered the room in which she was now lying, she was in a state of complete collapse, caused by fear, exhaustion and shock. Under the kind and intelligent ministrations of Mrs. Bell these painful impressions had passed away, and she had sunk into a delightful slumber, or rather an ecstasy of relief, in which all consciousness became lost in a succession of dreamy impressions of goodness. This was succeeded by a heavy slumber which lasted until after 12 o'clock noon, when nature asserted herself, and she slowly awoke to a comprehension of her situation. For a long time she lay with her eyes closed, while the events of the past three days and nights passed slowly in review before her mental vision. Her conversation with her aunt, the horror of her expulsion, her adventures on the street, her attempted suicide and her rescue by Loma and the doctor, seemed to her like the phantasmagoria of an awful dream. They did not disturb her, and so complete was her sense of present safety that they merely formed a dark background to the sweeter impressions of her interview with Mrs. Bell.

Slowly the blue eyes opened, and as she became accustomed to the dim light which came through windows which had been carefully shaded by the faithful Nora, in order that her sleep might last as long as possible, Myrtle became conscious of the fact that she was lying in a sumptuously furnished apartment, the appointments of which reflected luxury, combined with exquisite taste. Every incident of the furnishings seemed to be a part of a harmonious assemblage of restfulness, comfort and hospitality. Myrtle was so completely impressed with this fact that she abandoned herself once more to the sense of luxury and safety which overwhelmed her, and turning over in the bed, which seemed to be itself charged with a benediction, she sighed:

"Oh, this is heaven itself."

"Are yez awake, darlint," said a pleasant voice, and opening her eyes once more, Myrtle recognized the face of the maid who had attended her the night before.

"Oh, yes, and I have had such a delightful dream. Oh, this is so nice, and you are all so kind."

"Bless your swate face, who could be unkind to the likes of you. It wouldn't be Nora O'Grady, an' bad 'cess to the likes of them that ever caused you the trouble that brought the tears to your swate eyes last night. But yez are all right now. Would yez like to slape some more, or will I be afther helpin' ye with yer twilet?"

"Thank you, Nora; you may wash my face if you like, and comb my hair, before that dear lady comes in who was here last night. I presume she is your mistress."

"Indade she is, an' sure its mesilf wouldn't be livin' to-day, if it wasn't for her and the doctor, her son, he is. Ah! but he's the swate gintleman! an' sure, all he has to do is to look at a body, and they gets well in spite of themselves, I'm thinkin'."

Amused at the intense loyalty of the maid, but at the same time mentally conceding that the praise was well placed, Myrtle submitted to her manipulations with a further sense of sympathy and comfort. When Nora had bathed her face, and had bound back her luxurious tresses with a ribbon, she paused and looked admiringly into Myrtle's face and said with genuine Irish approbativeness:

"There now, you look as if you were ready to meet the finest lady in the land, an' sure that's what's comin'. Oh! but isn't your hair purty. But the missus left orders, as how I was to get your breakfast as soon as ye waked up, an' if yez like, I'll be after gettin' it at wanst."

"Thank you, Nora. I am really hungry, I believe. I did not eat anything yesterday, and I begin to feel as though I would enjoy a breakfast."

The maid withdrew, and in a few moments returned with a tray containing a tempting arrangement of simple food. A dish of toast, a small piece of steak, done to a turn, an omelet and a small urn filled with steaming liquid, all delicately served in beautifully decorated small dishes. A bunch of Concord grapes and an orange completed the repast, which Myrtle regarded with the interest of an artist.

"This is delicious," she exclaimed as Nora poured out a cup of the liquid from the urn. "What is this, Nora? It is not coffee."

"That's restoria," said Nora. "It's something Mrs. Bell invented a long time ago, and we all like it. Sure, you'll never get a drink of coffee in this house. They don't have anything here that's any harm to any one. There's no liquor in the cookin', nor in the house, for that matter, and the missus wouldn't let me cousin, what comes to see me, light his pipe in the back yard.

The whole premises, as the doctor calls 'em, is sacred to health and goodness, he says, and sure it's himself that does be spakin' the truth, for not a bit of sickness has any of the family or the servants had since I've known 'em, and that be six years, come next Christmas."

While Nora was thus volubly sounding the praises of her employers, Myrtle finished her breakfast and leaned back against the pillows of the luxurious bed, with a delightful consciousness of strength regained. Nora removed the tray, and said:

"Now, I'll go to tell the missus, that yez have had a good breakfast, and that yer as well and as smilin' as a basket of chips."

Nora departed, and Myrtle awaited the coming of Mrs. Bell with an impatience born of love and gratitude. Nora had opened one of the windows, and the sunlight was streaming in and falling in a broad ray across the bed. To the mind of the girl, raised so suddenly from the darkest despair to the brightest of hope, it seemed a promise of happiness, and she felt her whole being warmed with the magnetism of its rays. While she was breathing a prayer of thankfulness and hope, the door opened and Mrs. Bell advanced to the bedside. Myrtle threw up her arms, and clasping her benefactress about the neck, kissed her again and again, finally burying her face on her shoulder and bursting into a flood of tears.

"Oh, I love you so! I love you so!" she exclaimed when her emotion had calmed sufficiently for her to speak. "I am so happy, and I have had such sweet dreams. My mother came to me last night and kissed me and told me not to fear anything in the future. She said that you would be my mother here on earth, and that I should love you and trust you as I would her, and I do. Oh, I would love to be as good as you are."

"You shall be my own sweet daughter, Myrtle dear, and you may call me mother if you like, for you shall remain with me henceforth, and it will be my loving duty to protect and cherish you as you deserve," said Mrs. Bell, as she kissed her tenderly and, as Myrtle thought, reverentially.

"I will be your daughter, and I will love and respect you in all things," said Myrtle, "for you have certainly been a mother to me when I most needed love and sympathy."

The compact was sealed with a long and loving kiss, and Myrtle lay upon the pillow, holding the hand of her new found mother, caressing it tenderly.

"My dear child," said Mrs. Bell, after a pause, "are you as well and strong as you appear to be, this morning?"

"Oh, yes, indeed. I never felt better in my life. I don't believe I ever felt as good. I am so happy I cannot express myself."

"Then you are well enough to have some important information conveyed to you, and to know something which will still further increase your happiness?"

"Oh, yes, indeed. I will listen to anything you wish

to say, for I know it could only be good," and Myrtle looked inquiringly into the eyes of Mrs. Bell. "But tell me how you knew my name. I do not remember having told you."

"You did not tell me, dear, but since you went to sleep I have learned your whole history, and that from a very unexpected source. You have nothing to be ashamed of, but, on the contrary, your destiny is so high that you will be accounted as one of the most blessed of women, by reason of the very facts which have seemed for the time to bring you into misfortune. You have been in love with an excellent young man who is now dead, and in the expression of your love for him, you did something which your uncle and aunt thought was very disgraceful, and for that they turned you out of your home. I know all about how you tried to get work, and how you found the world all against you, and how you at last tried to find relief in the lake. I tell you these things so that you will know that I know all about them, and you may dismiss them from your mind, for I do not want you to think about them any more than you can help. I also know who your father and your mother were, and you have every reason to be proud of them. Your aunt and uncle are good people, only they have been wrongly taught, and they are the victims of the false philosophy of the religion they profess. They thought they were doing right to treat you as they did, but they were mistaken, and it is your duty to forgive them, and love them, and perhaps, some time, you may teach them the great and glorious truth."

"It seemed dreadful for them to treat me as they did," said Myrtle, "but I could not help feeling that they were laboring under some horrible mistake all the time. They liked Albert, and seemed to think that he was an excellent young man, and I heard my uncle say once that he was a perfect gentleman. They never told me anything about what we did, and I was perfectly ignorant. I knew Albert would not do anything wrong and I trusted him. If he had not been killed, I do not think there would ever have been anything said."

"You are quite right, my dear, because you would have been married, and the form of Christian religion which your aunt and uncle profess teaches that marriage is the only state in which such actions as you and Albert performed are permissible. If you are married, you may do all such things, even regardless of health and safety, but if you perform that act outside of marriage, you are forever disgraced in their eyes."

"Then why did they not tell me about it, so I could have avoided it," exclaimed Myrtle, with some indignation. "Neither myself nor Albert would have thought of doing anything of the kind if we had known it was wrong."

"That is one of the peculiar inconsistencies of Christianity," said Mrs. Bell. "While they condemn such actions as the vilest form of sin, and visit the most condign punishment upon the violators of their very singular code of sexual ethics, they consider it almost equally vile for any one to impart any information upon the subject, and some of the best men and women of this country have been imprisoned and many more have been socially ostracized for endeavoring to teach the truth in regard to such matters. This seems all the more singular, when you consider that Jesus Christ, whom they profess to worship as God, and whose mother they venerate as the most blessed of women, believed and taught an entirely different doctrine, and Jesus himself was born as a result of the violation on the part of his mother of this very same custom."

"Is that what they mean when they say that Jesus was born of a virgin?" asked Myrtle wonderingly.

"Certainly. Mary, the mother of Jesus, had a lover, exactly as you have had Albert. Like you they had indulged in intercourse without marriage. Subsequently when Mary was betrothed, according to the custom of her country, to a man named Joseph, she was discovered to be in the same condition that you are now, that is, she was about to become a mother. Joseph, being a kind-hearted man, did not wish to disgrace her, and he was about to break off the engagement privately, when he had a dream in which he received the impression that he should not only overlook her condition, but that he himself would be greatly honored by becoming her husband. He did so and became her protector, and when her child was born he kept it as his own. You are probably familiar with the rest of the story."

"Oh, yes; I have heard it in Sunday school and in church many times. But they never explain that part of it."

"No, that is the singular part of it; and while they worship an illegitimate child, as they term it, they drive into dishonor and starvation all mothers of similar children to-day. Now, my dear, you must understand that here, in this house, you will be taught a different doctrine. If this were not true, we would have turned you out last night like all the rest. We believe in and practice a different form of religion. We believe that motherhood is the highest and most sacred duty of woman, and that marriage is simply an expedient invention of society. We believe that love is the real law of reproduction, and that as you and Albert loved each other dearly, that you committed no crime, but merely violated a social custom of which you were ignorant. The son, of which you will be delivered in due time, will be a lovely child, and a thousand times better in every element which makes a good man than the average child that is born in wedlock. Jesus was an example of the same fact. Now as Nature sets her seal of approval upon such offspring, we believe that man has no right to condemn them for sins they never committed."

"I could not see how it could be a crime for Albert and myself to enjoy each other, when we loved so dearly," said Myrtle.

"It was not a crime, in fact, my dear, and the worst wrong which any one has committed has been in leaving you in ignorance and then condemning you, when you had no chance to even know their sentiment. I wish you to get all the idea of guilt out of your mind as soon as possible. Believe in your innocence and virtue, and cultivate your self-respect to the utmost, for you have a glorious destiny. And now, my dear, I must tell you that a most extraordinary thing has happened in your case. Do you remember the gentleman who took you out of the water last night?"

"Not very well. I can only remember that, when I jumped into the lake, I was immediately seized by a strong arm, and I was dazzled by what seemed to be an electric light all around me. I felt something like electricity go all through me, and then I have a confused memory of voices and some one carrying me into this room. I remember you best of all." And so saying, Myrtle smiled and kissed the hand of Mrs. Bell which she still held.

"Very well. Then I must tell you that the gentleman who rescued you is now in the house as our guest. He is a distinguished scientist from another country, and it is through him that we have learned all about you. This gentleman is of the same religion that we are, but he is infinitely more advanced; in fact, he is, without doubt, the greatest teacher now on earth. He has all the wonderful powers that you have been taught were possessed only by Jesus Christ and his disciples. These powers are natural to all men, but few men become good enough to ever learn to use them. Now I come to the most wonderful part of my announcement to you. This gentleman, whose name is Loma, says that you have been destined, from the moment of your conception in your mother's womb, to be the mother of a child which shall develop into the grandest teacher the world has ever known. This child you are now pregnant with has been conceived by you at a time when your love for Albert reached its purest and best expression, and it is destined to be as perfect as it is possible for a human being to be at this stage of the world's history. Loma says that your whole history, up to this time, has been according to a pre-arranged plan, and that your meeting last night was not accidental, but controlled by the same great power which molds the destiny of the universe. His mission is to teach you everything that is good and true and beautiful during the remaining months of your pregnancy, and by so doing he will be able to implant in the forming brain of your child the germs of the great truths which he is hereafter destined to teach to the world. Myrtle, my beloved daughter, is it not glorious?"

Unable to control her emotions longer, Mrs. Bell rose and walked the floor in a transport of sublime exaltation. Myrtle, who had listened with wonder and amazement, now sprang from the bed in an ecstasy of delight and threw herself into the arms of her foster-mother, crying out, "Oh, mother, my darling mother, what happiness this is! Oh, Albert! Albert! if you could but have lived to hear this! Oh, it was not wrong, it was not wrong! Our love was the truest guide after all."

Clasping the palpitating form of the girl in her arms, Mrs. Bell rained kiss after kiss upon her forehead and upon the golden hair, which had become loosened from its ribbon and now flowed at will in a bewildering mass of gold around the queenly head. The loose robe which enveloped Myrtle's slender form slipped from her shoulders and fell to the floor. In all her life Mrs. Bell had never gazed upon a vision of such enchanting loveliness as Myrtle presented as she stood upon the floor, arrayed in nothing but the garb of her own complete personal beauty.

With a quick movement of her left hand she disengaged the cord which fastened the wrapper she wore about her own person, and in a moment she also was without adornment other than her own splendid personality. Placing her arm around the waist of Myrtle, she led her toward the east end of the room, which was composed of two large folding doors.

"Take me to Loma!" cried Myrtle, as she clung to her benefactress in a transport of joy. "I know that I will love him and that he will love me."

"LOMA IS HERE!" said a voice, which fell upon their ears like a deep-toned bell sounding amid the rush of a cataract of sweet waters. There was a strain of entrancing music, the folding doors opened noiselessly, and revealed the conservatory, in the midst of which stood Loma, with arms outstretched in an expression of welcome, his body illumined by the magnetic glow which seemed to radiate from him in all directions in the form of a halo of glory. As Myrtle and Mrs. Bell entered the conservatory, the folding doors closed noiselessly behind them, and Loma, advancing, embraced them. Myrtle felt the wonderful thrill of his personal contact, and then as his lips met hers, she closed her eyes and sank upon his breast in blissful unconsciousness.

CHAPTER VII.

MYRTLE'S FIRST LESSON.

"And it came to pass, that when Elizabeth heard the salutation of Mary, the babe leaped in her womb; and Elizabeth was filled with the Holy Ghost."

The introduction of Myrtle into the conservatory, and her first impression of Loma, had been carefully planned. Doctor Bell had informed his mother of the remarkable character of Loma's mission to the earth, and the important part which Myrtle was destined to play in the advancement of civilization. With superb tact, Mrs. Bell had conducted the announcement to Myrtle of her glorious destiny, and just at the moment when the delicate and impressionable nature of the young mother was at the highest point of its receptivity, the introduction had occurred. That it was in the highest degree dramatic, and that it was accompanied with all the accessories of music and the beautiful scenery of the conservatory, where æsthetic taste combined with wealth had produced the most surpassing effects, were all elements which combined to impress upon Myrtle's unborn child the happiest conditions of organization. Myrtle, as the reader has already been informed, was in the first period of her pregnancy, when impressions of physical beauty can be most successfully made. Her association with Loma was designed to impress upon her offspring the most desirable physical and mental conditions. Loma had been introduced to her as a dazzling vision of human perfection. Himself the embodiment of all that is good and beautiful in human character, both in physical and mental attributes, which are always inseparable, and imbued with a lofty conception of the dignity and grandeur of his mission to the earth, it is not strange that he should have glowed with the highest intensity of the magnetism which was a part of his glorious nature. In her first sweet embrace, received from the being who had traversed the space of worlds in her behalf, Myrtle received a charge of magnetism which permeated her whole being and thrilled her in every nerve and cell of her organization. In an instant of time, the superb personality of Loma entered into her being and became incorporated with it, never to depart. In after years the memory of that sweet moment was sufficient to set every center of her brain vibrating with intense and delicious ecstasy. At the same time, the sensitive embryo within her womb received the impression of Loma's character, and thenceforth all of his grand attributes became a part of the nature of the unborn child. The quickening effect of Loma's magnetism was such, that, at the moment of contact, the child leaped in the womb of its mother, and from that time Myrtle was conscious of its presence.

The conservatory in which this extraordinary event took place was itself a bower of beauty. It was built upon an elevation in the rear of the doctor's residence, level with the second floor, and connected, as the reader already knows, with the room in which Myrtle had slept by folding doors, which were operated by electricity. It was also reached by the door at the head of the stairs in the hall through which Loma had been introduced. It consisted of a broad dome of stained glass, so arranged that by means of sliding panels any desired quantity of sunlight could be admitted or excluded. Artificial heat was supplied from a furnace in the room beneath, and cold air connections enabled the doctor to command any degree of temperature that might be desired, in any condition of weather. In the center of the conservatory a fountain continually played and filled the air with the music of falling water. Rare plants and flowers from all parts of the world, arranged with that skill which only is exhibited by those who have long studied the laws of beauty, shed their delicious fragrance and filled the room with exquisite combinations of harmonious colors. Adjoining the conservatory, and really forming a part of it by an extension, was a music room containing a magnificent pipe organ, a grand piano, and several portable musical instruments. Doctor Bell had been seated at the organ when Myrtle and his mother entered, and had accompanied their entrance with the sublimest strains of which his musical skill was capable. He had controlled the movement of the folding doors with an electric button, at a signal from his mother, and had been largely responsible for the dramatic effect of the introduction, having received his instructions from Loma, as to the effect the latter desired to produce. He remained at the organ until he finished the march, when he left it and joined the interesting group at the fountain. He, also, was entirely nude, and as he joined his mother, who leaned upon his shoulder with infinite pride, he presented a striking picture of manly grace and physical beauty.

Loma held the unconscious form of Myrtle for several moments in a loving embrace. Then he placed her upon a couch near the fountain, and pressing one long kiss upon her brow, stood for a moment contemplating her with an expression of unspeakable love and tenderness. Mrs. Bell and the doctor stood upon the opposite side of the couch, and gazed entranced upon the exhibition of beauty before them. Loma's body continued to glow with his incomparable magnetism, and so great was its fervor at times that it completely dazzled the two witnesses. Gradually it subsided until it was evidenced only by a halo of magnetic glory around his head. When he had reached this stage, he lowered his hands, which until this time he had held over Myrtle in an attitude of benediction. Myrtle opened her eyes with an exquisite smile.

"Oh, I thought I was in heaven last night, but now I know I am. You all wear halos, just as I have seen in the pictures of Christ and the angels. You look like angels. I am one myself. I am happy. This is Life. It is Love. I love everything. Everything loves me."

Loma took both of Myrtle's hands in his, and bending

over her in an attitude of superb grace, spoke in a tone which mingled with the music of the fountain in exquisite harmony:

"Beloved, receive the Truth. Nature is Love's highest, sweetest expression, as Love is Nature's supreme law. Everything which is natural is good. Evil is only the antagonism and repulsion of that which is contrary to Love. Humanity must learn to love, before it can be natural or good, in a complete sense.

"It is impossible to love that which is unnatural. It is impossible to love completely that which is not completely revealed. As long as humanity is presented to the senses in an unnatural way, love is impossible, and it can never be complete until humanity is completely revealed.

"The religions of the past have degraded humanity, and priests and kings have taught that humanity is vile, in order that it might lose self-respect and be more easily enslaved. Men and women have been taught to regard their bodies as vile, and that those members of the body which were directly used to reproduce humanity were especially to be held in dishonor. Men have been ashamed of their manhood; women have blushed for the evidences of maternity; all have covered themselves with the garb of disgrace. The belief that these organs and functions were dishonorable has caused them to be put to dishonorable uses. Men and women will not cherish and cultivate that which they have been taught to despise. Because of this fundamental error, man has received the impression that his mother conceived him in sin and disgrace, and hence he has not respected his mother nor her sex, but as a consequence woman has been held in slavery to man. This degradation will continue as long as woman is ashamed of her person, or is ashamed of maternity, for slave mothers never yet produced a race of freemen.

"The long night of slavery, ignorance and superstition is past. The glorious dawn of liberty is at hand. You are, at this moment, enveloped in the first rays of the advancing sunrise of intelligence. The experiences of this moment will never be forgotten by you, and will be received by your sweet offspring in embryo, to be by him developed and expanded and transmitted to a world which is hungry for the Truth. From this supreme moment you will be proud of your body, and of the maternity of which it is the beautiful and appropriate instrument. Your child will never blush for his manhood, and he will revere and love the body of his mother, and through her, the body of all that humanity it is his mission to bless.

"Nature has scourged humanity with a long train of frightful diseases, caused by the reabsorption of the excreta, thrown off by perspiration, which is absorbed by the unnatural clothing so universally worn and reabsorbed by the skin. The covering of the body has made it unduly sensitive to changes of temperature, and many of its sweetest and best powers have been lost. Men have become careless as to cleanliness, for it has been easier to cover filth than to remove it. Frightful and distorted fashions have been invented and the original beauty of the form has been destroyed. But the worst and most degrading fact, in the whole train of calamities, is the false conception of human nature which has taken the place of the true standard of manhood and womanhood. The children of men do not know what a true man or woman is, and hence they form no true ideal of character, and do not strive to attain to any. The conception of womanhood which exists in the minds of most men, is a dress, a face and a bonnet. With equal force it may be said that most women think of a man as a cloth suit, surmounted by a face and a hat. True manhood and womanhood lies buried beneath the product of the tailor and the dressmaker. Until manhood and womanhood can be revealed in its completeness no conception of it can be formed by the fathers and mothers of the coming generations, and a correct generation is impossible.

"Generation can only be accomplished by the transmission of magnetism. This transmission is accomplished by personal contact, at the time of conception, and during gestation. It is impossible to completely transmit magnetism when the bodies of the parents are insulated in clothing. Yet most of the conceptions of humanity on this earth take place when the parents are at least partially robed, and under the cover of darkness, when it is impossible for a true conception to result, hence most men are only fragments of the humanity they misrepresent.

"Conception is not confined to the time of the impregnating intercourse. The mother receives new impressions daily from those with whom she comes in contact. Unless she receives impressions constantly from the free and untrammeled forms of good men and women, she cannot endow her offspring with their attributes. Unless she is free and untrammeled herself, her capacity for receiving magnetic influence is destroyed.

"Rise, beloved, and enjoy your liberty. Embrace those who, like yourself, have passed beyond the degrading influences of conventional laws and customs, and who are pure, as their thoughts and motives are pure. In these delightful surroundings, and amid these sweet and pure associations, submit your own fair body to the reception of the germs of truth it is my mission to implant!"

So saying, Loma raised Myrtle from the couch, and embracing her and imprinting upon her lips a rapturous caress, delivered her to the no less enthusiastic and affectionate congratulations of the doctor and Mrs. Bell. Love reigned supreme, and mingling with the perfume of the flowers and the music of the fountain, in one delicious harmony, was the exquisite aroma of human magnetism in its highest and best expression.

When the first enthusiasm of this transcendent experience had in part subsided, the doctor arranged four luxurious easy chairs near the fountain, and the four friends, who were so closely united in the development of a higher civilization, held an earnest conversation. Notwithstanding the exciting experiences she had passed through so recently, Myrtle's mind was well balanced, and while she was only beginning to realize her high destiny, she was neither unduly exalted nor in any manner removed from the sweet womanliness which was a very conspicuous part of her character. She received the caresses of her friends with a hearty reciprocation of affection, but she also preserved her dignity, and when Loma made any suggestion, he found in her an attentive and earnest listener.

"I love to hear you talk," she said to Loma. "I do not think I have ever met any one like you. You seem to be like a person from another world."

"I am from another world," replied Loma, and in a few brief sentences he conveyed to her the information, which is already in the possession of the reader, regarding his origin. Myrtle accepted his statement as a matter of fact, for his extraordinary character and the peculiar impression of truthfulness which was a part of his manner left no room for doubt.

"This is all so new to me," she said to Loma after a pause, "that I am not sure that I fully comprehend it. Of course it is all so different from what I have been taught. Now that I comprehend that everything that I learn from you will be implanted in the brain of my child, I am anxious to have a clear impression. I understand from your statements, that it is natural to be nude, and that we are unhealthy because we are not. But how is such a custom to be maintained in this climate? Do the inhabitants of Venus remain in a nude state at all times?"

"In tropical countries, on this planet," said Loma, "the natives who live naturally, remain nude most of the time, and spend a great deal of time in the water. Man is originally a native of the tropical zone, and it is only as he has moved north that the necessity for clothing became apparent. His excursions were first of a limited extent, and of short duration, and he availed himself of the covering of the skins of beasts, to protect him from temporary discomfort. Subsequently, as he increased the extent of his excursions northward, he allowed the habit to become fixed and disregarded the law of nature that would have provided him with abundant natural protection, if he had been content to go more slowly and allow his body to become adapted to the climate. It is true, that when the continent of South America was explored, whole tribes of natives were found at the extreme southern extremity, where the climate is much more rigorous than is the climate of Chicago, who were entirely nude at all seasons of the year and who enjoyed excellent health. The advent of Christian missionaries wrought a sad change in the condition of these natives. They were persuaded to adopt the custom of wearing clothing, and in a short time hundreds of them died with consumption and various forms of catarrh. The almost universal prevalence of catarrh in this climate, and the hundreds of deaths from consumption, are due to the same cause. Until your people learn to expose the body and allow the skin to have its natural action, you cannot become clean. The ex-

creta which is thus arrested is reabsorbed and must
be thrown out of the body in some other way. The
lungs and the mucous linings of the various canals of
the body become overtaxed, and the result is the
numerous and offensive diseases which afflict mankind.
In Venus we have advanced to that degree of civilization that the energies of men and women are not
absorbed in the conquest of land or finances. We have
a limited population and we inhabit only the best
climates, and as we have abundant leisure for enjoyment, we are habitually nude. If it becomes necessary
for any purpose to expose the person to the rigors of
an unaccustomed climate, a sufficient protection is
worn, but such conditions rarely occur, and are only
experienced by the adventurous portion of the community who desire to make explorations, or those who
are engaged in transportation. The regular apartments of dwellings, workshops and other places of
habitual resort are all kept at such a temperature as
is approximately the mean average temperature of the
atmosphere. Under such conditions the body is
allowed its full liberty. We are universally a healthy
people, and disease is regarded as a disgrace."

"My experience as a medical practitioner has confirmed all that you say," said Doctor Bell, "and I must
give my excellent mother here the credit for having
first called my attention to it. This doctrine is not
taught in the medical colleges, but I have always been
able to cure catarrh and incipient consumption whenever I could persuade a patient to live in pure air, in an

equable temperature. and be habitually nude and practice bathing to the fullest extent. Our sanitariums benefit patients very greatly by energetic baths, massage and various forms of exposure, but it is only recently that these methods have had any standing as therapeutic agents."

"The hardest thing that I have encountered in my efforts to introduce this practice," said Mrs. Bell, "is the apparent impossibility of persuading patients to do enough of it. Patients do not like to be alone, and they cannot be persuaded to be nude in a sociable way. If men and women could recover from the awful sense of shame which seems to beset them when they are exposed to the view of others, it would not be difficult to insure healthy conditions."

"I have always been taught," said Myrtle, "that this sense of shame was natural, and that it was the chief guard of virtue, and that if I did not have it I was very immodest. I must confess, however, that I could never see any good reason for it, and if it were so, why should babies be exposed. Mothers are always proud of the chubby arms and legs of their babies, and frequently expose their beautiful bodies to the admiring gaze of their friends of both sexes, and no one thinks it is wrong. But these same mothers would be awfully ashamed to expose themselves in the same way. And I have noticed another peculiar thing. Young girls, who would faint if their gentlemen friends saw them in their underclothing only, will go in bathing in suits that are made on a pattern that exposes more of the body than the underclothing does and think nothing of it. They expose their breasts and arms in full evening dress, but are filled with consternation if a tear in another style of dress should expose half as much of the person in the same locality."

"The exposure of the person," said Loma, "is entirely a matter of fashion. As soon as it becomes fashionable to wear a style of dress which last year was condemned as indecent, the devotees of fashion are eager to adopt it. Let the enlightened conscience of a people declare that it is unfashionable to wear health-destroying clothing, and as soon as people became accustomed to it, you would hear no more of this false modesty. True modesty consists in being ashamed of that which is wrong. If the sense of shame were naturally associated with the condition of nudity, children would manifest it as soon as they began to be conscious of their surroundings. As a matter of fact they do not until they are chided and shamed into manifesting it, and it generally takes some time to establish it then. There are some sensitive natures which seem to show it very early, but they are the offspring of mothers who were ashamed of the condition of maternity, and such offspring usually pass through the world apologizing for their existence.

"The most remarkable fact in this condition is the strange prejudice with which people of all religions founded upon the Bible view the subject. The Bible contains abundant authority for the defense of habitual nudity, and it is strange that some vigorous expounder of so-called sacred history has not immortalized himself by exposing the true meaning of certain well-known passages. The circumstances of the planting of germs of thought for the advancement of civilization are well recorded in the Bible if the correct interpretation were understood."

"Do you mean that this process has been repeated before, and that other citizens of Venus have visited this earth for this purpose?" asked Myrtle, wonderingly.

"Certainly," said Loma. "Every important advance in civilization on this earth has been brought about in this way. In every case, it was necessary for the parties to be brought together in a nude state, just as we are, for it is impossible for the communication to be made when the magnetisms of the communicants are insulated in clothing. To receive a communication of this kind, it is necessary for the parties to be in a state of perfect purity, and to have their minds above all forms of disagreeable, indecent and lascivious thought. As soon as the element of lust is present, the communication is destroyed. It is not always necessary for the whole person to be nude in order to get a communication of minor importance, but if the communication is of great importance, nudity is essential, because it is necessary that there should be a complete and powerful transmission of magnetism. Only those persons who have attained to such a degree of magnetic perfection that the rays are intense and highly visible are capable of being translated from one

world to another, or of making the sublime impression
which is necessary to the transmission of germs of
thought. The magnetic glow which you see at times
radiating from my person is the badge of my office, and
the evidence of my fitness for my mission. When I
am engaged in some great effort you see that the glow
becomes intense. When the effort is less intense the
glow diminishes, but it is never entirely absent. My
translation from Venus to the earth was accomplished
over an electrical conduit, one end of which was at
the summit of the mountain of Alusia in Venus and the
other in the end of Lake Michigan near Chicago. When
I caught our beloved Myrtle from the lake, I was in a
glow from my transit, which made the doctor think
I was using an electric light. You have seen a similar
exhibition of its power here to-day. If I should approach you at such a time when you are arrayed in
your customary clothing, the resistance to my magnetism would be so great that an intense heat would be
generated which would burn your clothing and prove
fatal. When you are nude, as I am, the transmission
of the magnetic current is uninterrupted, and you are
not injured, but on the contrary delighted and strengthened. In Venus, the transmission of pure and highly
cultivated magnetism is the highest art of social intercourse. It is not necessary for me to argue with you
that this can only be attained while the parties are in
a state of perfect health and the correct use of all their
faculties. Now, if you will bring me a copy of the
Bible, I will call your attention to certain passages

which are more or less familiar to you, but upon which I shall be able to throw some new light."

Doctor Bell withdrew from the conservatory for a moment, and quickly returned with a copy of the Bible in his hand. Loma received it and opened it while his three auditors drew near with breathless interest.

CHAPTER VIII.

NEW LIGHT ON THE BIBLE.

"Seeing then that we have such hope, we use great plainness of speech."

"The first instance of a communication between this planet and Venus which is recorded in the Bible," said Loma, as he opened the book, "is found in the second chapter of Genesis. The story of Adam and Eve in the garden of Eden, while subject to a great many erroneous impressions among those who accept it literally, as here recorded, is far from being the myth which it is considered by some. The real facts are these. Adam and Eve were two highly cultivated and advanced persons who had been selected and trained, by the powers who have selected us for a similar purpose, to be the receptacles of germs of advanced thought. For that purpose they were isolated in the garden, and were delightfully cared for and educated, by persons selected for that high office, as you have been for the education of Myrtle's offspring. In order that they might be pure, healthy and happy, they had been nude from childhood. The story opens in this chapter, at the time when the representative of advanced civilization from Venus began to communicate with them. In the Bible this personage is called the

Lord God, because he represented to them a guardian of all good. The words literally mean, 'Ruler for Good.' Adam and Eve continued to receive his communications and to live in happiness and purity. The Bible says:

"'*And they were both naked, the man and his wife, and were not ashamed.*'

"They had not reached the time when sexual intercourse was permissible, for under the laws of nature, properly understood, the sexual act must be prefaced by a long period of culture, in order that it may be in the highest degree enjoyable, and that the best results may flow from it. The 'serpent' spoken of in the third chapter was one of the inhabitants of the earth, of the lower strata of society, who was fascinating in manner, and 'more subtle than any beast of the field.' He invaded the garden and succeeded in seducing Eve, and in arousing her passions to an extent which rendered her desirous of continued intercourse. Her seducer having departed, to obtain relief, she appealed to Adam and succeeded in inducing him to share in her unholy pleasure. This intercourse, participated in by them prematurely, for the mere gratification of desire, and not for its high and legitimate functions, caused a serious weakening of all the functions of the sexual organs, producing disease, and so changed their appearance that Adam and Eve became frightened, and thus discovered that the 'fruit of the tree,' that is the fruit of their unholy intercourse, was to give them a knowledge of the difference between good and evil, for whereas they had up to this time lived perfectly virtuous lives, and hence knew not the effects of evil, this unfortunate action showed them the consequences of a violation of Nature's law. Realizing, in part, the consequences of disobedience, and afraid to meet their instructor and friend in a condition which they knew he must detect, they hid themselves and resorted to fig leaf aprons. The consequence of this disobedience was, that they lowered their mental and moral status to such a degree that it was impossible for them to fulfill the high mission to which they had been called, and they were rejected, and sent out of the garden, and were compelled to associate with their fellow men and women on an equal plane. Hence, thereafter, they were compelled to toil for a living, and eat bread in the sweat of their faces."

"How very interesting," exclaimed Doctor Bell.

"There are a number of cases of similar communications related in the Bible," said Loma, "but the circumstances are not always set forth in detail. One of the best, however, is this one in the third chapter of Exodus, in which one of our citizens was sent to instruct Moses, to prepare him for the movement which resulted in the exodus of the Jews from Egypt, which has had as much to do with the advancement of civilization as any event in the history of the world. In the second verse of this chapter, it says:

"'*And the Angel of the Lord appeared unto him in a flame of fire out of the midst of a bush, and he looked, and behold, the bush burned with fire, and the bush was not consumed.'*

"You, of course, understand why the bush was not consumed by the magnetic glow, which emanated from the person of the 'Angel,' which was mistaken by Moses for fire. But mark the sequel:

"*'And when the Lord saw that he turned aside to see, God called unto him out of the midst of the bush and said, Moses, Moses. And he said, Here am I.'*

"*'And he said, Draw not nigh hither; put off thy shoes from off thy feet, for the place whereon thou standest is holy ground.'*

"Moses, according to the custom of shepherds in that climate, was already nude, except shoes or sandals for the feet, and the inference is, that he lost no time in obeying the warning, for he was afraid, and he hid his face. The incident, however, shows that nudity is a necessity in such communications, for the reasons I have already stated. It is amusing, however, to see that 'The Lord' does not tolerate the wearing of clothing in his presence, and then see the efforts made by those who profess to be his followers to claim that it is necessary to decency. It simply shows that those who attempt to interpret the Bible as a system of worship and theology have entirely mistaken the nature of the persons who have from time to time appeared as 'The Lord' and as 'Angels,' and that their whole system of interpretation, theology and morals is rotten and utterly unfounded on fact.

"Passing over numerous other instances found in

the Old Testament, we come to one which more nearly concerns us, as it furnishes the immediate precedent for my own mission, and was accomplished under very similar circumstances. I allude to the case of Jesus Christ.

"In the highest and best sense, Jesus was the son of God. But since the beginning of time, God has never violated a natural law to accomplish the designs of His creation. He always works according to His own great eternal principles, and in the case of Jesus, while the circumstances of his conception and birth are marvelous to the mind of man, who does not comprehend the extraordinary conditions which accompany the transmission of germs of good influences from precedent planets to succeedant ones, yet, in every case, natural laws are obeyed.

"Before you can comprehend the extraordinary character of the conception and birth of Jesus, you must know that this tremendous presence which men worship under different names as God, is the great, universal creative Energy, which molds the destinies of stars and planets with the same unerring righteousness with which it deals with the growth of vegetation and the evolution of animal life. With the first glimmerings of reason, man realizes his dependence upon this power, and he personifies it, ascribing all his good fortune to the beneficence of a Good spirit and all of his troubles to an Evil one. As he advances in intelligence and learns, that everything in nature is good, and that his troubles are only the corrective influences of goodness toward him, he eliminates the devil from his theology and learns to cast himself trustfully upon the goodness of an Infinite Heavenly Father, whose best expression comes to him in the natural processes of the universe which surrounds him. It is natural, therefore, that he should forever keep in his mind a high conception of a Great Power which is infinitely good, infinitely just, omnipresent, omnipotent and omniscient.

"The higher man advances in the scale of intelligence the more perfect becomes his knowledge of his Creator. He learns to divest Him of the puerile attributes of the personality with which he first expressed his conception of God, and to acknowledge his inability to define the Infinite. When he has reached this stage he is ready to study God as He reveals himself in Nature, and then it is that he begins to be able to comprehend the working of the great law of interplanetary transmission. I will briefly explain the working of this law, by saying that every good and perfect gift, originating with the center of Creative Energy, is transmitted by it to every super-solar center, by them to solar centers, and from them to their attendant children, the planets and satellites. The universe, filled with starry constellations, thus becomes a grand machine for the distribution of the unfathomable goodness of God, and all that man should do, instead of disputing over dogmas and doctrines, is simply to look above him, and hold out his hands to receive to the limits of his capacity the blessings which will come as the reward of his faith and expectancy.

"In Venus we have reached this stage. We do not have any churches or priests to quarrel over disputed doctrines. We have learned to seek the kingdom of God and His righteousness, by living perfectly natural lives. Recognizing that God is Love, we have learned the science of love and practice it. And when, in the course of nature, an extraordinary wave of Love, coming down from the center of Creative Energy, reaches us, we have learned to recognize it and to accept it.

"Jesus Christ was the product of such a wave. The same wave of Infinite Love which produced such marvelous effects upon this planet at the birth of Jesus, permeated the entire universe with beneficent effects. But you must realize that upon a world as far advanced in growth as our sun, the conditions of life and growth are as far in advance of our conditions as the radiation of his superb magnetism exceeds in power that which we may receive from another planet of our own solar system. Compare the heat and light developed by magnetism received by this planet from Venus with that developed by magnetism received from the sun, and you have a fairly accurate idea of the difference in the conditions of life and growth on the two spheres. Grand as are our conditions upon Venus, as compared with conditions existing upon this earth, yet we realize that there are conditions yet to be reached in the progress of growth that are as entirely beyond our present comprehension as the glory of the sun is beyond the comprehension of the human eye. We do not, therefore, attempt to explain the methods by which God deals with His children, but accept His mercies with simple, child-like faith. This faith, however, gives us the power to reach a better comprehension of the natural phenomena that accompany the manifestations of the extraordinary impulses of His goodness that we from time to time receive.

"To explain, therefore, the natural phenomena attending the conception of Jesus, I will say that just previous to that conception an extraordinary impulse of Divine goodness was transmitted to Venus through Mercury and the sun, which culminated in the most marvelous growth of the virtues among the inhabitants of our planet. In fact, we passed into a condition which has been quite accurately described by the writers of your sacred books as the millenium. The millenium spoken of in the Bible is at hand, and the mission of Myrtle's offspring is to introduce it, and when it has worked out its grand results, it will send the germs of its goodness onward to Mars and the succeeding planets beyond the earth. Now, when this wave of goodness reached its height on Venus, all of its best and highest impulses were crystallized into the organization of a superbly perfect man named Manrolin, who was selected as the bearer of these influences to the earth, and he became the 'Angel of the Lord' who appeared to Mary, announced his mission and secured the conception by her of the greatest character in the history of the world.

"I have said that in the highest and best sense Jesus was the son of God. He was the natural son of

Manrolin, who represented in his personality the direct concentration of an extraordinary impulse of goodness from God, transmitted through the natural channel. Manrolin was the male vehicle of the germ of goodness, as Mary was the female receptacle. The product of their union was the first perfect man who ever appeared upon the face of this earth. In his perfection of humanity he was the representation of God to man, as the highest conception of God which can be formed in the human mind is perfect goodness, and this Jesus thoroughly typified. In so far as he was born of an earthly mother, he was earthly and human, as that word is applied to the inhabitants of this planet. In so far as he was the result of a conception of a germ borne to Mary from sources beyond the earth, he was super-human but not super-natural. He brought to the world the essentials of a complete philosophy which has never been successfully attacked. After passing through his remarkable history on this planet he returned to the source of Eternal Goodness from whence he came, and as a consequence of his successful performance of his mission now 'sitteth on the right hand of God,' by the operation of a perfectly natural process which it is my delightful duty to explain to you at a future time.

"In the first chapter of the Gospel according to St. Luke the circumstances of the conception and birth of Jesus are set forth with as much fidelity as could be expected of a narrator who wrote many years after the occurrence of the facts he relates, with a vivid imagination, somewhat inflamed with religious zeal. It will be seen that the communication was given by an 'angel of the Lord,' and tradition gives us a description of this personage, as he was probably described by Mary In the paintings produced by devout artists this 'angel' is represented as a man of great personal beauty, surrounded by the magnetic halo, which was undoubtedly true. The inference from this chapter, as related by Luke, is, that the communication was made to Mary when she was in bed, and nude. The facts of the case, as related in the histories used in Venus, are, that Manrolin was intrusted with this delicate mission, and came to the earth at the time of the conception of Jesus, and managed it with consummate wisdom and skill. First he introduced himself to Mary, as recorded in this chapter, and finding her in bed, and nude, he gave her a communication with such superb manifestations of power that he completely won her confidence.

"*And Mary said, Behold the handmaid of the Lord, be it unto me, according to thy word.*'

"Having thus completely secured the affections and coöperation of Mary, Manrolin presented his credentials and assured her that he was the man whom God had selected as the father of the coming prodigy, and they being complete complements of each other's natures, love at first sight was a natural consequence. In this way Manrolin produced the conception of Jesus, and the rest was a comparatively easy task. Joseph, who was in every way fitted to become the protector and guardian of the child and his mother, was selected for that office, and only required one visit from Manrolin to secure his hearty coöperation. It frequently happens that the person who is selected as the father of a child is not permitted to raise it, as many persons who have the gifts required in a certain character it is desired to secure are not fitted for the responsibilities of child culture. It was so in the case of Jesus, and was so decided in the case of Myrtle's offspring. Joseph, however, being a man of advanced ideas, accepted the trust and discharged it with great fidelity, and with the coöperation of these parties, Manrolin succeeded in implanting in the offspring of Mary and himself the seeds of the brilliant and humane philosophy which was afterward preached with such fervor and success by Jesus. The teachings of Jesus are the purest and best the world has had up to the present time, and have been the source of great progress, but have often been obscured by the distorted use which has been made of them by political machines, known as churches. In all ages, however, since his triumphant mission, there have been those who have comprehended and taught some of the true doctrines inculcated by him, and Manrolin's success won for him an enviable immortality in the annals of illustrious achievements. So great was his success, that his son and protege, Jesus, was enabled to attain to the eminence of being himself translated, and came to Venus at the close of his illustrious career on earth, where he was received with the greatest enthusiasm and where he finished his life in great felicity."

"It is commonly believed," said Doctor Bell, "that Jesus died upon the cross at the time of his crucifixion, at least by those who do not accept the Bible version of his death and resurrection."

"Neither of the commonly accepted beliefs in regard to the resurrection of Jesus are true," said Loma. "The facts are, that Jesus, when he had suffered upon the cross for several hours and mastered all the depths of human sensation and misery, which was necessary discipline, being a master of hypnotism, induced in himself the condition of catalepsy, which so closely resembles death that the Roman soldiers were completely deceived. None of the wounds inflicted on him were fatal, and after his supposed dead body had been delivered to Joseph, he was placed by the latter in the sepulchre, where he remained until the third day. At this time he recovered from the catalepsy and was released from the sepulchre, and appeared to the disciples as stated in the Bible. He subsequently departed for Venus, in the sight of a number of persons, as I hope you will have the privilege of seeing me take my departure when the time comes. Jesus succeeded in developing a great deal of magnetic power before his crucifixion, and at one time held a consultation with two distinguished men from our planet, who met him on top of a high mountain, at which time his powers were tested, but were not deemed sufficient to attempt the flight. Subsequently by the discipline incident to his sufferings he developed the powers of his mind to such an extent that he was able to evolve sufficient magnetism to accomplish the wonderful results which marked the close of his earthly history. If the true facts in regard to the life of Jesus were known, man would learn the value of discipline. The grandest acts in the history of the world have been performed by men and women who developed the ability to perform them by the discipline of great sorrows. Inactivity and self-indulgence are the greatest destroyers of mental power. The circumstances of this test are related in the ninth chapter of the Gospel of Mark, and the men were mistaken by the disciples for Moses and Elias. They were, in fact, two of the distinguished electricians of our planet, who had managed the translations of Manrolin, and who succeeded admirably with Jesus, a few days after his crucifixion. They were also largely instrumental in aiding him in his recovery from the catalepsy, and were the two men in shining garments mentioned in the twenty-fourth chapter of Luke. These gentlemen succeeded in producing some peculiarly brilliant electro-magnetic phenomena, in connection with Jesus, on various occasions. At the time of the so-called transfiguration, and at the baptism of Jesus by John, they succeeded in establishing the first telephonic connection between this world and Venus, and on both of these occasions the venerable Manrolin, who had returned to Venus long before, was permitted to send his voice reverberating though many million miles of space, exclaiming with all the fervor of his great paternal love and solicitude, *'This is my beloved son, in whom I am well pleased.'* It may interest you to know that Manrolin lived twenty years after Jesus reached Venus, and that the closing years of his life were enriched by his society. Jesus himself lived about seventy years in Venus after reaching society in which he was appreciated.

"So you see, my dear Myrtle," said Loma, affectionately, as he concluded this remarkable narrative, "the occurrences you have been taught to regard as the most wonderful and miraculous in the history of the world are susceptible to a perfect solution under natural laws. I am anxious that you should receive this fact as a permanent impression, for your child can never be the teacher or philosopher we desire him to be unless you succeed in liberating him from the last vestige of belief in the supernatural. Nature is sufficient. There is nothing supernatural, and there is no need for it."

"I am thoroughly convinced of that," said Myrtle, "and I am sure my child will be free from everything which can in the least enshackle his reason. But tell me, has any one else ever attained to the degree of eminence necessary for translation, and is there any hope that my child could progress to that degree?"

"There is every hope," replied Loma, "and one of the inducements you may hold out to him is the great reward which awaits him if he proves faithful to his trust. Adam and Eve could have attained to translation if they had not permitted unholy lust to mar their prospects for further advancement. Several persons besides Jesus have attained to translation from this earth to Venus. Enoch was one, but the circumstances are not set forth with any degree of detail in the Bible. Elijah was translated as related in the second chapter of the second book of Kings, and Elisha mistook the magnetic glow of the occasion for a chariot and horses of fire. You will also see in this narrative, that the translation occurred when Elijah was nude, for his mantle fell upon Elisha, when he had no further use for it."

"Taking all of these facts into consideration," said Myrtle, "I think it is wonderfully stupid on the part of the ministers of the gospel and others who pretend to study the Bible exhaustively, that they have not recognized the fact long ago, that the higher powers which have caused the events recorded in the Bible to happen have always recognized the nude state as the only one conducive to health and happiness. If the churches would teach this truth, it would not be long before health and happiness would be the rule, and sickness and misery the exception. But how much time is wasted on useless subjects, and no real information given to the suffering and starving people."

"Exercise patience, my love," said Mrs. Bell. "All will come to pass in due time. Truth, like everything else, must have its growth, and your mission will do its part toward impelling the world toward that glorious perfection which it seems is our ultimate destiny."

Loma turned to Myrtle and Mrs. Bell and embraced them affectionately, saying,

"My treasures, you must now retire to your rooms.

and find in blissful repose for one hour, that which will strengthen memory and enable you to retain all that you have received. May all good influences be with you while you rest."

As the ladies withdrew from the conservatory, the doctor played a beautiful air of his own composition. The folding doors opened at their approach, and closed as noiselessly after them as when they entered the conservatory. Then the doctor arose, and drawing Loma's arm through his own, conducted his distinguished guest to his own bedroom.

CHAPTER IX.

AN UNEXPECTED MEETING.

"Forgiveness is a virtue born of heaven,
The highest attribute of gods and men."

When Doctor Bell and Loma retired to the bedroom of the former, the auspicious beginning of the series of impressions which Loma was commissioned to make upon Myrtle was naturally the topic of their conversation. The doctor was enthusiastic; Loma, as usual, quiet and dignified, but evidently pleased with the development of the situation.

"A better woman than your mother, my dear Edward," said Loma, affectionately and familiarly, "never lived upon this planet. I heard much of her through my preceptors, before I left Venus, but I must confess that they did not more than do her justice. We are especially fortunate in having such a person to supplement my efforts in behalf of Myrtle's offspring, for it would be impossible for any one human brain to entirely comprehend the depth and scope of what I have to impart. Now that I have in some measure realized the extent of the aid which I may confidently expect from her and you, I have no doubt of the complete success of my mission. I am, of course, anxious that my work should in no degree fall short of that of Manrolin; and when you comprehend the tremendous influences that have been brought to bear upon civilization through the teachings of Jesus, you will understand what an undertaking lies before me, when I tell you that the powers expect fully as much, or more, of the present object of our solicitude."

"It is well that the outside world does not comprehend the nature or extent of your undertaking," said the doctor, "else this house would be besieged by a curious mob, and it is probable that the chances would be about equal for you to be worshiped as an angel or crucified, or, what amounts to the same thing in these times, lynched as a criminal."

"Manrolin had to contend with the same conditions," said Loma, "and we must be sufficiently politic not to allow any untoward circumstance to happen which could possibly interfere with my purpose. Now that my most important communication has been made to Myrtle, I desire that she should have the utmost freedom, and I do not wish to weary her with long and tedious lessons. Whenever I have an impression to make of paramount importance, I will meet her in the conservatory, under similar circumstances to those of this day's interview. At other times I desire her to receive impressions of less importance, in ordinary conversation, by contact with desirable persons, and particularly by hearing conversations between us and those of good abilities who hold contrary views. By these means she will herself become very much brightened in intelligence and in the scope of her understanding. All of this will have a desirable effect upon her offspring, and I expect much of you and your mother in aiding me in carrying out those designs. In order to do this it is necessary that for part of the time I should adopt some kind of costume, and while I am very averse to burdening myself with the conventional costumes worn upon your streets, which would, in a measure, interfere with my health, as well as my comfort, I must wear something, at least when we go in public, to avoid the opposition of the vulgar and the ignorant."

"I have already considered that problem," said the doctor, "and I will endeavor to solve it to your complete satisfaction. I have already told you the views which both my mother and myself entertain upon the question of nudity. Now I have endeavored as far as possible to conform to what I consider the best conditions of health and hygiene, and so in this house, after my professional labors are over, and I have no further occasion to go out, I am in the habit of being nude as much as possible. I have, however, found, that, owing to inherited conditions, my ancestors for so many generations having violated the laws of nature in this respect, my skin is too sensitive to permit of my being entirely nude to the extent that you would probably find agreeable and safe. Moreover, I have induced some of my immediate associates to follow the same custom for the benefit of themselves, and as some of them are ladies, and all of them to a great extent afflicted with the absurd fear of being considered immodest if they appeared before persons of the opposite sex in a nude state, I have effected a compromise which has been attended with the happiest results. I have imported from China a number of the most elegant silk gowns, which, being made loosely, do not interfere with the circulation nor distort the body, and simply serve the purpose of a covering, which satisfies the vulgar notion of so-called decency, and at the same time preserves the comfort and health of the wearer. I dispense entirely with underclothing while wearing these gowns, except a suit of the lightest cotton netting, and those being changed every day, the result is approximately perfect cleanliness, and at least the most comfortable and cleanly conditions that can be established short of a complete return to natural conditions. Now I suggest that you make these costumes your habitual wear, on the street or in the carriage, and at such times as we have guests in the house who are unaccustomed to our more radical views. I will to-day place the bedroom at your disposal, which is on the opposite side of the hall from Myrtle's, from which you will have completely free access to the conservatory. On that floor you may be habitually nude, as no one will ever intrude upon your privacy who would be objectionable, as my mother and myself occupy these front rooms, as you and Myrtle will occupy those in the rear adjoining the conservatory. The only other person who will come upon this floor without my special permission is Nora, and as she owes her life to my doctrine and treatment in this very particular, you will not have occasion to consider her. You will notice that she, as well as my mother, wears only a light silk gown while in the house. Myrtle will adopt the same fashion to-day, and we will all be as comfortable and congenial as it is possible to be. In regard to yourself, I will introduce you as a distinguished physician who has spent a great deal of time in the East, and who has adopted the customs of those countries. You will be the object of some well-bred curiosity among my friends, but as I am already regarded as something of a crank, it will not be considered strange that I have such a personage in my house. In that way you will be able to enjoy all the privileges you desire, and also to meet without reserve such persons as you may desire to bring into contact with Myrtle, which I presume will only be a select few."

"Admirable, my dear Edward; admirable," exclaimed Loma. "You have exactly anticipated my wants, and, as usual, left nothing to be desired."

"Now, I will show you my resources," said the doctor, opening a large dressing case. "These robes have never been worn, and as we are about the same height, I presume these will fit you without alteration. Here are also several pairs of Chinese shoes, which are more healthful than our own. Although they treat the feet of their women shamefully, it seems their lords of creation show better sense in regard to their own. I prefer our Indian moccasins, myself, and if you should desire to wear them, here are several new pairs. I also have some sandals, which are better than our shoes, but the thongs with which they are tied on are not comfortable to me, and they impair circulation, so I seldom wear them, except in very warm weather."

"I shall be able to get along excellently with these," said Loma, as he donned one of the richest of the robes and surveyed himself in one of the mirrors, "but I cannot say that I believe with the most of your citizens, that the dress improves the appearance of a man. I certainly would not have been willing that Myrtle should have received her first impression of me while I was thus arrayed."

"It does not add to your appearance," said the doctor. "On the contrary, it hides just that much of a personality which must be seen in its entirety to be appreciated. I have often thought that Jesus must have had this subject in his mind, when he said, *'Consider the lilies of the field. They toil not, neither do they spin: And yet I say unto you, that even Solomon in all his glory was not arrayed like one of these.'* "

"You are right," said Loma, "and if you will read the next verse, you will be impressed still more with the fact, that Jesus was striving in some degree to correct this error. His own raiment was very simple, and at no time exceeded what you have so generously provided for me. He wore clothing for the same reason that I shall wear these gowns, and by so doing postponed his crucifixion, until he was ready to endure it, but he did not hesitate to declare himself, in the very words you have quoted and what follows:

" '*Wherefore, if God so clothe the grass of the field, which* to-day is, and to-morrow is cast into the oven, shall he not much more clothe you, oh ye of little faith?'"

"'Therefore take no thought, saying, What shall we eat? or, What shall we drink? or, Wherewithal shall we be clothed?

"'(For after all these things do the Gentiles seek:) for your Heavenly Father knoweth that ye have need of all these things.

"'But seek ye first the kingdom of God, and his righteousness; and all these things shall be added unto you.'

"In the light of our recent discussion, these words of Jesus are very plain," continued Loma. "In his enthusiasm, he appeals to the patriotism of the Jews, which he knew to be one of the strongest influences he could use, urging them to be different from the Gentiles. He uses the faith they had in their God also, and yet he introduced an appellation which shows how strongly he implied that all good gifts come from the eternal source of supply in older planets toward younger ones. 'Your Heavenly Father knoweth that ye have need of all these things.' He urges them to take no thought wherewithal they shall be clothed, for Nature will provide a covering. It is equally true that men should not 'take thought' to provide so many varieties of unwholesome foods and drinks. Nature supplies an abundance of natural food and drink in every climate which man should inhabit. Jesus classes all of these evils together, and in the strongest language implores his countrymen to live naturally. His climax comes in the sublime words of the last verse I have quoted. 'The kingdom of God' is the natural life, in which man lives according to the laws of the universe. When man comprehends 'his righteousness,' which is simply living according to the immutable laws of equity and justice, 'all these things,' to-wit, all the blessings of a natural life, health, wealth, beauty and happiness, will b...'

"It is wonderful," exclaimed Doctor Bell, "how priests and kings and unscrupulous politicians have distorted those sublime teachings of Jesus into a mass of contradictory rubbish, apparently designed for no purpose but the stupefaction of the human intellect and the enslavement of their devotees. I have heard those verses preached from as texts, by renowned preachers, many times, but I have never comprehended what was meant until this moment. Do you suppose, my dear Loma, that Jesus comprehended and taught the sublime doctrine of the origin of this world which you unfolded to me this morning, and that he understood the doctrine of the translation of germs, from parent stars to their children, and from them to younger generations?"

"Certainly. He not only understood it and taught it, but his disciples did also. Listen to this sublime passage from the Epistle of James, which shows the grasp he had on this subject, and that he perfectly comprehended the condition of the center of all our systems, the center of our super-solar system, which, as I explained to you this morning, is the parent of all that surrounds him, and is therefore at rest, in perpetual darkness, cold, and equilibrium, while he diffuses magnetism to all his children. The seventeenth verse of the first chapter of the General Epistle of James reads as follows:

"*'Every good gift, and every perfect gift is from above, and cometh down from the Father of lights, with whom is no variableness, neither shadow of turning.'*"

Doctor Bell dropped into a seat and regarded Loma with fixed astonishment. "And this is the Bible," he exclaimed, "which half the Christian world reads with eyes blinded by an idolatrous trust in the interpretation of stupid priests, and the other half treats with complete indifference. Why, the words you have quoted would not make sense in the light of any other explanation."

"Certainly not," said Loma. "But then, you know, the priests do not want anything to read with sense, for that would tend to educate their dupes beyond their control. However, if you will read the whole of the chapter, you will find that this superb writer was one of the free-thinkers of his period. In the twenty-fifth verse he says:

"*'But whoso looketh into the perfect law of liberty, and continueth therein, he being not a forgetful hearer, but a doer of the word, this man shall be blessed in his deed.'*

"And again, in the closing verse of this chapter, you will find a sentiment which you, my dear Edward, have most nobly exemplified, and which you may sometime have occasion to quote to Myrtle's Presbyterian uncle:

"*'Pure religion and undefiled before God and the Father*

is this, To visit the fatherless and the widows in their affliction, and to keep himself unspotted from the world.'"

"Thank you, my dear Loma. I am most happy in having deserved that compliment, and I assure you that I shall continue to live according to the noble principles that have been instilled into me from my youth by the mother I adore. Now we will appropriate of these costumes those which blend most harmoniously in color, and prepare to meet the ladies at dinner, after which I promise myself the felicity of a drive with all of you over our incomparable boulevard."

"I shall be delighted to view Chicago," said Loma, "for I have heard much of it through my instructors, as it has from the first been regarded as my field of operations."

"I presume you will find much to criticise," said the doctor, "for I imagine that your civilization is so far advanced that much that we endure with complaisance would be regarded by your citizens as intolerable."

"Perhaps so; but as my mission does not relate to municipal ordinances, but rather to the inculcation of those doctrines which will, when comprehended and taught, elevate the tastes and refine the intellectual processes of mankind, I do not expect that I will have much to say on those subjects which are daily discussed pro and con in your newspapers. For instance, the whole subject of municipal, and I may add, state and national government, is embraced in the principle of social justice, which, when once considered in the light of advanced intelligence, will lead to the abolition of every trace of your present form of government, and the overthrow of your entire social and industrial system."

"I can readily see that such a revolution must come with advanced civilization, and our best minds now concede that there is a monstrous injustice somewhere, but as yet no one has been able to formulate a plan which promises complete relief. Of course, this must be a matter of growth, like everything else, but I assure you that I await with some impatience everything which you will say in my presence, for the experiences of the last twenty-four hours have awakened me to a realizing sense of the immense importance of your mission to mankind, and of the transcendent responsibilities you have imposed upon you, as well as those which rest upon us, who have been counted worthy to be your assistants."

Just at this point the doctor was interrupted by a strain of music, proceeding from a large orchestrion in the hall below.

"That is the way my steward announces dinner. If you are ready, we will proceed to the parlor, where the ladies are awaiting us."

The doctor escorted Loma to the parlor, where they were met by Mrs. Bell and Myrtle. Both ladies were arrayed in gowns of the finest Chinese silk, somewhat different in style from those worn by the gentlemen, but made perfectly loose, and of such colors as were harmonious with each other and with the complexions of the wearers. Mrs. Bell took the arm of

Loma and led the way to the dining room, while the doctor escorted Myrtle, the orchestrion meanwhile playing a lively march.

The dining room was under the conservatory, and here also all the details reflected the refined taste of the owner. Everything was arranged with reference to comfort, hospitality, and the combination of lights and colors into one general delightful effect.

It was a happy and a merry party which sat down to the repast which was served by the doctor's steward in most approved style. Myrtle was radiant in her new-found happiness; Mrs. Bell genial and smiling in the capacity of hostess; the doctor, divided in his admiration for Myrtle, devotion to his mother and enthusiasm in behalf of Loma, while the latter was charming in his courtliness, in gallantry to the ladies, and in the wit and sparkle of his conversation. The table was beautifully decorated with flowers, and the dinner consisted of the choicest vegetables and fruits in the market, elegantly served and supplemented by a small roast, of which all partook but Loma, who excused himself on the ground that meats were not permissible to him, for reasons which he would explain at another time.

Occasional bursts of melody from the orchestrion relieved the conversation, which was itself punctuated with frequent peals of merry laughter from the quartet of friends, provoked by some sally of wit from the doctor or Loma, or some bright saying of one or the other of the accomplished and versatile ladies.

When dinner was over, the friends returned to the parlor, where conversation was resumed for a half hour. Then the ladies retired to dress for the ride, and the gentlemen repaired to their own rooms for the same purpose.

An hour later they were rolling along the famous boulevard, in the vicinity of Lincoln Park, behind the doctor's team of black beauties, in which he took especial pride. The ribbons were in the hands of Thomas Flannigan, a young Irishman whose skill in driving was only equaled by his devotion to the doctor himself. The carriage was a handsome landau, and the doctor and Myrtle occupied the seat next to that of the driver, while Mrs. Bell and Loma faced them at the rear.

The day was drawing to a close and the sun was setting behind the western hills, through a maze of Indian-summer clouds. The balmy breezes from Lake Michigan tempered the heat of the early autumn into a delightful warmth, which was grateful to the senses and invigorating to the body.

The four friends were enjoying their ride with all the exuberance and zest which comes from clear consciences and happy and congenial natures pleasantly associated. Myrtle's hand nestled confidingly into that of the doctor as she remarked:

"We are all so happy, and it seems to me that Nature herself is expressing enjoyment in its full fruition at this time of the year. Why is it that human beings, who are accounted the most intelligent beings on earth, should be so universally unhappy? Nine out of ten of the faces we meet are not cheerful."

"Human beings are not as intelligent as they believe themselves to be," replied the doctor. "In proportion to the volume of brain carried, the average individual should be able to show more than ten times the amount of intellectual energy that is actually displayed in order to compare favorably with the results attained by the best classes of animals, in their natural state. I attribute this result to our defective education, and the further fact, that mankind has not yet progressed sufficiently in the evolution of its faculties to establish that harmonious co-relation which animals, having a smaller number, and hence less complicated cerebral development, have been enabled to reach."

Just at this moment Myrtle caught his arm, saying, "Oh, Edward, look! There are my uncle and aunt, in their carriage! They will pass us in a moment. Shall I recognize them?"

"Certainly, my dear," said Mrs. Bell. "That is, if you wish to forgive them for the way they have treated you."

"Oh, I do forgive them!" exclaimed Myrtle. "In my happiness, I cannot harbor ill will toward any one. I am sure they did not know what they were doing."

As the carriage containing her relatives approached, Myrtle leaned forward and smiled and bowed most affectionately to her aunt, who was looking toward her. The woman recognized her, but without returning the salutation, turned to her husband and caught his arm.

He also turned, and recognizing Myrtle in the handsome carriage of the doctor surrounded by her friends, stared in astonishment and frowned. Then giving no further sign of recognition, they passed on. Myrtle's eyes filled with tears.

"Never mind, my dear," said the doctor, affectionately passing his arm around her waist. "I have recognized your uncle and know him well. He will doubtless call on us in a short time to continue his persecution of you, at which time we will turn him over to mother, for a lesson in religion and advanced civilization. When she finishes her instruction, he will have learned several important truths."

Mrs. Bell and Loma smiled, and Myrtle dried her eyes. Her elastic temperament soon overcame the depression caused by the slight her relatives had imposed, and the drive was finished by the entire party in the best of spirits.

CHAPTER X.

THE PHILOSOPHY OF LOVE.

"These things I command you, that ye love one another."

The life of Myrtle Burnham, after the events detailed in the preceding chapters, flowed on like the placid current of an untroubled stream. In the delightful society of her new environment, her mind expanded, and as she was no longer bound by the conventionalities of the narrow society in which she had before been placed, her growth was rapid and sure. In the exercise of her new liberties, however, she was guilty of no impropriety, and her natural self-poise always asserted itself, and the buoyancy of her temperament, and her rare gifts of intellectual accomplishments, added to the sweetness of her affectionate nature, soon endeared her beyond measure to every member of the household.

Under the wise administration of Mrs. Bell, guided by suggestions from Loma, Myrtle's time was well occupied with pleasant occupation and agreeable company. She was altogether absorbed in the exalted mission to which she had been called, and like most enthusiastic natures, would soon have exhausted her vitality, if her excellent preceptors had not compelled her to observe a wiser course. As it was, she usually devoted about two hours each morning to special instruction from Loma in the conservatory, in which delightful interviews she was generally, but not always, attended by her devoted friends. It was a part of Loma's plan, that the doctor and Mrs. Bell should also hear his instructions, as he desired that they should become thoroughly familiar with his doctrines, in order that they might be competent to act as instructors to Myrtle's offspring after he had taken his departure for Venus. Consequently they were rarely absent from his morning lessons to his protege, and the morning session in the "holy of holies," as the doctor called the conservatory, became a delightful experience to which they all looked forward daily with most pleasurable anticipations.

In addition to these pleasant sessions for instruction, much time was devoted to music. The four friends were all accomplished musicians. Mrs. Bell possessed a contralto voice of great sweetness and power; her son was considered one of the best baritones in the city, and had frequently distinguished himself in concerts given for charitable purposes, by the elite society in which he moved. Both were masters of the organ and piano, and the doctor was also an amateur violinist of considerable note. Myrtle possessed a soprano voice of surpassing compass and extraordinary quality, and it had been carefully trained by the best teachers in Chicago.

But it is impossible to describe the musical abilities

of Loma. As he had mastered the language and literature of the earth, before undertaking his great mission, so he had also mastered music. And in its performance he not only expressed the abilities of an earthly musician producing the best effects of the masters in the stage of the development of the art now known on the earth, but he added to it much of the beauty and higher expression he had learned at home. When joining with his friends in the rendition of some of the classical music in which they all delighted, he sang the tenor with the skill and expression of the best earthly performers. But at their request he frequently sang alone the melodies of his native planet. At such times his body glowed with strong emanations of magnetism and his voice assumed a quality unknown to earth. His hearers became enraptured to complete ecstasy, and Myrtle frequently lost consciousness of everything but the heavenly melody which thrilled her whole being.

At other times she surrendered herself entirely to the pleasures of social intercourse. Toward both Loma and the doctor she became conscious of the most devoted emotions of love, arising within her own nature and craving a free expression. She regarded them both as representatives of the highest types of manhood, and whenever they approached her, she felt that each was impelled by the highest motives of love for her, and consideration, devotion and purity of intention. In a short time she learned to treat both of them and Mrs. Bell with the most hearty expressions and demonstrations of affection, which were always warmly reciprocated.

On one occasion, when she met Loma in the conservatory, she threw herself into his embrace with more than usual fervor. She imprinted several ardent kisses on his lips, and as he sat down beside her on a divan and affectionately encircled her waist with his arm, she inquired:

"Tell me why I love to kiss you and Edward so much. I never kissed any man but Albert until I kissed you, and I was always told that it was wrong. But now I feel and know that it is right, and moreover my nature seems to crave these expressions of love from those whom I feel truly love me."

"In the first place," answered Loma, "you are now for the first time really living in a natural way. Love is natural, and the unfortunate woman who is not surrounded by those whom she can unreservedly trust and upon whom she can freely express her affection is robbed of the sweetest and best food which nature provides for growth and development. It is just as natural for a woman at your age to crave the loving caresses of pure and affectionate men as it is for her to breathe and to crave the pure air of heaven. You are fortunate in possessing two loving friends, whom you can implicitly trust, with whom you may freely indulge your natural desire. It would be just so much better, if, instead of two, you had twenty, for love is a thing susceptible to growth, and the more you love, the stronger and sweeter it becomes. It is necessary, however, for you to discriminate, for it would not be wise to lavish your affection on unworthy objects, and you would be contaminated by their impure association. With the knowledge which I shall impart to you, however, you will be perfectly safe, for you will learn to discriminate with intelligence. Your son will also possess this power, and wherever he goes, he will be surrounded by pure and virtuous women, who will sustain him with their affection and caresses as Jesus was sustained by the delightful friendships which he had with Mary and Martha, and the many unfortunate women whom he rescued from the degradation of their time. There is no question, from the accounts given of Jesus in the Bible, without referring to other sources of authority, that he continually surrounded himself with good women, and that his affections were gratified by them in the highest degree.

"There is another reason, however, why you are more than usually affectionate at this time," continued Loma, while his voice thrilled with peculiar tenderness, "and that is, that at just this stage of your pregnancy, your child is forming the rudiments of those portions of his brain which preside over the affections and give him the capacity to have affection himself. At this time you have an unusual craving for the expressions of love, and if you were not gratified, your child would come into this world without the ability to develop those energies which give the sweetest and most attractive traits of human character. It is perfectly easy to distinguish between the offspring of loving and much-loved mothers and those who have had but little desire and satisfaction of these faculties. Those who love much, and are satisfied by the loving expression of friends and consorts, develop the posterior portion of their brain, and the head becomes symmetrical, and those features of the face, and, in fact, of the whole body, which are in sympathy with and controlled by that portion of the brain, become much more harmonious and beautiful. While the unfortunate offspring of mothers who do not call out these demonstrations, by a lack of affection in themselves, or who are deprived of a natural satisfaction by the coldness and indifference of those who surround them, are uniformly lacking in the essential elements of manhood and womanhood. Their heads are badly formed, especially in the occipital region, and every feature of their unfortunate bodies shares the misfortune and reflects deformity in just the measure that these conditions of growth have been denied. The eyes are small and lack luster; the chin is small and retreating, and even the walk is ungraceful, and the voice disagreeable in its tone.

"So, my sweet girl, whenever you feel the desire to give expression to your feelings in these directions, remember that we love you, and that it is our highest privilege to minister to you the gratification which will not only cause you to thrill with happiness, but will endow your child with the highest social graces, and enable him to bless untold thousands who may come within the radiance of his sublime magnetism."

As a response to this fraternal declaration, Myrtle bestowed another rapturous kiss upon Loma's lips, and Doctor Bell happening to enter the conservatory at this moment, she ran to him and greeted him with corresponding ardor. The doctor placed his arm around her, and led her back to the divan, where, seated between himself and Loma, she surrendered herself to the full measure of their warm and magnetic influences.

"Tell me," she exclaimed, as she entwined her arms around her friends, and rested her golden head upon the doctor's shoulder, "why is it that humanity has never recognized the benefits to be derived from such loving associations as we have, and why is it so universally considered to be wrong? Now, my teachings in the past have been very meager upon all of these subjects; in fact, I was often reproved for even asking questions on those topics, but the impression I received generally was, that it was wrong to let any one kiss me, and that even in marriage some things would be done which were mysterious and dark, and which in that state might be permissible, but were even then to be covered with secrecy. I know that once or twice my aunt went to visit some of her lady friends who were said to be 'in a delicate condition,' and when I asked what that meant I was reproved, and told to wait until I was married, and then I would find out. I never could understand why, if marriage was the most blessed state in existence, there should be such an unwillingness to let us know anything about it. Moreover, when I went to church, I heard the preacher read a great deal from the Bible commanding the people to love one another. But it seemed to me that the moment any one tried to carry the precept into practice, a great scandal arose. If a married man or woman even expresses a great deal of love for any one of the opposite sex, by words or writings, it is considered proof that something is wrong. I remember that one of our Sunday school superintendents was compelled to resign, because a letter which he wrote to a married lady, who was one of his teachers, contained the words, 'I love you dearly, and I believe that you are the best woman I ever met. Your kisses are the sweetest in the world.' Her husband found the letter and he made a commotion, and the lady was disgraced and lost her position in society, and the man resigned the superintendence of the Sunday school and left the church. Now, if the Bible is right, and it says 'Love one another,' I do not see why this should have happened. Another thing I wish you would explain. We are expected to love our husbands, and yet it is the prevailing doctrine that a young lady should not allow any gentleman to kiss her, and even after she is engaged, she is urged not to allow her fiancé to take any liberties with her, as it is called. The most that is considered consistent with prudence is to allow him a very formal kiss once in a while. I did not see any good sense in this, and as no one ever gave me a satisfactory reason, but only a warning command which seemed to be contradictory to the impulses of my nature, I violated it with Albert. Now I would like to know, if a young woman is to be thus restricted, how she can ever find out whether she really loves a man or not. It seems to me that love is something which comes to us by experience, and that the closest possible intimacy is necessary to enable any one to decide, whether it is possible to love the object in view."

"You have stated the case with the ability of a first-class lawyer, my dear," exclaimed the doctor. "Now, let us hear what Loma's answer will be."

Loma was thoughtful for a moment, and then began to answer with earnestness and gravity.

"The trouble is, that love is not as yet understood upon this planet. Your poets sing of it, your teachers and preachers prate concerning it, but your citizens have not as yet comprehended what it is. To understand love it is necessary to study the human constitution. When we do this intelligently, we find that man has a large number of mental faculties, each one of which is devoted to the acquisition of a different kind of sensation and knowledge. It is the possession of all of these faculties in a good degree of condition and capacity which distinguishes a bright and intelligent man from the idiot. It is the possession of a larger number of these faculties and a higher degree of educability which is the principal distinction between man and the animals by which he is surrounded. Some animals seem to have only a single faculty, others have more, but man seems to have more than twice as many as any animal with which we are familiar. Our best mental philosophers now estimate the number of faculties possessed by man as sixty-four, and we have, correspondingly, sixty-four departments of knowledge obtainable by man. Each mental faculty possesses four distinct powers, to wit, attraction, repulsion, satisfaction, and memory. Each mental faculty is derived from the action of an organ in the brain corresponding to it. You will also understand that the mental powers of individuals will vary according to the growth and development of the brain and the consequent size and physiological condition of those organs. Thus one man has more musical talent than another, because those organs which relate to music are larger and in better condition in his brain than they are in the brain of his less fortunately endowed brother. As a consequence, he will be more strongly attracted toward good music, more powerfully repelled from discord, will derive greater satisfaction from a satisfactory performance, and will remember more about it. As you are all musicians, you, of course, understand this.

"I have chosen music as the basis of my illustration, because it is one of the departments of knowledge which have been brought to a high degree of perfection on this planet, and is so universal that it will be more readily understood. Now, the ability of a man to love music, and to delight his friends with his performances, depends, first, upon his possession of the musical faculties; second, upon his education in the art; third, upon his possession of an excellent instrument of expression; fourth, upon his willingness to play, and lastly, upon the appreciation of his audience. It is not necessary for me to enlarge upon the fact, that his audience must in some degree be as cultured as himself, in order that the appreciation may be complete, and that the highest degree of mutual pleasure may be experienced.

"What I have stated as being true of music applies with equal force to every faculty of man, and to every department of knowledge which is represented by a faculty. In order to have a complete man, it is necessary that every faculty should be insured by the creation of a complete brain. This can be done by complying with the laws of reproduction. It is only as man violates these laws that he is punished with offspring which are fragmentary, and so far idiotic. When a complete brain is produced, it is then necessary that a complete education should follow. The education of the citizens of this planet, at present, is confined to less than half of the actual capacity of the brain, and this is so faultily administered that your students get but little benefit, and your industrial system is so unjust that the great majority of your children are entirely neglected. Assuming, however, that reform in education is established, and that your citizens are completely educated, it is still necessary that each one should have the largest opportunity for the exercise of his faculties, by being provided with instruments and occupation, and that he should have the liberty to enjoy his powers. When these conditions are established you will have the highest expressions of goodness in all departments of human effort, and the appreciation of the efforts of each individual by his fellows will follow as a matter of course.

"It follows, necessarily, that while there will always be diversity of human character, there will also be diversity of talent, and diversity in the expression of the various forms of love of which man is capable. One individual will love music above all other occupations, another will love architecture, a third may devote himself to mathematics, and so on through the whole catalogue. While this is true, there is no reason why all persons should not be required to reach that degree of perfection in the social graces which will make them fit objects for association and affection.

"I will now proceed to answer Myrtle's questions, by saying, that those faculties which are concerned in the expression of all forms of personal attachment, are entirely neglected in the curriculum of education, as at present administered on this planet. It is true, that man has, as prime faculties of his mental powers, the faculties which enable him to take cognizance of gender and the act of reproduction, of attachment for offspring, animals and parents, of friendship for man and woman, independent of sexual association, and also the love of home and the associations of patriotism. The natural growth and education of those powers would cause him to experience the largest possible happiness to himself, and the highest ministration of gratification to others. Instead of obtaining this development, however, the selfishness of mankind has produced a distortion of these impulses, into the most barbarous sentiments, until the natural language of these faculties has been almost entirely obliterated, and actions which are, in fact, the most outrageous of crimes have come to be considered the exemplification of the virtues.

"The fundamental error was the chaining of the reproductive sense of gender by the institution of polygamous marriage. As long as men and women were free to choose their sexual affinities, the race improved by the operation of the law of natural selection. When marriage was given enforcement by law, woman was enslaved, and in a few generations it became an easy matter to enslave her sons. Consequently, we find in an early period of the Jewish civilization, from which the present Christian stage is descended, that a tyrant like Solomon could revel in debauchery with three hundred concubines and seven hundred wives, while his slaves toiled at the building of the temple for his glorification, without any wives at all, and hundreds were even deprived of the means of reproduction by mutilation, as eunuchs.

"The natural sense of justice in man has asserted itself, until in the later development of civilization the practice of emasculating men has been discontinued, and all men are free to have one wife, provided they are able to persuade one to submit to the relationship. The idea of the dominion of man over the woman is still the central one, however, in the Christian form of civilization, and the barbarous form of marriage is still practiced, with all of its humiliating and degrading implications. It is to the infinite credit of your humanity, that it has outgrown the ceremony, and that it is in a large measure only a mere formality, which society takes for granted will only be considered subject to the modifications which good sense and the enlarged liberties of mankind have imperatively demanded. However, as long as the present form of matrimonial obligation is practiced among you, it will remain as a partial barrier to the development of correct sexual relations and good morals, because it continually educates the minds of the people to false conceptions of duties and privileges, and engenders jealousy, promotes selfishness, creates wrong desires, and, worst of all, prevents the development of love.

"The earlier forms of marriage required only the expression of allegiance and devotion on the part of the wife to the husband. She became his slave and surrendered all of her liberties to him, hence the pledge of the woman, to love, honor and obey her tyrant, destroyed in her the ability to discriminate as to what was lovable, honorable or capable of being obeyed without sacrificing her own honor. As an abject slave she was not supposed to consider these things. It was sufficient for her that her lord and master commanded. She obeyed. It is easy to see how, in this condition of things, the selfishness of her master soon dictated to her that she must not under any circumstances love, honor or obey any one but himself. Here we have the origin of the sentiment that it is wrong for a woman to allow herself to love any man but her husband. The enslavement of woman naturally led to another disastrous consequence. She ceased to become an object of love to man, except as she ministered to his carnal desires. The idea of love became dissociated from every relationship but the sexual. Considered solely as the vehicle for the satisfaction of the inflamed and unnatural desires of man, the desires having become inflamed and unnatural through the abuse which followed the enslavement of woman, she was, of course, degraded in his eyes, and was considered unworthy of education, or participation in any of the higher walks of life.

"To the infinite credit of your manhood, it is true, that gradually, though slowly and painfully, it has struggled from beneath the burden of these errors, until at this time, in the more enlightened communities, the proposition to advance woman to full and complete equality with man is being seriously considered, and will eventually occur. One by one her privileges have been restored to her, until her condition is infinitely more tolerable than in the past, but complete results will not be attained until the last barrier is removed, and she is recognized as the companion, and not as the slave of man. She will then become the mother of a generation of freemen, and the advance of civilization will be rapid.

"The first step in the line of reform must be the complete emancipation of woman. As soon as this is accomplished, and she receives the benefit of her liberties, so that she can think and act with freedom, she will escape from the present impression that she is merely the vehicle of man's passions. She will cease to regard her possession by a man as essential to her existence, and she will act independently. The next step will be the industrial equality of woman, and she will demand and obtain the same wages as man. Being by this fact placed in possession of the mastery of her own person, she will yield it only on the dictates of love. The best men will then be able to obtain sexual favors, regardless of money, while those who are nonattractive, vicious or depraved will be compelled to go without altogether. In the meantime, the advancement of woman and the reorganization of the industrial system will have decreased prostitution to a minimum, and with the generation of better men and women and the advancement of education as to the proper use of the sexual functions, it will eventually disappear, and there will exist on this planet a greatly improved type of humanity.

"When humanity reaches this stage of development, marriage will be regarded as it is in Venus, as a barbarous custom of savage nations, as polygamy is already. Men and women will then begin to study love as a science, as you now study music. The act of reproduction will not be considered as it is now, the only basis of association between a man and a woman. Neither man nor woman will be under a pledge to love one person to the exclusion of all others, because the fact will be generally recognized, that such a pledge is destructive of morals, and is practically the suicide of the love faculties. Such a pledge will then be regarded as you would now regard the pledge of a musician to play only one tune. Whenever civilization advances beyond the selfishness of man, the principle will be recognized that the largest growth and the grandest expression of human life is in universal love.

"When Jesus commanded his followers to love one another, he meant exactly what he said. It is not only the right but the duty of every sane man and woman to cultivate and express love for as many individuals as possible. The larger the number of lovers, the richer becomes the life. This does not mean promiscuous love, nor promiscuous sexual association, but it does mean the largest possible freedom in social intercourse. It means that if a woman loves a man, or a man loves a woman, that they should have the privilege of meeting as often as they please, where and when they please, and expressing their love for each other in any language they choose, whether it be spoken, written or expressed in kisses, caresses, or merely friendly greetings. This right is inalienable, according to all dictates of sound public policy, and any contract which deprives a man or woman of this liberty is void. Under your present conditions, if a man and woman meet each other freely, or a married man or woman is seen to any great extent with some other person of the other sex, you assume that they have met for sexual intercourse, and a scandal is the result. This is greatly augmented if there is the slightest evidence that they have kissed or caressed each other. All of this grows out of the degraded conception of love which has been forced on the human mind by the fact that man has been trained to regard woman as solely an object for the expression of sexual passion, and your men of the present generation cannot understand any other relationship.

"As soon as woman escapes from the bondage of marriage, she will regulate this matter herself. She will demand that men recognize the purity of her motives, and she will teach them that if they wish to find favor in her eyes, they must be capable of enjoying all the other pleasures of life with her, without associating her with the gratification of mere passion. When men and women learn to associate on this plane the espionage of woman will cease. As it is now, a man is suspicious of his associate, because his own conscience tells him in many cases that if she is not unfaithful to her marriage vow, it is not because she has not ample provocation. Men establish an espionage upon women, because they are suspicious and selfish. Women assist in this espionage with incredible zeal, because they are jealous and selfish, and every woman who can be crowded off the social stage makes that much more room for the degraded slaves who do the spying and gossiping. When this slavery and degradation is abolished with marriage, and men and women associate upon an equal plane, the artificial crimes of adultery and fornication will disappear, friendship and love will be cultivated, better men and women will appear, and harmony will exist where discord now prevails."

CHAPTER XI.

A LESSON IN ETHICS.

"And Jesus said unto her, Neither do I condemn thee; go and sin no more."

A few days after the recognition by Myrtle of her relatives on the boulevard, as the friends were about to repair to the conservatory for the morning session of instruction, a visitor was announced in the parlor, and Nora presented to Mrs. Bell a card salver bearing a card upon which was engraved "Mr. J. C. McDonald." As Mrs. Bell read the name aloud, Myrtle exclaimed, "That is my uncle!"

"Sure enough!" said the doctor. "Well, as I suggested before, we will have mother attend to him, while Loma entertains us in the music room. When you have finished his instruction, mother, you will find us in the conservatory eagerly awaiting to hear the result of the interview."

So saying, the doctor led Myrtle to the conservatory, where Loma awaited them, while Mrs. Bell proceeded to the parlor to meet her visitor. She found a tall, dark-complexioned man, of an intellectual but somewhat melancholy appearance, whom she at once recognized as the gentleman she had seen in the carriage on the boulevard.

The formal greetings over, Mrs. Bell requested her visitor to be seated. He complied, and with evident embarrassment began the conversation.

"Mrs. Bell, I have come to perform a very disagreeable duty, but one which I am compelled to face in the discharge of my obligations as a Christian and a member of society, and one which, however painful it may be to both of us, you will doubtless thank me for not delaying."

"Indeed, sir, you astonish me. I hope it may not be as painful as you anticipate."

"Would to God, madam, that it were not. But as it is always painful to recognize depravity in any of our fellow creatures, it becomes doubly so when we find it in our own household and in the hearts of those we have learned to love and from whom we have reason to expect better things. To come directly to the point, however, madam, I have learned recently that you have in your house, and, as I am informed, as your guest, a young woman by the name of Myrtle Burnham. Is this true?"

"It is true. She is my guest, and I am sure a sweeter and more lovely associate could not exist. Are you interested in her?"

"It grieves me beyond measure, madam, to destroy the conception you have of the character of this person. It is my Christian duty to inform you that she is utterly depraved, an outcast and a reproach to her sex, and that, as you value your own good name, it is imperatively necessary that you should expel her at once from your house."

"Impossible! My dear sir, we regard Myrtle as the embodiment of everything which is good. By what right do you bring these accusations against her? I beg you to be careful what you say, for remember it is easier to accuse than it is to prove guilt."

"Alas! madam, the proof is only too easily obtainable. We have her own confession and her own condition to substantiate everything I say. This person is, or rather was, my own niece, and until a few days ago resided at my house, where she had every inducement to lead a pure, virtuous and upright life. I say she was my niece, for since the discovery of her dishonor, she has been dead to us. She has had all the advantages of the church, the Sabbath school and a Christian home, and the purest and best of associations. She was engaged to be married to a young man who was considered a most eligible and wealthy connection, and who was a perfect gentleman. Such, however, was the depravity of this girl, that she allowed herself to be seduced by her fiancé, and what is still worse, she became pregnant, and is now plainly in that condition. The young man paid the penalty of his sin by being killed in an accident to a cable car in the La Salle street tunnel several weeks ago, which circumstance we are obliged to confess a direct visitation of Providence. A few days ago this girl confessed to my wife that she had been guilty of the worst of crimes, with her intended, and when my wife informed her of her condition she did not have sufficient sense of shame to even profess remorse. We, of course, expelled her from our home, and we heard no more of her until my wife recognized her in your carriage on the boulevard a few days ago. We were at first dumfounded, but later inquiry developed the fact that she was here as your guest. I do not know by what measure of deceit she has succeeded in imposing herself upon you as a respectable person, but I presume that this explanation, for which I hold myself responsible, will enable you to see your way clear to her immediate expulsion."

"The circumstances of her admission to my house are simply these," said Mrs. Bell, quietly. "After being driven from your home, she wandered three days and two nights upon the street, when, in her misery and despair, she attempted suicide by throwing herself into Lake Michigan from the pier at the foot of Van Buren street. She was rescued by a gentleman who is also our guest, and by him and my son brought to this house, where she has since remained."

"How unfortunate," groaned the visitor. "Would to God, madam, she had succeeded in her attempt, for living, she can only be a source of misery to herself and a disgrace to those who are unfortunately associated with her. My wife has been almost crazy with grief since this calamity, for our position in society is among the best, and my wife is president of the missionary society of one of our leading churches, and you know how seriously such an occurrence affects one's social standing."

"I infer from your remarks, sir, that your wife's grief and your own discomfiture arise mainly from the fear of disaster to your social position. You do not seem to have any consideration or sympathy for the unfortunate girl."

"Why, surely, madam, you would not expect me to show sympathy toward a depraved and unchaste person, where the honor and social standing of my family are concerned," exclaimed Mr. McDonald, warmly.

"I expect you to show justice, at least," said Mrs. Bell. "You have not proved, as yet, that Myrtle Burnham is either depraved or unchaste. Before I reach a decision in this case I desire to know all the circumstances, that I may act intelligently, and place the blame, if there is any, where it rightfully belongs."

"Madam, I fail to understand you. Have I not told you that this young woman has been seduced, that she is even now pregnant, and that she has confessed these circumstances to my wife. As a respectable, Christian woman, what more can you demand?"

"I am not a Christian," said Mrs. Bell, with dignity, "but I will discuss this matter with you from a Christian standpoint, if you please. As far as you have proceeded with your statement, you have only brought two facts in evidence, namely, that she is a young unmarried woman, and that she is now pregnant. Have you any other evidences of her depravity?"

"I do not see that more could be required."

"I differ with you. Mary, the mother of Jesus, was in precisely the same condition at one time, yet you consider her the most blessed of women, and worship the fruit of her womb as your God. You surely would not claim that a depraved mother could bring forth such a son as Jesus."

"But, my dear Mrs. Bell, that was different."

"In what respect, pray?"

"Why, he was God."

"Very well. If he was God and was conceived in that way, then if there is any distinction between being conceived in or out of wedlock, it is more godlike to be illegitimate than it is to be legitimate. If you regard him simply as a man, then the only criterion by which we may judge is his character and works. But if he was really God, by coming into the world in that way he manifested in the clearest manner his disapproval of the barbarous custom of marriage, which then, as now, was simply the badge of the enslavement of woman. I find that he still further exemplified his disapproval of marriage by remaining single himself."

"Madam, you astonish me. You surely do not mean to claim that the Son of God approved of adultery and fornication."

"Certainly not. But there is a vast difference between adultery and fornication and the expression of pure love, in a natural way. When you exalt marriage as the only test of purity, you are making a stupendous mistake. There is as much prostitution in marriage as there is out of it. Love existed in the human constitution before marriage laws or customs, and it will survive after they have perished."

"Do you not believe that marriage is a divine institution, and that fornication and adultery are the worst possible crimes?"

"By no means. Marriage is simply the invention of priests, kings and politicians, used for purely political purposes. Applying the tests of the highest Christian standards, the actions of Jesus and his blessed mother, I find that both condemned the custom by their actions, and Jesus by his express words refused to condemn a woman taken in adultery. I do not find that he ever approved the custom by any action or word. I honor his judgment, and from the standpoint of one who is not a Christian there are far worse crimes than either adultery or fornication, and I do not hestitate to tell you that one of them consists in turning a defenseless girl from a home, where she has a right to protection, out upon the street without resources, where she is exposed to every temptation that can beset mind or body, and likely to fall into the most horrible evils that exist. There are conditions that are worse than death, and to expose a young, innocent, and defenseless girl to them is worse than murder."

Mrs. Bell's visitor regarded her in silent astonishment. He sat nervously clasping his hands and biting his lips, which were dry and colorless.

"Now, Mr. McDonald, we may as well come to the vital point in this matter at once. I believe that you are a man of good impulses, and naturally upright and kind, but you are laboring under a horrible mistake, and you have committed an act of the greatest inhumanity, while you believed you were doing your duty. I do not blame you, but I do hold in utter contempt and detestation the execrable philosophy which has blinded you to the dictates of affection and justice. Now, sir, if I am correctly informed, you became guardian for Myrtle when she was ten years of age, and since the death of her mother, which occurred at that time, you have directed her education, her father having died seventeen years ago."

"That is true."

"Now, will you please inform me to what extent Myrtle has been instructed in the details of physiology, especially that part which relates to the sexual nature and the processes of reproduction?"

"Why, madam, I do not consider that the topics you mention are fit subjects for a young and unmarried female to study at all. We never mentioned them in her presence, much less made them a part of her education."

"Just so. And yet you exposed her to the society of a young and amorous man, where she was sure to be confronted with the temptation to indulge in sexual intercourse, without the slightest information or knowledge as to its nature and consequences. You required her to continue chaste, when you never gave her an opportunity to know the difference between chastity and unchastity, or in what unchastity consisted. Without the slightest preparation for the ordeal, you exposed her to conditions which have, in all ages, proven too much for the established principles of the wisest and best of men, and because she ignorantly transgressed a social custom which she had no opportunity to understand, you consider her vicious and depraved. Do you think this accords with justice or reason?"

The visitor was silent, but his face changed color and he was evidently very much disturbed. Mrs. Bell paused a moment to give him time to think, and then resumed:

"There is another aspect in which we ought to consider this question. Suppose we admit, for the sake of argument, that Myrtle had willfully sinned. What should we do with a sinner? What did Jesus say we should do? You said that you came here to discharge your duty as a Christian. Can you find the place in the Bible where Jesus ever persecuted any one? Did he follow the woman who was taken in adultery to see that she did not associate with decent people, and to warn them against her? Nay, do we not find, on the contrary that he gave even his own loving companionship to the Magdalen, out of whom he had cast seven devils? Suppose that Jesus had been present at your house when you expelled this dear girl and sent her forth from your home to wander on the streets of Chicago, do you really think he would have approved of your action?"

Mr. McDonald's lips trembled while he muttered the words, "But Jesus was different."

"Yes, Mr. McDonald, he *was* different from the average Christian of to-day. If he had come into your Bible class last Sunday, you would have regarded him as a tramp. If he had brought with him the women he associated with when he was on earth, you would have sent for the patrol wagon. But your religion professes to encourage you to follow him and be like him. My religion permits me to admire him and imitate his actions as near as I can in my humble way. I do not expect to meet him at the judgment seat, but you profess that you do. Assuming that you are right, what are you going to say when he asks you what you have done '*unto the least of these*,' the girl who was intrusted to your education and protection?"

Mr. McDonald groaned. He wiped his eyes with his handkerchief and said nothing. The philanthropist continued:

"I read in your Bible this definition of true religion:

"'*Pure religion and undefiled before God and the Father is this; to visit the widows and the fatherless in their affliction, and to keep himself unspotted from the world.*'

"Now, my dear brother, the very worst that can be said of Myrtle when your wife discovered her condition last week, is, that she was in affliction. She had done no willful wrong, for she knew nothing of the consequences of her act, and her ignorance was the direct result of education. She was the fatherless and in affliction. How did you visit her? What account can you render of your actions toward her at the Christian day of judgment? Are you without sin yourself in this direction? Are you able to cast the first stone at an unchaste woman, admitting that she is willfully guilty of fornication?"

Mr. McDonald could stand no more. He rose abruptly and took his leave, saying:

"Madam, I do not understand this. Perhaps I have done wrong. I must have time to think. I will call again."

He went out wiping his eyes and pulling his hat down over them, and as Mrs. Bell closed the door she noticed that his steps were unsteady as he walked away from the house.

Mrs. Bell returned to the conservatory, where Myrtle, Loma and the doctor listened eagerly to her report of the conversation. Myrtle was much affected.

"Oh, I wish they would learn the truth, and let me love them," she exclaimed. "They were always good and kind to me, until this happened, and I would be perfectly happy if they would only see their mistake and trust me as they did before. Of course I do not wish to return to their home, for I am much happier here, but it would relieve my mind to know that there was no ill will between us. In my present surroundings I cannot bear to think of any enmity or harshness toward any one, and I do not want it expressed toward me."

"You are rapidly developing the Christ spirit, beloved," said Loma, as he embraced her and imprinted a kiss upon her forehead. "I hope that your wishes may be gratified, and from what our dear mother here tells us, I think we may confidently hope that your uncle may soon be converted. Let us celebrate her victory with a song."

The friends repaired to the music room, and a moment later the perfumed air vibrated with the harmonious blending of human voices in an expression of triumphant love.

CHAPTER XII.

RECONCILIATION.

"For if ye forgive men their trespasses, your heavenly Father will also forgive you."

While Loma was thus engaged in implanting in the mind of Myrtle the germs of the great truths which her offspring was destined to teach to the world, his devoted assistants were no less conscientious in the performance of their duties in preparing her for the physical ordeal through which she was about to pass. Both the doctor and his mother were enthusiastic students of gynæcology and had for years made a specialty of conditions favorable to the best results in childbirth. Now that a lively personal interest was joined to professional pride, in the case in hand, they made elaborate arrangements to procure for Myrtle every influence which would secure her comfort, safety and happiness, as well as conduce to the perfection of her offspring. In all of this they were warmly assisted by Loma, who brought to their aid not only the immense stock of new ideas he had imported from his native planet but also the inventive genius and artistic talent of his superb intelligence.

Her diet was the first consideration. Mrs. Bell explained to her that now that the bones of her child were beginning to form, it was necessary that she should avoid all such food as would result in hardening them to such a degree as would render her parturition painful. She was instructed that it was necessary that her own bones should be subjected to a softening process, in order that they might be rendered pliable and thus decrease the resistance to the passage of the child from the internal cavity, through the opening of the pelvis. She was assured that if these precautions were carried out, she would not only pass through the critical experience of labor with little, if any, pain but that her offspring would be greatly protected, and that by a proper course of diet after birth, his bones would be rendered sufficiently strong before he would have any occasion to support himself upon them, and that her own system would quickly recover its necessary rigidity. Myrtle submitted to all of these arrangements with a ready compliance, so perfectly did she repose confidence in the skill and superior wisdom of her devoted friends.

Accordingly, all the water that she drank was carefully distilled to remove the lime and other earthy material held in solution, and all articles of food containing the same principles were carefully excluded. She was provided with an abundance of the best fruit on the market, and several barrels of apples were secured for her especial benefit. These she ate, either raw or cooked, as she desired, and grapes, tomatoes and melons, were freely provided. A limited quantity of lemons and oranges were added to this, but as the doctor believed and Loma confirmed, it was not considered best to indulge in any great degree in fruits that were not indigenous to the climate of her residence. These were supplemented with onions and green vegetables, with a limited quantity of rice, sago, tapioca, figs and raisins. Potatoes were excluded, and turnips, beets and such vegetables as consisted of roots were not favored. The general principle adopted in this diet was, that whatever grew above the ground, as the fruit of the plant, was acceptable, while roots and tubers were not. The single exception to this was onions, and as these were only used as a relish in small quantities, and were valuable for their antiscorbutic qualities, they were considered desirable. Pure honey, molasses, sugar, butter, oils and vinegar were allowed in such quantities as she desired, but all bone-hardening and muscle-producing foods were rigorously excluded. Hence she used no bread, either of corn or wheat, and very little meat of any kind. An occasional indulgence was permitted in meat, but when used it was usually fat, and of limited quantity. On the subject of meat eating, Loma expressed himself as follows:

"In the present stage of your civilization, the consumption of meat is a necessity to many of your citizens. Meat is nourishing and stimulating, and incites the consumer to the display of great energy, and often to cruelty. Meat-eating nations are usually cruel and selfish, and as long as you have to contend with cruel and selfish conditions, your citizens will need the stimulating effect of a meat diet. But when you reach the perfect form of civilization which exists in Venus, the consumption of all animal food will cease. Consequently, for myself, I desire to follow an exclusively vegetable and fruit regimen, but I do not consider that you have reached the stage when you can safely do without meat."

Myrtle was kept in a state of absolute cleanliness by frequent baths in tepid water, and occasional sponge baths in cold water, for which services the trained skill of Nora was enlisted. The exposure of her body in the equable temperature of the conservatory, and the action of the sunlight on her skin, produced a peculiar strengthening and beautifying effect, and at the end of the second month of her stay at the residence of Doctor Bell, she was more beautiful than at first.

During all of this time she had been subject to a thorough but not fatiguing course of gymnastics. Mrs. Bell was an enthusiastic teacher of physical culture and had a large class of young people whom she had personally instructed, and who were enthusiastic converts to all of her physiological and social theories. Myrtle was introduced to these young people, and immediately became a general favorite. Among these liberal minded and thoroughly enlightened people, her condition, instead of being regarded as a disgrace, entitled her at once to generous love and consideration. Social parties and clubs were organized in her honor, and she was constantly made to feel that she was an honored guest. Dancing parties occurred at least twice a week, and while she indulged in this exercise with moderation, she was permitted to have a full and complete enjoyment of her strength, and was not encouraged to consider herself an invalid merely because she was pregnant.

In this way the time passed agreeably, and she was sufficiently employed at all times to obtain the full use of all her faculties without becoming fatigued, and in all of her social engagements she was carefully guarded against the possibility of an unfortunate accident. She enjoyed a ride in the carriage every pleasant day, with one or more members of the family, and took frequent walks through the parks and streets, accompanied by the doctor or Loma, all of which she enjoyed with all the enthusiasm of her elastic temperament.

Under the careful tuition of Loma, she was daily engaged in those forms of physical and mental culture which were considered desirable, having reference to the formation of the brain of her offspring. Loma had explained, that there were three distinct stages of educational influences, the conditions surrounding the mother at the time of her impregnation, the impressions received by her during gestation, and the training imparted after birth. The conditions surrounding her at the time of her impregnation had been most favorable, owing to the fact that she had conceived her child at a time when her whole system was glowing with a pure expression of love for its father. The first three months had been passed by her in great activity of mind and body, which was most favorable for the operation of the second class of educational influences, to wit, the impressions received by the mother during pregnancy. Loma explained that, during this period, those organs of the brain which were occupied with the faculties of observation, the objective intellect, physical energy and physical love, were being rudimentarily developed, and by the fact that the mother during these months was kept very active in the expressions of the same faculties, they would be strengthened and developed in the child. By this means she also escaped all of the distressing symptoms of "morning sickness." Mrs. Bell had always believed and taught her patients, that this unpleasant symptom of pregnancy was simply the revenge of nature for the general inactivity which was practiced by most ladies as soon as they discovered themselves to be pregnant, and often induced by the confirmed indolent habits of the patient. She was glad to find her doctrine corroborated by Loma, and as Myrtle yielded to the advice of her friends, and performed heartily all of the exercises and duties assigned to her, which she realized to be for the welfare of herself and her child, the results were highly satisfactory. It was arranged that the general activity of her bodily exercise should be gradually reduced during the fourth and fifth month, and that her energy should be directed more toward intellectual and constructive employment, involving the subjective intellect, the cultivation of prudence, the love of the beautiful and the sublime, and the extension of her social pleasures. This arrangement corresponded with the second period of brain formation, and involved the faculties that would be represented in those organs of the brain that are located in the middle portion. The last three months of her pregnancy were to be devoted to the higher forms of logical and subjective reasoning, the cultivation of sympathy and dignity, and special exercises in benevolence, mirthfulness, hope, faith and reverence. During this time she was also to be impressed with the firmness and justice of the eternal truths she had received from Loma, and the dignity and importance of her exalted office, with the full and adequate realization of the renown which must inevitably accompany it.

As she was now passing through the stage when impressions of beauty were desirable, the doctor arranged that every morning, as soon as she awakened, her eyes should be feasted with some object of exquisite perfection. For that purpose he ransacked the art stores and the collections of his friends, and provided a new object of beauty at least twice a week. Sometimes it was a beautiful painting, at other times a choice piece of statuary, and as often some lovely floral design in which colors were blended in perfect harmony. These were taken into Myrtle's room and covered with a beautiful curtain, just at the foot of her bed. While she was asleep, the curtain was removed and the lights arranged so as to produce the most desirable effect in the morning when she should first behold it. Each article was permitted to remain as long as she desired it, and when her senses had thoroughly comprehended it, she was supplied with something new. Her expressions were carefully watched, to see that she was not wearied by this process, and occasionally when she had a decided attachment to some particular work of great beauty, it was presented to her by some of her devoted associates, so that the gift might always be a reminder of friendship or love.

One day Loma came in from a walk with the doctor, and finding Myrtle in the parlor, advanced and presented her with a beautiful diamond ring, at the same time paying her a delightful compliment, and congratulating her on having reached in safety the middle day of her pregnancy. "This is a custom on Venus," he said, as he placed the ring on her finger, "and I hope that whenever your eyes are pleased with the brilliancy of its rays, you will think affectionately and gratefully of the brilliant star whose rays are always directed toward you in paternal benediction."

Myrtle was deeply affected, and embraced him with great ardor. "I love the beautiful planet, every time I see it above the horizon," she exclaimed. "I love it because it is beautiful and good, and because it has sent you to me. I love it because upon it humanity is free and maternity is honored. But tell me one thing. Are all pregnant women upon Venus treated as I am treated by you and these dear friends?"

"Yes indeed," said Loma. "Only upon Venus we have infinitely better facilities than are even furnished by the munificent hospitality we are at present enjoying. In a few days I shall begin the discussion of subjects in which the advanced methods we pursue upon my native planet will be explained to you, and I promise you that you will be delighted to know them, and that when you realize the tremendous advance which must occur upon this planet, from the teaching of the same principles by your son, you will feel that your mission is indeed an exalted one."

"I have often wondered," said Myrtle, "which afforded the most happiness—to live in a place where all the conditions were perfect, or to feel one's self a potent factor in evolving good conditions out of evil. When I was a child I used to read of the struggles of those brave men and women who led the battle for liberty in behalf of the African slaves on this continent, and I frequently wished that I had been born a generation sooner, in order that I might have had a part in it. But it seems that there are battles of greater magnitude to be fought to-day, and I am highly favored in having a share in them. But my situation is so much more pleasant than those who fought those battles. I do not think that it takes much heroism to be placed in such delightful surroundings and be ministered to in this way."

"My dear child," said Loma, smilingly, "the highest test of heroism is the willingness to do one's duty at the right time and in the right way. Your duty falls in pleasant places, but it requires great strength of character to endure your present situation without becoming selfish and indifferent to the rights and wrongs of others. I have carefully watched your conduct, and you have invariably returned a full measure of love for all of the favors you have received, and your mind has been constantly on the alert for the best possible use to be made of your opportunities. As long as you maintain this high standard, you will be performing the duties of a heroine, and you will fight and win a battle which was lost by Adam and Eve, and by many others since the civilization of this world began."

At this point in the conversation, the door bell rang, and Loma and Myrtle retired to the library. The visitor was shown into the parlor, and Mrs. Bell was summoned. When that lady reached the parlor she recognized in her visitor Myrtle's uncle, Mr. McDonald. He looked haggard and worn.

Mrs. Bell greeted him cordially, and endeavored to place him at his ease. She invited him to be seated, but he remained standing and gave every evidence of being in a state of mental distress. Finally he exclaimed: "My dear madam, I have come to tell you that I am the most miserable of men. Your conversation of a few days ago has opened my eyes to the utter injustice of my action toward an innocent and unfortunate girl, who had a claim upon my protection which miserably failed her in the hour of need. I have confessed my sin upon my knees in the presence of my God, and I have come to acknowledge my transgression before you, and to beg for you to intercede with her to forgive me. Thank God, she is yet alive, and my ignorance and uncharitableness has had no worse effect than to expose her to perils, from which by the mercy of God she has escaped. I can never express my gratitude to Him, and to you and your friends as his instruments, for saving me from the commission of a crime which I now believe with you, to be worse than murder. Will you grant me the favor to say to the dear girl, that I have not slept since I was here from remorse, and that unless I can obtain her pardon I will never see another happy moment."

"It will not be necessary for me to intercede for you, my dear sir," said the philanthropist, gently. "Without solicitation on the part of any one, Myrtle has declared that she bears you no malice, and only awaits the first indication on your part of a desire to resume affectionate relations, to meet you more than half way. Such is the beautiful and forgiving nature of her character, that I do not believe she is capable of harboring a thought of revenge or enmity against any one, not even those who have wronged her. Shall I tell her that you wish to see her?"

Mr. McDonald sank down upon a sofa, covered his face with his handkerchief, and burst into tears. "And this is the girl I thought was vicious and depraved!" he exclaimed. "She is an angel, and I am not worthy to touch the hem of her garment. Send her to me that I may confess my inhumanity, and if she forgives me I will know that God has done likewise."

Mrs. Bell withdrew from the parlor, and in another moment Myrtle entered the room. She advanced to her uncle's side and placed her arm around his neck, and imprinted a kiss upon his cheek. " Dear uncle," she said softly, "I know what you would say, and I have forgiven all. Do not think of it again, but love me as you always have and let us be happy. It was all a horrible mistake."

Her uncle caught her in his arms and kissed her passionately. "My child, my precious child!" he exclaimed, "can you forgive the ignorance and inhuman conduct of your poor, weak, blind uncle? I was blinded by prejudice, and by the slavish adherence to conventional beliefs. I was selfish and inconsiderate, and I allowed my pride in my social and religious position to destroy the spirit of the religion I professed. Forgive me, and I will be your protector and guardian henceforth in the face of the world, and of my wife."

"Is Aunt Sarah still against me?" asked Myrtle.

"Alas! my child, for the hollowness and insincerity of religious profession. Your aunt is entirely absorbed in her social position and in the prestige she obtains from the presidency of a missionary society which spends thousands of dollars annually on the heathen in foreign lands, and which is powerless to soften the hard hearts of the heathen in its own membership. I know now that I was entirely dominated by her in my treatment of you, fool, coward and hypocrite that I was. I have read the Bible, argued, wept and prayed with her, and all to no purpose. But I have realized my own duty, and in spite of her threats and curses,— yes, she cursed me when I told her I was coming to beg your forgiveness,—I am here to offer you my protection and my love, and to say that I despise the teaching of the formal religion which has caused me to do this great wrong to you. I have seen your Aunt Mary, and she rejoices in my changed views. She sends you her love, and offers you a home with her, and I will say that you shall never need for anything while I live, and in my will you shall be remembered as my own daughter. This is all I can do at present to atone for my great wrong, but if you will accept it, I shall be happy once more in the performance of my duty to my sister's child."

"Dear uncle," said Myrtle, as she kissed him on the forehead, "you have made me very happy, and I will be able to relieve you from all embarrassment in the matter. These dear friends with whom I now have a home, have adopted me as a member of the family, and I am very happy. If I should go to Aunt Mary's now I would be thrown among those who look at me in very much the same spirit as Aunt Sarah does. The people of your church, and the class of society in which I formerly moved are all blind on this subject, and it will require the coming of another Messiah to convert them. Here, I am surrounded by those who love and respect me, and my child will be born and educated under the most favorable circumstances. If you will give me the comfort of your society occasionally, and Aunt Mary will come to see me here, I shall be perfectly happy. I love you both, and I love and forgive Aunt Sarah, and I only hope she will also see her mistake some day and be converted to the glorious truth. Now kiss me, and know that I have forgotten all the unpleasant things that have occurred, and we will never mention them again. I want to introduce you to my friends, and show you what a beautiful home I have."

Pressing an ardent and forgiving kiss upon her uncle's lips, Myrtle left the room and soon returned with Loma, whom she gracefully introduced. Doctor Bell soon entered, and Mr. McDonald took occasion to feelingly thank both gentlemen for their rescue of Myrtle, whom he now referred to in terms of the warmest affection. Mrs. Bell was the recipient of a graceful tribute from the thoroughly reformed pharisee, and when he had recovered his ease of manner and felt secure in the respect of Myrtle's friends, who were too liberal to hold his mistake against him after he had confessed his fault, Mr. McDonald proved himself to be a warm-hearted, accomplished and lovable man. An hour was spent in delightful conversation, and then he took his leave, after accepting an invitation from Mrs. Bell to bring his sister and dine with her on the following Tuesday.

Myrtle was radiant with joy after her uncle left, and was warmly congratulated by her friends on his conversion to her defense.

"I owe it all to you," she said, gratefully, to Mrs. Bell. "I believe you would convert Aunt Sarah, too, if you could meet her personally as you did Uncle John."

"I admire his courage," said Doctor Bell. "Considering his education and prejudices, and the character of his associations, it is a remarkable exhibition of courage, conscientiousness, independence and intelligence for him to do what he has done to-day. An ordinary man can go forward in what he knows to be his duty, when he has never committed himself to a contrary course. But it takes a brave man to acknowledge a wrong, to apologize or ask forgiveness of one he has wronged."

CHAPTER XIII.

THE CODE OF GALLHEIM.

> "Alone he stands,
> Girt with the flawless armor of the Truth,
> And in one hand a torch whose light dispels
> The mists of superstition, as the sun
> Drives doubts and shadows from the face of morn.
> The other holds a sword whose keenest edge
> Is turned against the mortal heart of Error,
> A trenchant blade, and wielded by an arm
> That knows not fear, nor halts at criticism."

Doctor Bell had followed with rapt attention every lesson which Loma had delivered at which he could possibly be present. The young physician was a bright student and had made very copious notes of every one of the short lectures delivered by Loma, being fully resolved that nothing should escape him which would add to his ability to perform successfully his part of the great mission of instruction to Myrtle's son, when he reached the age at which he would be committed to his charge. Loma had planned that the childhood of the coming prodigy should be spent under the maternal instruction of Mrs. Bell and Myrtle, and that when he reached puberty, his education should then be directed by the doctor. These matters had been fully discussed and agreed to by the friends, and all their energies were harmoniously directed toward the consummation of the great plan.

More than two months had passed rapidly and pleasantly away, since the arrival of Loma upon the earth, and the time had been most thoroughly utilized. Myrtle was now in the second period of her pregnancy, and according to the laws of gestation which Loma had explained, she was building in the brain of her child those organs which related to the constructive powers, the reasoning faculties, and the instincts of preservation and sociability. She became more cautious and prudent, for her increasing size and weight constantly reminded her of her condition and the care necessary to prevent accidents. The select circle of friends to whom she had been introduced by Mrs. Bell became still more solicitous and interested in her daily. Never a day passed but she was reminded of the affectionate interest of some one of the circle by a personal visit, usually accompanied by some loving token or gift, most frequently some beautifully fashioned garment designed either for herself or the little one who was soon to bless her with his appearance. Every manifestation of this character caused Myrtle to thrill with the sweet sensations of love and pride, for they were nearly all the work of the hands of the givers, and bore to Myrtle the delightful assurance that she was loved and cared for. In this way her mind continued to expand and grow, until one day when some special tribute of affection had aroused her enthusiasm to a high degree she exclaimed: "If this continues I shall feel that I am the best loved woman on earth, and I shall glow like Loma with the magnetism of its reciprocation."

"That is precisely as we wish you to feel, my love," said Mrs. Bell, kissing her. "And if you feel that way now it will become the permanent condition of your child, and he will be a worthy representative of Loma, as Jesus was of Manrolin."

Myrtle became, during this period, intensely interested in art, especially in its constructive forms, and in the expression of the beautiful. Sometimes her rapture over these subjects became sublime, and she wrote articles and poems, which were gems of literary construction and artistic conception. Much time was now devoted to music, and here, also, she displayed her constructive and perfective powers by producing musical compositions of a high grade. Under the tuition of Loma, she progressed rapidly in the study of philosophy and logic, and entered into debates with her friends with extraordinary spirit and lofty courage. Loma was delighted with the progress made by his pupil, and when he had thoroughly satisfied himself that she had mastered all of the preliminary instructions he had designed for her, he thrilled her and his two other auditors, one day in the morning session in the conservatory, by announcing that he was now ready to relate the substance of a description of civilization as it existed on his native planet.

Myrtle clapped her hands with pleasure, while Mrs. Bell exclaimed, "How delightful! I have been dying with curiosity to ask you about the condition of society in Venus, but we have been so thoroughly entertained by what you have told us on other subjects, that I have not found the opportunity, and, moreover, I was afraid if I did ask, that you might decline on the ground that we were not ready to comprehend it."

"All in good time," said Loma, smiling. "You were not ready for it two months ago, but now that I have criticised some of the conditions which exist here on earth, you have a right to know how things are managed with us, who have developed beyond your present stage."

"The civilization of Venus," said Loma, as he began his narrative, "while it is many centuries in advance of this, is not so essentially different from what you will attain to in a short time as you may suppose. To make myself clearer, I will say that while a people are engaged in advancing from ignorance to intelligence, there is great rapidity of progress, but when complete intelligence is reached there is no progress necessary. Our people reached a solution of the problem of existence many centuries ago, and since that time they have been living right, and in accord with nature, hence there has been no change except the slow growth toward higher forms of intelligence as new senses and faculties have been evolved. These only occur with the changing conditions of natural surroundings, which you will understand are not rapid.

"The essential difference between your people and ours, at present, is, that your citizens are impelled forward by resistless energy toward progress, while ours are contented and happy as they are, because they are enjoying correct conditions, while you are straining every energy to develop better conditions than those you now have. Now, some of the animals on this planet have developed to perfectly correct conditions, according to the limit of their faculties, hence they live perfectly contented lives and make no remarkable progress, because progress is not necessary. Man will continue to struggle toward correct conditions until he reaches them, and you have already reached a comprehension of them in a large degree, in some of your faculties, and your complete civilization will date, as ours does, from the time when, as a race, you recognize the principle of mathematical equity in all the departments of action, and the true nature of the constitution of man. You have the means of the solution of the problem in your hands already, and if I can impress upon you, and through you especially upon Myrtle's offspring, the comprehension of the true solution, he will be able to teach it to mankind, and thereafter it will only be a matter of a few generations of men and women created upon correct principles, which will enable you to reach a plane of life substantially the same as now exists upon Venus."

His auditors drew closer with breathless interest. Loma rose from his seat and requested them to do the same. He then formed a circle by joining hands and raising his eyes toward the sun which glowed through the opening in the dome of the conservatory, exclaimed: "Source of Power and all Goodness!

give me strength to perform my duty! May the words
of this hour be uttered in wisdom, and may the effect
be the elevation of mankind to happiness in the domain
of universal love!"

As he spoke this invocation, his body glowed with
magnetism until it was as bright as the sun, and the
glow communicated itself to the bodies of Myrtle, Mrs.
Bell and Edward, while they thrilled with the delicious sensations which Loma's magnetism always imparted. He then released their hands and seated himself to begin his instruction.

"The foundation of a correct civilization," said
Loma, "begins with the rejection of the belief in the
supernatural. As long as our people believed in the
existence of ghosts, gods and devils, they attributed
all phenomena to their agency and neglected the study
of the natural. Our civilization properly begins with
the teaching of a great and good man by name of Gallheim, who declared, as I hope Myrtle's son will teach,
that everything is natural, that human character is
a matter of growth and culture, and that all problems
can be solved by applying the principles of mathematics. He was at first persecuted and ridiculed, but
his power was so great, that he established a respectable following, who lived strictly according to his
teachings. They organized themselves into a society,
from which, as a nucleus, arose a growth of humanity
which ultimately conquered the planet and established
the civilization which we now enjoy.

"The fundamental doctrines of Gallheim were:

"First—That man is an aggregation of atoms that are all governed by the same laws which govern the material universe, and that his intelligence is the result of growth and the formation of his constitution, the aggregation of the power of the associated atoms composing his organization and depending for its complete manifestation upon the completeness and complexity of his structure.

"Second—That the character of any individual can be determined by an inspection of his physical constitution, and adapted to its proper sphere of growth and enjoyment of existence.

"Third—That by the study of the laws of nature and by conforming thereto in the generation and culture of humanity, as well as all other organisms, approximately perfect results can be obtained.

"Fourth—That the laws of mathematical equity which have been found to produce harmony in music and art, can be applied to every other of the sixty-four departments of knowledge and the spheres of action pertaining thereto.

"As soon as these doctrines took root and began to form the rule of action in the lives of Gallheim's followers, the following remarkable results were attained: First, his followers abandoned the delusion of future lives, which had consumed their energies to the neglect of the present, and began to study and order their lives so as to produce the greatest amount of happiness for themselves and their associates in the present. His second great doctrine taught them the true worth of human character, and the study of themselves from a scientific standpoint enabled them to form a true conception of their talents and how to use them, and their faults and how to correct them."

"That is what the magnificent discoveries of our own Gall and Spurzheim will do for us as soon as Phrenology is accepted," exclaimed the doctor, with enthusiasm.

"Certainly," resumed Loma. "I told you a moment ago that you had the means of the solution of the problem in your hands already, and as soon as the science of Phrenology is developed, in accordance with Gallheim's first great doctrine, instead of making it subservient to the old errors concerning mind and soul, you will be half way toward the correct result.

"The great light shed upon human character by these two doctrines led to the enthusiastic development of the third, which, as has also happened on the earth, had already in a measure been applied to the culture of animals and vegetation. As soon as man comprehend his weaknesses, as exposed by Gallheim's system of character study, which was essentially the same as the Phrenology of Gall and Spurzheim upon this planet, he began to conscientiously cultivate himself toward perfection. The result was that, in seven generations, approximately perfect organizations had been reached, and during this transition marriage and all other barbarous customs were abolished, for as soon as intelligent culture was attempted, it was found that perfect love was essential, and as love could not exist under compulsion and slavery, marriage disappeared and love was the universal law. The most remarkable result attending this development was the fact, that, as soon as liberty was declared and people became accustomed to it, the tone of public sentiment rose so high that those persons who attempted to be selfish, or who would not conform to the best conditions of development, were held in such universal detestation that they immediately reformed, or else went out of the new society and associated with the barbarians, who were at last entirely crowded off the planet. Because as the new society grew in numbers and in the perfection of its members, it rapidly obtained control of all governments, and the remainder of the population were gradually educated to a comprehension of the benefits, so that they were rapidly absorbed. The new society began by limiting the increase of population among themselves, producing only as many citizens as were required, and these only of the best quality. It followed, as a matter of course, that even among the barbarians those who wanted offspring followed the teachings of Gallheim and produced good citizens, who became members of the new society, while those who were indifferent failed to reproduce, and thus at last died out. The new society gained at last complete possession of the planet by peaceable means, and with the use of no other weapon than its own superb intelligence."

"Admirable!" exclaimed Doctor Bell.

"But the crowning glory of the teachings of Gallheim is found in his fourth great doctrine," resumed Loma, "and it is to this especially that I wish to direct your attention, for it is the essential doctrine which is necessary to the completion of your civilization. The most advanced minds among you are quite ready to accept the others, but unless the fourth doctrine is enforced, the best results will be delayed until it is. The great doctrine of mathematical equity is all that is needed to make men honest and unselfish, and you will agree with me that dishonesty and selfishness are the great barriers which stand in the way of the progress of all reforms.

"I can best illustrate this doctrine by again referring to music, because you understand it, and it is one of the departments of human knowledge and effort in which you have already applied the principle with superb results. Now, music has been reduced to exact mathematical principles. A half note is just twice as valuable as a quarter note, and pitch is regulated by a mathematical position of the note upon the staff which corresponds exactly with the position of the tone it represents in the musical scale. Our beloved Myrtle, here, being an accomplished musician, can compose an entirely new work, express it in musical notation and send it to Germany, where an equally accomplished and intelligent person who has never heard it will play it exactly as Myrtle has intended it should be played. The piece may be rehearsed by an orchestra in Germany, and by another in Chicago, and if they are all well-trained musicians, the two orchestras may be brought together, and upon meeting, they will be able to play the work together with such harmony that other cultivated musicians will be constrained to applaud. The same result has been substantially attained wherever mathematical equity has been brought to bear upon the working of any of the human faculties, but it has only been applied to a few. But you have reached superb results through these laws in music, art, architecture, mechanics, engineering, and accounts, and fragmentary results of great value in some other departments. The application of precisely the same principle will give you the same perfection of results in the administration of every form of action of which a human being is capable. Right here I wish to call your attention to a remarkable fact. It is, that the comprehension of the harmony which results from the application of mathematical principles incites men to righteousness. The musician loves to play correctly, and in the case of the orchestra I have used as an illustration, if one of the musicians willfully played wrong and destroyed the harmony, he would be regarded as insane by his brother musicians. *Such conduct does not occur* among refined musicians, because they are trained by the application of these laws and constrained by ambition and love of applause to do exact justice. As soon as these laws are understood and applied in other departments of human effort, *wrong conduct disappears*. You can hardly conceive of a first-class artist daubing a beautiful picture, or of an accomplished architect willfully destroying the strength of a building, or of an expert accountant falsifying an account, unless some element is introduced which will make it appear profitable. Now, when all the human faculties are educated on this principle it becomes impossible to commit an unrighteous action without outraging some sense which is thoroughly well trained, and hence a complete equilibrium is established and maintained. When you understand that there are only sixty-four faculties to educate, if you will consider the amount of effort it takes to train the single faculty of *time* to correct action, and multiply that by sixty-four, you will have a conception of the effort it takes to educate a child in Venus to a complete use of all his abilities, which leads to the establishment of a basis for absolutely correct moral conduct in every department of life. In subsequent lessons I will give you a further insight into the operation of these doctrines as they were developed on our planet and as they are now responsible for the measure of happiness we enjoy. But the knowledge of this principle, and its application in the present instance, admonishes me that my beloved pupil has received as much instruction to-day as justice will permit. Let us adjourn to the music room and rest the faculties we have been using, by the employment of others no less enjoyable."

CHAPTER XIV.

THE LABOR PROBLEM.

"Phrenology! The word is like a charm,
To cure the ills of life. An omen sure
To cheer the toiling masses on their way
To higher aims and brighter hopes withal,
When Love shall tear aside the blackened pall
Of misery and let the daylight shine
Upon the birth of Justice and of Truth.
When Reason shall prevail and men shall bow
Before the shrine of Wisdom, learning there
The lessons sweet of beauty and of health."

"The first sweeping revolution which was accomplished by the adoption of Gallheim's teachings was the effect it produced upon the labor problem," said Loma, as he began his next lesson, on the day following. "Previous to the advent of this great philosopher upon our planet, we were in exactly the same dilemma, as to the disposition of human labor and the accumulation of wealth, that now besets your society. The increase in the productive power of machinery, the great advance which had been made in the arts and sciences, and the development of new territory, produced the same conditions upon Venus that you have experienced here. Enormous fortunes were made and enjoyed by the few who possessed financial skill, while those who were not organized upon that pattern went hungry, as they do here. The great majority of men and women were slaves to those who possessed wealth, and the aristocracy were the only people who enjoyed even a small measure of the conditions of correct growth. Even they did not receive the benefits which were possible to them, for selfishness and ignorance are always the greatest enemies to happiness, and the rich suffered, in common with the poor, from the results of a pernicious industrial system, which condemned the great majority of mankind to enslavement and to the performance of unnecessary toil, with the consequent loss of development, while the rich, by reason of being relieved from toil altogether, failed to obtain the development which comes from a correct amount of wholesome labor. We had precisely the same conditions upon Venus which now confront you, and while, on the one hand, large numbers of our citizens were impoverished, for lack of wealth, and thousands starved in the sight of plenty, another class of idlers was created who died miserably for want of enterprising occupation.

"Gallheim's followers began by organizing their society on the basis of exclusive association, as far as it was possible. They kept their wealth within their own society by producing everything they needed and patronizing their own institutions exclusively. They early advocated the abolition of marriage, but as public opinion was very strong in favor of the ancient and venerable mistake, they did not antagonize the barbarians by whom they were surrounded by disobeying the laws, however erroneous they considered them, but they secured their end by marrying among themselves.

When they had been organized fifty years, they had produced such an improvement in human development, that they began to attract universal attention by their superior beauty, and it was impossible to find a follower of Gallheim who would consider the proposition of associating in marriage with a barbarian. So thoroughly did they practice the doctrines of their distinguished founder, that their marriages were almost universally agreeable, and as we had liberal divorce laws at that time, even among the barbarians, when any marriage was found to be unhappy for any reason, it was quickly dissolved, and that without scandal. One of the curious facts about the early followers of Gallheim was the reform they introduced into the marriage ceremony itself. We had, up to that time, the same absurd implications in the ceremony that you have here. The woman promised to love, honor, and obey her husband; the man promised to love, honor, and cherish his wife. Gallheim himself called attention to the absurdity of these promises, and showed so clearly that they were void on their face, that they became ridiculous even in the eyes of the most conservative barbarians. He argued that love and honor were consequences that flowed from lovable and honorable conduct, and could not be pledged in advance without the stultification of the party making the pledge. This was so clearly evident, that a reform in the ceremony followed at once, and thereafter the parties promised to be lovable and honorable themselves, instead of requiring a pledge of love and honor to be rendered, regardless of the conduct of the other party. The result was, as might have been expected, that as soon as loving and honorable conduct became the rule and not the exception, the pledge itself fell into disuse, because it was so universally understood as implied.

"As soon as love and justice began to be developed, through these influences, a better conception of human rights and privileges began to obtain. The followers of Gallheim had in the meantime become immensely wealthy. But as they were committed to the doctrines of their great founder, as soon as they began to accumulate a surplus of wealth they applied the doctrine of mathematical equity to its use. The members of the society who were gifted with financial skill realized that they could not accumulate vast riches and allow their brethren to starve, without sacrificing the benefits of the third great doctrine of their order. It became necessary for them, in order to improve themselves to the highest degree, to practice the most exalted forms of benevolence and justice. The ambition which the members of this remarkable society possessed, to improve the society, itself, so that it would be able to fulfill its exalted mission of the subjugation of the planet to their high ideal of civilization, caused them to use their wealth to the fullest extent in improving every member in the order. Thus, in a short time, those who possessed great financial skill came to be considered merely as the stewards of the order, and their social standing was made to depend on the ability and fidelity with which they discharged this obligation.

When a member was found who did not possess the ability to gather riches, he was in a large measure relieved from financial responsibility, and was only required to perform such work in that direction as would tend to develop him, if he was a young man. If he was advanced in years, he was relieved altogether from any kind of labor which he was likely to fail in performing, and was permitted to expend all his energies where he had talent. This was one of the secrets of the great success of the movement and the remarkable power which they developed. It was largely due to the recognition of Gallheim's code, and especially to his method of character study, which enabled them to measure the capacity of an individual with accuracy, and to assign him to his proper vocation in advance.

"The new society continued to grow in wealth, numbers and popularity, until, some thirty years before Gallheim's death, they numbered about three million. We had at that time upon Venus nearly the same political conditions you have here, and strange to say, there was a nation which was in all respects analogous to the United States of America, in which Gallheim's work had originated. His followers, acting under his advice, settled in such numbers in one of these states, which was in size, productiveness and natural situation very much like the State of Illinois, that they were able to buy all of the real estate in the state, and establish such laws and customs as they desired. From that time all obstacles to the new civilization seem to have disappeared, and its progress was as rapid as the growth of humanity itself. Within one hundred years, from the time of the organization of their first state, they were in possession of all the desirable portions of the globe, and the barbarians were eagerly submitting to their laws and customs and becoming absorbed into the new society.

"As soon as the great principles of Gallheim's code were understood, humanity realized that the end and purpose of existence is enjoyment. In the study and application of the third great principle embraced in the code, it was found that those persons who enjoyed life most produced the most desirable and perfect offspring. Another great fact was, that those persons who experienced the greatest amount of pleasure in the sexual act, itself, produced the strongest and most perfect offspring. The enjoyment of existence then became the most enthusiastic study of the populace. Here again the majestic character of Gallheim displayed itself. He impressed upon his followers that the development of pleasure would come, not from dissipation and the indulgence of desire but in cultivating perfect self-control, and in displaying the most perfect harmony in the use and development of the mental faculties. In a word, the effect of his teaching was, that every member of his society strove to the utmost to secure as quickly as possible that development of the sixty-four organs of the brain, the action of the sixty-four corresponding faculties, and such education in the sixty-four departments of human knowledge as would enable them to order their conduct with the same degree of righteousness that had already been obtained in music. The results were marvelous. Gallheim lived to realize the complete success of his philosophy, and died at the close of his long and illustrious career, blessed, honored and revered by every inhabitant of the globe he had so thoroughly reformed."

"And do you consider it possible, that my son may be able to make an impression upon the inhabitants of this earth, similar to that which Gallheim made upon the people of Venus?" exclaimed Myrtle, as Loma paused at this point in his narrative.

"Certainly," responded Loma. "Unless he does, I shall be completely disappointed, and shall be compelled to consider my mission a failure. But there is no fear of such a result. The principles I have announced to you, as constituting the code of Gallheim, are very simple, and you have comprehended them yourself sufficiently well to begin their inculcation to-morrow. But when they are presented by your son, with all the force and magnetism with which he will be endowed, by reason of the pains we are taking to make him a complete specimen of manhood, there can be but one result."

"Oh, this is perfectly glorious!" exclaimed Myrtle, while Mrs. Bell encircled her waist with her arm and held her in a warm embrace of sympathy, while Loma continued his narrative:

"As soon as the conduct of the new society became regulated by the principles and teachings of Gallheim, and men became accustomed to living for enjoyment, instead of the pursuit of wealth, some very extraordinary changes occurred. The study and practice of the third article of his code soon developed the fact that the greater portion of the labor which had been performed up to that time had been worse than useless. For as soon as it became known that great happiness could be attained by studying and conforming to the laws of nature, a great deal of energy was expended in that direction, and, of course, the laws of health and correct living soon became established in the intelligence of the people by the results of the experiments that were made. Of course, it was soon established what articles of food were desirable and what were injurious. All injurious articles of food were at once discontinued and their manufacture ceased. You would be astonished, if you knew what an effect would be produced on your own market, if the knowledge which we have in Venus could be enforced in this direction alone. Over half the stock of your provision depots would be condemned, and, of course, the people engaged in the manufacture and sale of these articles would be liberated, or, as you would express it, 'thrown out of employment.' You will not be astonished to know that all such articles as alcoholic liquors, tobacco, opium, and other purely injurious articles, went by the board in the early stages of the development of this new civilization. Only such quantities as were needed for purely chemical and medicinal uses were tolerated, and these were soon greatly reduced by the excellent health of the inhabitants under the new order of things.

When you consider that in the United States you spend more money for these injurious articles than you do for food, you will understand how many people were released by this change. The next advance occurred with the development of the fact that every one had been consuming too much food, and food of poor quality, and the reduction of the quantity to just that amount which was required by the individual, and the production of only the purest and best foods, released another large contingent. With the abandonment of the habitual use of clothing, and the discontinuing of harmful and useless forms of dress, another great burden was lifted from the shoulders of toiling humanity.

"The improvement in the growth of humanity, itself, and the development of the sense of justice, abolished crime and contention among the members of the new society, and a vast army of lawyers, judges, policemen and officeholders were relieved from their wearisome duties. The change in the system of the administration of wealth made insurance unnecessary; banking, speculation, and all forms of gambling were discontinued, and the offices occupied for such purposes were closed, and their owners, with their legions of overworked clerks, typewriters and cashiers, walked out into the sunshine of liberty. The decrease in the demand for commercial commodities, and the destruction of the competitive system of the accumulation of wealth, liberated the merchants and their hordes of employes and those who were connected with them. In short, the introduction of the new system destroyed the necessity for nine-tenths of the distressing labor under which humanity had groaned for centuries."

"And this grand result was accomplished by the recognition of the single fact, declared to the inhabitants of this earth centuries ago, but never understood, that wisdom is better than gold," exclaimed Doctor Bell.

"That is very true," said Loma; "but humanity, enslaved under the conditions which then existed, was unable to comprehend the utterance, much less put it into practice. It is doubtful whether the philosopher who uttered it had the faintest conception of what it implied. Our humanity had to go through the same conditions of growth, and it is impossible to reach perfection in any other way."

"It is not quite clear to me," said Mrs. Bell, "how such a large number of persons were organized into correct methods and habits, without the demoralization which must surely arise from idleness. Will you please explain."

"It was a matter of gradual, though very rapid growth. You must understand, that this movement began with a small collection of persons who were under the direct tuition of the great Gallheim, and who were by him instructed in the full meaning of his code. They increased very rapidly, as soon as he was able to demonstrate the results of his system, for we had then on our planet, as you have here, a large number of very advanced and intelligent persons who were seeking earnestly for a better method of living. As soon as they solved the money problem—and the solution, as you have seen, consisted simply in having the commonwealth administered by those members who were best endowed with financial sense, and holding them to the application of the rule of mathematical equity, which they dared not violate, because they would not only outrage their own consciences, but would lose the inestimable benefits of the society by being cast out among the barbarians,—then everything else became comparatively easy. As fast as new members were received, they were kept busy, first in learning the principles of development, and secondly in doing whatever work was necessary to be done, while the older members of the order were granted complete immunity from labor, except when their services were required as teachers. During the first two generations, the teachers had plenty of employment, and there was so much to be done in clearing away the evils of the old system, and in devising and putting into operation the improvements which were made, that there was plenty of employment for every one within the limits of the hours which Gallheim had established as the maximum amount of labor which should be required of every member of society. But as a large amount of unnecessary labor had been abolished by the new system, so, also, a large increase was the immediate result in those departments of labor which minister directly to human enjoyment and improvement. There was a tremendous demand for teachers and workers in every department of literary labor. The sense of justice and discrimination having been highly developed, there was an overwhelming sentiment in favor of good literature, and everything which was vicious, obscene and demoralizing was soon condemned. The universal demand was for that which would elevate, refine and purify society and enable the members to reach, in the shortest possible time, the highest culture of every faculty. Brilliant authors and writers, lecturers, artists and musicians, had only to demonstrate their abilities, and they were at once lionized in society. The architect who could improve a building, the engineer who established a swifter or a safer mode of transportation for the myriads of emancipated men and women, who were for the first time enabled to enjoy the delights of travel, the actor who could present a realistic portrayal of that which was good or beautiful, in fact, any one who could add to the sum total of human happiness, was hailed as a benefactor, and accorded the praise and social position which he merited. It was no longer a question of money or of the ability to make money. The test of a man's popularity was simply the voice of the people, testifying to the benefits he conferred upon them. The effect of all this upon the energies and ambitions of the people was simply incredible. Some of the critics of Gallheim had urged that the adoption of his system would destroy progress and annihilate the energy and ambition of the people. These men were probably honest in their belief, for they could not comprehend the existence of energy without the commercial stimulus. The truth of the matter was, however, that under the old system no one was energetic, except those who were gifted with the acquisitive sense, or who were stung into action by the privations of poverty. The first class were the only ones who succeeded. The second class made spasmodic efforts, but usually sank into the apathy of disappointment, after a number of failures, and it was only after the new system was adopted, that the political economists realized what a vast amount of energy had been paralyzed by the evils of the old.

"Under the new system, instead of having a half dozen incentives to human activity, we now have sixty-four. As matters now stand in this world, the great majority of your citizens have no conception of business except as a means to accumulate money. Ask the first one hundred men you may meet in Chicago, what they would do if they had a million dollars, and the majority of them will answer, 'I would retire from business and have a good time.' By a good time, they mean the indulgence of every form of human selfishness. This is proved by the fact that nearly every man who does accumulate enough money to do some good in the world fails to employ it for any purpose except the gratification of his own selfish desires. If your average citizen of wealth, say those who possess from one hundred thousand dollars up, could be translated to Venus to-day, and be endowed with the same power that they have here for the amelioration of human misery, and they lived as they do here, they would be held in universal execration and contempt. Under the development of the entire list of faculties, as we are now educated in Venus, there is constant employment in the practice of good actions, and as it is one of the laws of health and development that a man must exercise every faculty in some degree, every day, you can readily see that life in Venus is not idleness, but a continual round of healthful, enjoyable and life-developing duties.

"One of the remarkable principles which Gallheim inculcated under the application of the fourth article of his code was the limitation of population. In Venus, you will understand, the principle of mathematical equity is applied to everything. Accordingly, as the members of the new society possessed themselves of those portions of the globe which were desirable places of residence, the exact number of inhabitants which each territory would sustain under the very best conditions of growth was carefully calculated, and the population was limited to that number. In applying this principle, Gallheim enforced upon humanity the same degree of forethought which an intelligent husbandman exercises in regard to his crops. He has learned by experience that in the successful growth of corn, for instance, the hills must be just so many feet apart, and there must not be more than a certain number of stalks within a certain territory. If he violates this law of mathematical equity, his crop suffers in proportion to the extent of the violation. This law was vigorously enforced by Gallheim's followers, and, as a consequence, their offspring were uniformly vigorous, and as the barbarians were gradually crowded upon the most undesirable and least fertile portions of the globe, and as they paid no attention to the great laws of reproduction, they very soon died out. The development of the study of human improvement, under the stimulus imparted to it by Gallheim's code, soon enabled his followers to establish a complete code of sexual ethics, under which it became possible for them to not only regulate the number of offspring but to determine the sex at will, and to endow them with whatever talents were most needed by the society, and to insure their health and personal beauty. This threw the physicians out of employment, and most of them became teachers or devoted themselves to the development of special branches of scientific study.

"In future lessons I will tell you all about the system of education as it is practiced in Venus, and also explain, at length, how the domestic relations have been brought to their present stage of perfection."

CHAPTER XV.

THE NEW EDUCATION.

"It is a long way from the charcoal to the diamond, but every element that is in the diamond is also in the charcoal. It is a long way from average humanity to Jesus, but the virtues and graces which shine with such resplendent luster in Him lie hidden and undeveloped in us.

"What do these facts indicate? Not that we are ruined, but that we are incomplete."

When the four friends assembled in the conservatory, for the next session of instruction from Lonna, Mrs. Bell began the conversation by saying:

"Whenever these reforms have been discussed among advanced thinkers on this earth, we have always been met by the following questions: 'If marriage is abolished in society, what will prevent the race from relaxing into complete licentiousness? How will the sexual relations be regulated? How will a father be able to recognize his own child? What will become of the children? What will become of parental responsibility? Who will take any interest in education?' These, and a thousand similar questions, are propounded to the advocates of reform, and I must confess that, so far, they have never been satisfactorily answered."

"They cannot be satisfactorily answered until the code of Gallheim is adopted and practiced in its entirety. As long as humanity is dominated by selfish motives, slavery must exist in some form. Some years ago, in the United States, you practiced four leading forms of slavery. You now have three conspicuous forms remaining. You have abolished in a degree, and wholly as a matter of law, the slavery of the African to the Caucasian, but you still enforce the slavery of of the poor to the rich, the slavery of woman to man, and the slavery of children to their parents. You have yet to learn that each of these classes have rights which those who rule over them are bound to respect. I might also speak of the slavery of animals to man, but that subject properly belongs to another discussion. I think I can best answer all of your questions by tracing the operation of the code of Gallheim at the present time upon our planet, and showing you how it affects the life of an individual from the time the germ of his life originates in the loins of his father, to the time that he reposes in the everlasting arms of the universal mother, Space, when his organization is dissolved in what you call death.

"To understand the working of society on Venus, you must understand that every man and woman is completely educated. You will also understand, that, by reason of the perfect application of the third article of Gallheim's code, we have an almost universally perfect humanity. By this I mean that every one of our citizens is brought into the world with a complete brain and body, and while we have diversity of character and different types of humanity, yet we have completely eliminated idiocy, insanity, deformity, and all other unfortunate congenital conditions which arise from ignorance and disease. Occasionally, though very rarely, some accident occurs to a pregnant woman, or to a young child, by which a cripple is produced, but this is so rare that such persons are regarded as great curiosities when seen. They are tenderly cared for according to the degree of their misfortune, and secure as much happiness as it is possible for them to appreciate and enjoy. Now, if you will conceive of a society organized with such individuals composing it, and that all are equally free and independent, and that they are not hampered with the consideration of accumulating wealth, but are all living for the greatest possible enjoyment, and all actuated by the sincerest desire to promote the happiness of all that surround them, and particularly anxious to promote the happiness of posterity, and to leave a progeny which will be a credit to the last generation, you may comprehend what follows.

"There are always a large number of persons who do not wish to become parents. They are absorbed in other pursuits, and are persuaded that they can render the state a better service by not attempting to produce offspring. There are others who find in parentage the exercise of the highest privilege, and when a young man or woman decides to adopt that mode of life, they are enrolled in that class, after being carefully examined to see that they possess the highest degree of physical and mental perfection, and are accorded the special privileges of the parental division. This exempts them from compulsory labor and leaves them free to devote their whole time to the cultivation of the talents they desire to impress upon their offspring. The relation of sexual intercourse is established according to a system which I will describe in due season. I wish you, at this point, to simply realize that the conception takes place when both parents are in the highest possible state of perfection, and that the act is performed under such conditions as will insure the greatest possible gratification to both parents, which, as I have before intimated, has a corresponding effect of producing the greatest possible perfection in the offspring.

"When the female has conceived, she is at once made the recipient of special attention and honor, and the father of her child attends her through the whole period of her pregnancy, giving her the felicity of his society, and jealously guarding her from every possible accident or untoward circumstance which may possibly mar the perfect effect, which he is, of course, desirous of producing. He gives her at all times the warmest proofs of his affection, and any neglect at this time, or harsh conduct on his part, would forever disgrace him in the eyes of society, and possibly prevent his ever being selected for a similar office. In short, every pregnant female in Venus is surrounded constantly by the same conditions which we have been so careful to provide for the benefit of our beloved Myrtle, only on our planet the conditions are rendered more favorable by the fact that there are more persons who have a perfect understanding of the subject. We believe, however, that more education can be accomplished during the nine months of pregnancy by correct maternal impressions than can be reached in nine years of effort after birth where these important influences have been disregarded. Consequently, you will understand, that the citizen of Venus comes into his world with the first right of every citizen fully guaranteed to him,— the right to be thoroughly and completely created.

"In the meantime, the life of the mother has been so natural, and her diet and exercise has been so well regulated, that parturition takes place without pain, and the birth of a child is an event of great rejoicing and congratulation to the parents, who are invested with further honors with pleasing ceremonies. The father is now relieved from further duty toward his offspring and the mother, but the attachment is usually so strong that he devotes much of his time to her entertainment, and, as I will explain later, these attachments are usually of life-long duration, and greatly more felicitous than the most happy marriages you have on this planet.

"From the conception of the child until it is weaned the mother is an inmate of the palace of maternity, an institution especially maintained by the state for the entertainment of pregnant and nursing mothers. Here every condition is maintained which will conduce to her
14

happiness and the perfection of her offspring, and during the nursing period her food is specially prepared to give her strength and to harden the bones and increase the growth of her child. When the child is weaned her responsibility ceases, and the further care and education of the young citizen is assumed by the national educators. These are persons who have been selected by the state with reference to their especial fitness for the purpose, according to the superb system of character study introduced by Gallheim, and are those who are known to be most highly endowed with patience and love for the work of instruction. They assume the education of the child, and from the time it is weaned until it graduates from the highest educational institution on the planet, it remains under the jurisdiction of the various departments of education. Thus one department superintends the awakening of the faculties during the first year, another continues the process the second year, and as the child grows, he passes through all of the departments, on the same principle that you have in your graded schools, but in Venus we never sacrifice the first and most important years to the methods of incompetent mothers. On the contrary, as the state recognizes its most important duty to be the protection of its youngest and most helpless citizens, it provides that during each successive year of growth the citizen shall be placed in the most favorable environment, surrounded by the companionship of those of his own age, and under the jurisdiction of skilled educators, who have won distinction for their success in the management of pupils of that age. It has been determined, by experience, that those persons who give their lives to the office of reproduction have done enough when that function has been well performed. Therefore, instead of having the conditions which formerly obtained, and which still obtain here, where the children are conceived, nursed and governed during the first six and most important years by overworked, devitalized, impoverished and entirely incompetent parents, we secure for both parent and child the happiest possible conditions. In doing this we have only carried into effect the principle which you recognize in the establishment of the public school. If the state has a right to pass a compulsory education law,—and there are few of your citizens who do not concede this as necessary to the preservation of the state,—then it certainly has the right to make that education complete and effective. The difference in our system and yours is this: your educators have not yet comprehended that the chief end of education is, not to stuff the child with information but to teach him the use of his faculties. You begin your education at six years, because you are dominated by the idea that that is as soon as the child can begin to load up with information, and remember such things as the multiplication table and the forms of letters. You have lost the most important years of the child's life, because he has not been taught the true use of his faculties, and he has acquired pernicious habits and faults of character, under the jurisdiction of his impatient, incompetent and often unkind parents, which will remain to cripple him for life. Moreover, your teachers are not instructed in the art of character study. They do not understand the child, because they do not understand human nature. They proceed upon the altogether untenable and unscientific theory, that the child has a soul, regardless of the fact that such a thing has never been seen or demonstrated to exist since the beginning of the world. They do not regard the child as a creature of growth, and hence they do not inspect his growth. Many a child has been punished and degraded in your schools for inattention, when the fact was that the pupil was deaf. We might, with justice, say that the teacher was blind."

"I can readily see that such a system must result in the greatest possible culture of the child," said Mrs. Bell; "but do not the mothers suffer from this separation from their offspring, and does it not tend to destroy the maternal instinct?"

"Quite the contrary. You must remember that the mothers are granted almost complete immunity from other duties, and are left to the highest culture of themselves. They thus have abundant leisure, and they are not separated from their offspring. The children are under the jurisdiction of the educators, but as only a few hours each day are devoted to actual exercises of development, and the greater part of the time of the young citizen is passed in play and various forms of athletic exercises, the mothers have the privilege of being delighted spectators and participants in these sports, and they have five or ten times as much actual companionship with their offspring as the average mother has here. Moreover, as the departments of education are constantly needing new teachers, in all of the grades, a large number of the young mothers find it enjoyable to master the entire details of the educational system of certain grades, notably the infant and primary classes, and many of our best educators are those who have been the fathers or mothers of several citizens. The grounds of the departments of education are magnificent parks, and they are constantly filled with parents, who, in addition to participating in the games and sports of the young, are exchanging the most delightful social courtesies among themselves. You will remember that every citizen is instructed as the basis of his education, that he must exercise every one of the sixty-four faculties to some extent, and while the lives of our citizens are for the most part continually passed in the development of pleasure, there is no ennui and no dissipation. These evils are entirely prevented by the operation of the law of mathematical equity, which every citizen understands, and which he is trained to observe and regard as the foundation of his happiness.

"The period of education of a citizen of Venus extends over thirty years. This is divided into three decades. The first decade is occupied with the awakening of the faculties, which is simply physical culture. By an admirable system of exercises and drill, the child is taught the correct use of himself. He is first trained to observe. Then the faculty of language is aroused and he learns to talk. Meanwhile his social faculties have not been neglected, and he is made to realize that he is loved, and he at once reciprocates the affection. Then he learns to walk, and by calisthenic exercises and drill, he learns to walk gracefully and correctly. He is not permitted to do any of these things until he has developed strength, and hence we never have any bow legs, crooked knees, or other deformities such as are so common among your citizens from the neglect or ignorance of incompetent parents.

"This first decade is passed under the most favorable conditions of growth and development, which is, in fact, the rule of the entire life on our planet. There is no confinement, no close atmosphere, and no impatience or injustice practiced toward the young citizen. He passes his time with companions of his own age, and as the sexes are constantly associated, he has the advantage of the development of love from the very beginning of his existence. You will understand that I use the pronoun 'he' in its general signification, for there is absolutely no distinction in the matter of sex, except that the little girls are impressed with the dignity of motherhood, while the boys are instructed to observe and practice the virtues that lead to correct fatherhood. These subjects, however, are freely discussed in the presence of both sexes at all ages, and, therefore, there may be said to be no difference in the methods of education. It is a fact that the little boys love dolls as well as the little girls, and the girls love athletic sports as well as the boys. The greatest attention is paid, during this decade, to the development of social graces, the cultivation of physical energy, and the training of the objective powers of the intellect, so that, at the age of ten years, there is not a child among us but what is affectionate, sociable, active, observing and exceedingly graceful in all of his expressions.

"During the second decade all of these acquired powers are kept active, but more attention is given to the development of the subjective forms of reasoning, to composition and construction, to the development of prudence and executive ability, the forms of government and military discipline. The military system, by the way, is not organized for offense and defense, as on this planet, and guns and swords have long since become obsolete. A few of them are preserved in the museums as curiosities, and to show the great progress which has been made; but our military system is simply the orderly arrangement of governmental discipline. The evolutions of large bodies of persons is still practiced as a means of securing control, and it is one of the admirable illustrations of the application of the rule of mathematical equity. During this second decade all of the education which is attempted on this planet is accomplished, and a great deal more, in the departments of sociability and ethics, of which you do not, as yet, have the faintest conception. During this decade a great deal of productive work is accomplished, and all that is done for the benefit of society, in the line of actual production, is placed to the credit of the student.

"The progress of the student has been carefully watched up to this point, and the observations of the direction his growth is taking enable his preceptors to decide with absolute accuracy what line of work he is best adapted to, and to what extent his powers are limited. Usually, these powers have been given a definite direction by the desires of his parents, and the pains that have been taken to make the circumstances attending the conception and gestation of the citizen insure his possession of special talent for special services. But it sometimes happens that some unforeseen circumstance changes the character of the citizen, and some unexpected talent is developed, or perhaps some weakness is discovered, which will alter the calculation and change the destiny of the life. Gallheim's system of character study, embraced in the second article of his code, provides for this exigency, and whatever the character of the citizen proves itself to be, it is recognized and permitted to have its full development in the most profitable lines of action.

"At the end of the second decade the decision is made as to what profession, trade or occupation the young citizen will devote his efforts. It is, of course, his ambition to excel in some line, and render such important services to the state that he will be advanced to the highest grade of social position. The third decade gives him an excellent apprenticeship, in which he performs a large amount of profitable work, which is placed to his credit. He now devotes four hours per day to the work of his chosen profession, under the most competent instructors. The rest of his time is his own, and the most ambitious young citizens devote four more hours to the prosecution of the further study of such arts and sciences as they may have a liking for. Large numbers devote this time to music, and the number of trained musicians who are always at the service of the state, and who are engaged in giving private concerts at various places, would astonish you. There is a great demand for the services of musicians, for all of the athletic and calisthenic exercises of the young members of the two first decades are performed to the time of music, and this music must needs be first class, because their young ears must not be dulled with imperfect harmony. A great deal of time is devoted by all classes to dancing, and the military drill requires a large number of musicians of the highest grade. Grand choruses are constantly being organized, and every afternoon every park is converted into a feast of song, music, and dancing, according to the desires of the persons who frequent each resort. Thus, in the city of Rosalia, where I reside, which has only five thousand inhabitants, there are more than one hundred musical organizations of a private nature, beside the large musical section of the students, who are required to furnish a certain number of concerts every month.

"The student, therefore, after spending four hours per day in the labor of his profession and devoting four more hours to such arts and sciences as may suit his taste, is prohibited from any further severe form of labor by the law of mathematical equity, and is required to devote the remaining time to social pleasure, rest, or any occupation which may be wholesome and agreeable, provided that he appropriates at least eight hours of this remaining time to sleep. He has every opportunity for social pleasure, as the working hours for professional labor are from 8 a. m. to noon, and after that the young apprentice is practically master of his own time, provided he is able to give a good account of it to his prefect. The prefects are members of the educational body, and each one is responsible for the conduct of one hundred pupils.

"When the third decade is completed the citizen has completed his education, and at the age of thirty years he is inducted into his profession with appropriate ceremonies. He now devotes ten years to the service of the state, and is required to serve four hours per day, six days in the week, in the discharge of his professional duties. It has been found by experience that this amount of time is more than sufficient to place at the disposal of the state a splendidly trained and equipped body of workers in every department of labor required by society. Consequently, the government has at its disposal plenty of time to allow deserving workers frequent vacations, and it is a fact that the workers are, as a rule, so absorbed in the prosecution of their duties, and so thoroughly contented, that the government is obliged to employ a

large corps of fertile inventors to keep up a supply
of new enterprises upon which to employ the talent
at its command. In fact, at the present time the
highest honors have recently been won by those who
have been able to suggest some desirable enterprise for the employment of the regular professionals.
Every available piece of ground has been beautified
and cultivated, until the entire inhabitable portion
of the globe is a vast farm, garden and park. The
most superb examples of architecture abound everywhere, and as fast as there is the slightest sign of
decay or lack of safety, the old buildings are torn
down and replaced by new ones. Our engineers have
brought the problems of transportation and sanitation to the highest possible point of perfection. In
fact, there is hardly a branch of industry that can be
named, that is conducive to the happiness and welfare of mankind, which has not been brought to the
very best possible conditions.

"At the age of forty the citizen has completed his
services to the state, and thereafter his time is entirely
at his own disposal and he does as he pleases. His
social position is assured; he has earned his living,
and the amount of his services placed to his credit is
greatly in excess of the cost of his maintenance in
luxury, even to the age of one hundred and fifty years,
which is the greatest age which any of our citizens
have succeeded in reaching. His habits of industry,
however, are so thoroughly well fixed by this time,
that he probably continues to work in his profession,

either as a teacher or writer, or perhaps he devotes his time to the prosecution of some entirely new branch of study. For instance, my father, after serving the state for ten years in the capacity of editor of a daily paper, upon receiving his discharge, devoted his usual working hours to the study of astronomy, in which he became very expert and won two gold medals from the National Association of Astronomers, for the discovery of two new comets.

"One grand feature of our industrial system remains to be told," said Loma, and his fine countenance glowed with an expression of great pride and reverence. "We take care of our aged citizens with the same solicitude that is expended upon the young. As the shades of eternal night begin to gather, when the step loses its buoyancy and the eyes grow dim, there is no sadness, no neglect, no memories of ingratitude. As there are those who by nature are specially qualified to assume the control and direction of the first years of the young life, so there are those who are especially gifted in the ability to minister to the wants of the aged. Serene in the contemplation of a life well spent, jubilant in the retrospection of past triumphs, surrounded by the hale companions of his youth, and ministered to by loving hands, with no speculation on the present and no fears for the future, the aged citizen of Venus calmly awaits the dissolution of his powers. There are no honors too great to be rendered to the serene old man or woman, as they calmly review the procession of their descendants, who are enjoying the blessings bequeathed to them through their observation of the law of mathematical equity. And when at last the golden bowl is broken and the citizen is admitted to eternal rest, there is no grief, no mourning, no habiliments and trappings of woe. His body is quietly cremated, and all that remains of him is the sweet perfume of his perfect life and the memory of his excellent accomplishments."

CHAPTER XVI.

SOCIAL AND SEXUAL ETHICS.

"Phrenology! Best gift of Mind to man,
Before whom Evil hides her guilty face
And Superstition cries out in alarm.
Thy power will emancipate the race
And lead us on to joys intensified
A thousandfold beyond our present ken,
When we shall blend in perfect harmony
And Love's sweet offspring come in Virtue's power
To bless the world with fairer creatures still.
Phrenology! 'Tis thy triumphant hour!"

At his next morning session for instruction, Loma announced that he would proceed to interest his auditors with a complete exposition of the system of sexual association practiced upon Venus.

"To understand my remarks upon this subject you must bear in mind that our citizens have the advantage of many generations of complete and correct education. While Gallheim's system of philosophy was very complete in itself, yet the full benefits of its operation were not felt for many years. At first there was some friction, and this is always to be expected after a change, until the mental capacities of the people are educated to a full comprehension of it. But when you understand that all of our citizens are now created under the operation of his wise laws, and that the patriotism of each member of society is always excited towards making a record in behalf of the improvement of the race, you will be able to understand how we conquer some difficulties that might otherwise seem insurmountable.

"The first important fact to which I wish to direct your attention is, that our citizens are in a natural state, and that we do not have to contend with inflamed and unnatural passions. It is safe to say, that seven-eighths of the moral obliquity of which your citizens are guilty in the department of sexual ethics come from unnatural and injurious food, and the use of alcoholic liquors, tobacco and other stimulants, which are entirely injurious, and which, beside blunting the moral perception and destroying the balance of the judgment, actually inflame the desires to such an extent that they are uncontrollable. These conditions were all abolished by the adoption of Gallheim's code, and we have a class of citizens, as a consequence, who are able to control their desires and make them subject to the application of the law of mathematical equity.

"Another condition which is in our favor, is that the natural desires of the affectional nature are satisfied from infancy to old age. The very first impression that is made upon the young citizen is, that he is loved, and that his affection is desired in return. He is kissed, caressed and encouraged to exercise his own affection by both sexes from the beginning to the end of his life. Now, on this planet you violate the law of the development of love by instructing your young people that it is dangerous and indecent to express love freely. As soon as the young citizen passes out of his swaddling clothes he begins to despise the caresses of his mother, and he is taught that it is unmanly and babyish to be affectionate. Your girl is taught to absolutely strangle her affections until marriage, in order that she may then gratify the selfish whim of the tyrant who is to own her, by being what he calls 'chaste;' that is, that she has never given expression to a single impulse of love to any fellow-creature of the opposite sex, except his arrogant, ignorant and selfish self. As a consequence of this sentiment and doctrine, there are thousands of your young men and women who are in a state of sexual starvation, and as they have been starved from their youth up, they have no conception of what is right. With the larger liberties you allow your boys, the majority of them become rakes, and satisfy their passions whenever and wherever they can, without taste or discrimination, and after a few years of such dissipation they are utterly unfit for a pure sexual association with any woman. On the other hand, your girls either become sexually paralyzed, or, yielding to the dictates of strong impulses, they violate the customs of your society, and, if discovered, they are disgraced.

"Now, upon our planet we have no such conditions. The fact that love is made a subject of study, and instruction, the same as music or any other department of knowledge, has enabled us to obtain the same desirable results. The affection which exists between the parent and child is never allowed to grow cold. You will see a mother of advanced age surrounded by stalwart sons and beautiful daughters, and perhaps a score of grandchildren, and by actual count you will see that she receives as many, or perhaps more, demonstrations of affection in the course of a day as she received when she was a beautiful young baby in her mother's arms. As between the sexes, and persons of the same age, the same spirit of affection prevails. Young persons become attached to each other in infancy, and continue through life to give and receive kisses and caresses with the greatest freedom.

"As a consequence, we do not have the condition of starvation to contend with, and the affectional natures of our young men and women being satisfied by these conditions, they are ready to consider the sexual relations with sound judgment and to adopt that course of action which the experience of the race has proven to be in accord with the law of mathematical equity and the best practical results. Another fact which conduces greatly to the establishment of correct moral conditions is, that sexual intercourse is not considered forbidden fruit. It is regarded as a purely natural function, and the imagination of the young citizen is not inflamed by its being surrounded by the air of mystery which pervades all classes on the earth. The destruction of the belief in the supernatural, which was the first principle of Gallheim's code, rendered all subjects free to the investigation of the people, and as soon as the curiosity of the young citizen is satisfied with reference to his sexual functions, and he understands them, he dismisses the subject from his mind and engages himself in the pleasures which are suitable to his age, with the full belief, that, when he reaches maturity, he will have all of the enjoyment intended by nature in the exercise of those parts of his constitution.

"With these explanations, you can readily understand that it is not difficult to enforce the doctrine which is universally accepted on Venus, that sexual intercourse should not take place until the participants have reached maturity. We find that our male citizens usually become fully mature at the age of twenty-five, and the female citizens about five years younger. Hence the question of indulgence does not present itself to the consideration of the young members of society until they are sufficiently mature to meet it with sound judgment. It is firmly impressed upon the young citizen, that sexual intercourse before maturity is highly injurious, and destructive of enjoyment after that period, and the law of mathematical equity is again invoked with the happiest results.. But in the meantime the young citizen is instructed in the minutest details of the proper performance of the act, and as this, as well as every department of knowledge, is carried to the perfection of a fine art, when the time for indulgence arrives, the participants are prepared to obtain the highest form of enjoyment from the exercise of the function.

"The enforcement of the second and third articles of Gallheim's code has caused every citizen of Venus to be thoroughly instructed in the art of character study and the principles which underlie the improvement of the race. Consequently, all intimate associations are governed by the laws of affinity, and as the study of personal magnetism has been carried to the same degree of perfection as all others, we have learned what combinations of complexion, temperament, quality and phrenological development produce the best results in all departments of effort. You will remember that every citizen has been created with a definite purpose, and that that purpose has been kept in view at every stage of development and education. Each citizen is anxious to make the highest possible record, and consequently, as the act of sexual intercourse is recognized and used as one of the greatest powers of the individual, it follows that the selections that are made of companions for this exalted act are made with direct reference to the best possible effects on the happiness of the parties, and the results desired in the offspring, if any are contemplated.

"In order that you may comprehend the manner in which these selections are made, I must explain another feature of our social system. In the very nature of the constitution of man it is plain that some persons must be more agreeable than others to any given individual. While it is our duty to treat every living thing with justice and kindness, yet there are some we do not wish to be continually associated with, and many we cannot entertain to any extent. There are others we wish to manifest friendship toward, with more than conventional warmth, and there are others still upon whom we wish to lavish affection. Now, the capacity of any individual is limited in all of these directions, though under our system of culture of the affections, the number of persons that are fervently loved by some of our strongest and best natures would be incredible on this planet, where nothing of the kind is practiced, but rather suppressed.

"In Venus the social relations of every citizen are classified under seven specific degrees, as strangers, acquaintances, associates, brothers, sisters, lovers, and consorts.

"A stranger is a person whose relationship is unknown. This includes all persons not defined in the remaining classifications.

"An acquaintance is a person whose name, residence and social position are known, but who may not be related to the individual in any intimate way. An associate is an intimate acquaintance, and this relationship corresponds to that which your society maintains among those who have a visiting and cordial friendship, but who do not consider themselves bound by any special ties. The establishment of these relations is largely a matter of locality and convenience, sometimes of accident, but a man is not considered an associate until cordial social courtesies have been exchanged.

"When persons of either sex conceive a strong attachment for each other it is in order for either to propose a covenant of fraternity. This covenant is a pleasing ceremony, and is always celebrated with festivities in the presence of other members of society. When this covenant has been formally sealed, the parties are considered in an affectionate relationship, and they caress each other as freely as is agreeable. In this state there is an absolute guaranty of protection and fidelity, and a young woman in Venus never hesitates to accept a caress from a brother, because she knows he is sincere, and that it does not imply any sexual intercourse, or any temptation to indulge in that act. While sexual intercourse is not considered a crime, and if it were indulged in, it would not subject the parties to disgrace, but only to a parental admonition from a prefect, yet so thoroughly is the idea inculcated that this act must not be performed until the proper stage is reached, that the rule is never violated. A brother proposing such a thing to a young woman with whom he has celebrated this covenant would be regarded as insane, and it would probably produce the same effect upon her that would be produced upon Myrtle if I should ask her to rattle a tin pan while Edward was singing us one of his excellent compositions. Such is the effect of education and refinement, coupled with a correct understanding of the use of things.

"When, however, the citizen has advanced toward maturity, and the sexual senses have become thoroughly trained and subject to the dictates of enlightened judgment, the young man or woman becomes conscious that those persons who are his or her sexual affinities, according to the laws of human association, which have by this time been thoroughly mastered, are agreeable for a higher use. We will suppose that we are considering the case of a young woman of Myrtle's age, though, as I have said, there is no distinction in favor of either sex in the practical working of these customs. She has a large number of associates, and of these a number have been advanced to the fraternal degree. She becomes conscious that of her brothers there are not less than twenty who are of suitable age and temperament to be her sexual affinity. She must have time to discover which of these she prefers, and this can only be determined at last by very intimate association and the extension of fraternal greetings and caresses into those expressions which have a closer significance to the sexual act. She, therefore, advances to the degree of lovers those of her brothers for whom she has a strong personal attachment. This is probably five years before she expects to become a mother. But in the degree of love, she tests her feelings, and very soon discovers the one for whom she has the highest and most exalted sentiments and who reciprocates them in the highest degree. This matter of selection is purely mutual, and a rejection is not considered a slight to either party, for the law of mathematical equity requires each person to use the highest skill and best possible judgment in making the selection. When the selection has been made, it is announced, and the parties remain as betrothed lovers for several months, testing the effect of association in every possible way, and developing their powers together, so as to be sure before any sexual intercourse is attempted that they will be perfectly harmonious.

"When this period of probation is past they receive the congratulations of their friends, and begin their sexual association, with a ceremony acknowledging and recording the relationship. For at least one year no possibility of conception is incurred, and if at any time it is discovered that the relationship is injurious to either party, or that they do not harmonize in the highest degree, the relationship is at once dissolved and new relationships formed according to the same system. So perfect is the operation of the system of selection, however, that only a fraction of one per cent. of the relationships thus formed are ever dissolved. When a dissolution takes place, however, there is no scandal, and the parties suffer no more loss in the esteem of their associates than Myrtle would with us if she attempted to play a difficult piece of music and should make a mistake. The law of mathematical equity prohibits the visitation of any loss of social position upon the parties who have earnestly and conscientiously endeavored to do their best for the advancement of society, even though they may fail.

"It is usual for the parties to continue in the relation of consorts for a period of years, usually from two to five, before they produce offspring. When they have become perfectly attuned, they are admitted to the palaces of maternity, and here they generate their offspring according to the admirable system I have already described. When a child has been produced the obligation is at an end, and either party is free to return to single life, or to form a new relationship, if they so desire; but they have usually become so warmly attached to each other that the relation is continued at least to the full extent for which they are allowed by the law of mathematical equity to become parents. No woman becomes a mother after she is thirty-five years of age, and no man becomes a father after he is forty. So perfectly is the law of conception understood on our planet, that no accidents occur, and the man or woman who cannot regulate the matter of conception is unknown among us. After the age of conception is past the parties continue to consort together and enjoy their sexual relations, and, as I have stated, they seldom dissolve the relation. It is not compulsory, however, and after the parties have passed the age of parentage they are at liberty to do as they please. But by this time they have been so thoroughly satisfied, and what is decent and correct has become so thoroughly understood, that there is no indulgence but what is approved by our authorities as conducive to health and the best possible effects upon happiness.

"It has been determined that the best results are

attained by the exclusive sexual intercourse of one man with one woman, provided that it is accompanied by the highest expression of mutual love and reciprocated desire. Hence it is never attempted in any other way, and if the parties cease to be attractive and loving, which rarely happens, they are permitted to correct the mistake, and to form another relation, which is equally as exclusive while it lasts, and it usually lasts. Now, while it is found that sexual intercourse is more beneficial when it is confined to one consort, it is not so with the other expressions of love. When a man or woman ceases to exchange affectionate demonstrations with all persons except the consort, it is discovered that such persons become stale and flat in the exercise of love, and receiving no magnetism, except that of the consort, they soon become starved. Hence it is the custom for both parties to retain all of their lovers, and after a person has selected his or her consort, the lovers unite in contributing all their good influences to the benefit of the one who has favored them by advancing them to that degree. Hence, in the case of the young woman we have been considering, while she has sexual intercourse only with her consort, yet she is continually fed with the magnetism of her lovers and brothers, and the richness of the development of her love nature goes on without interruption. When she becomes pregnant she draws largely upon all of these resources for the sustenance and mental food she requires, and the result is, that her child reflects the combined excellencies of all her lovers in his constitution, instead of being the starved and puny production of two narrow natures.

"The foregoing observations apply to all those persons who have adopted the profession of parentage. The same system of selection obtains among those who have decided that they will not produce offspring, except that this fact is always mutually understood before they advance to the degree of consorts. In case both parties desire it, they may at any time adopt the profession of parentage, even though they do not contemplate it at the time of consorting. But in case one party develops a strong desire for offspring, and the other party does not, the relationship is then dissolved, and new relations formed, according to the wishes of the parties, for it is a cardinal principle in the law of reproduction that no person should ever become the parent of a child unwillingly, and that no one who is healthy and of suitable age should be denied that privilege when it is earnestly desired and can be indulged without violating the law of mathematical equity in its application to the welfare of the proposed offspring. Under the enlightened conditions which have been produced by the application of the full text of Gallheim's code, these matters are perfectly adjusted."

"It is clear from your exposition of the subject," said Mrs. Bell, "that your citizens use the act of sexual intercourse for more purposes than mere reproduction. Since the agitation of these subjects began on the earth, a certain class of reformers have developed, who argue that there should be no intercourse under any circumstances, except for actual reproduction. They have attracted a very respectable following by their arguments, many of which appear to rest upon reason. I would greatly enjoy hearing your opinion upon this subject."

"The same theory was advanced upon Venus when the subject was in the same stage of development," answered Loma, "and it was a healthy reaction from the unbridled license which had prevailed up to that time, under the system of marriage. While the wife was the slave of the husband, she was obliged to submit to his unnatural demands, and a long train of evils was the result. As is usual in such cases, there was a reaction when the wife began to obtain the control of her person, and those persons who did not comprehend the enjoyments of a perfect form of the act, began to advocate the theory you have mentioned. It was noticeable, however, that it had no strong adherents of either sex who were well developed in the affectional nature, except those who had been disappointed in marriage, and whose sexual passions had been in a measure injured or destroyed by some form of abuse. Those who really loved and copulated in purity and happiness, experienced such ecstatic joys that they were unwilling to adopt the theory, and those who were inflamed by unnatural desire ridiculed it and disregarded it. This led to a careful investigation at last, and under the application and practices of Gallheim's code, and especially of the third article, it was discovered that the sexual act consisted in an exchange of magnetism, and that when it was performed intelligently, it was a powerful force which could be used, not only for the reproduction of offspring but also for the reproduction and increase of all the mental and physical powers of the participants. The argument which was the strongest advanced by the advocates of the theory, that all other animals observed this supposed law except man, was completely overthrown by this discovery, because man was demonstrated to be the only animal who was sufficiently endowed with intelligence to apply it. It was shown that man was the only animal who could understand the laws of electricity and magnetism, and to compel him to forego the benefits which he could derive from a proper understanding and application of the laws of sexual magnetism and electricity was as absurd as to require him to abandon the uses of the same forces in the arts and sciences. Therefore, when man ceased to consider himself bound by the habits of the animals who were beneath him in intelligence and complexity of organization, and began to study himself, in the light of science, experiment and observation, the true laws of sexual association were rapidly formulated and comprehensively taught. I will make these laws the subject of a special session of your instruction."

"There is only one thing which I do not clearly understand in the operation of your system of sexual association," said Myrtle, "and that I can embody in a single question. When a young man or woman has a large number of lovers, do they become jealous and quarrel among themselves over preferences, as we do on this planet?"

"That is rendered impossible by the operation of the law of mathematical equity," answered Loma. "You understand that the fact that the young woman has advanced a number of her brothers to the exalted degree of lovers gives them no claim to exclusive possession of her under any circumstances. They are simply complimented by being assured that they have a share in her affections, and jealousy among them would be as absurd as jealousy among brothers in one of your present families concerning a sister. Jealousy never arises in such a relationship, even on this earth, unless the jealous person is insane. You sometimes have an example of a woman who is jealous of the affection of her husband toward his daughter by a former marriage, or of a wife toward her husband's sisters, or something similar, but in all of these cases you know that the condition is abnormal and you treat it as a form of insanity. A young man who would show jealousy, and make himself disagreeable, or attempt to interfere with the young lady's liberties in any way, would soon find himself dismissed from the coterie of her lovers, and sometimes such things have occurred, but so rarely as to furnish few examples. When a young man has been selected as a lady's consort he is very secure in her affections, and as all of her lovers now unite in showing how faithful and devoted they can be to her interests, he would be a fool if he manifested anything but the warmest appreciation of their efforts in her behalf. At the same time his lovers of the other sex are showing their devotion to him by every act which can promote his happiness in his choice, and his consort would be considered insane, and it would be considered good grounds for the immediate dissolution of the compact, if she in any way attempted to interfere with his liberties, or to require him to sacrifice any of the privileges which science and the experience of the race have decided are beneficial. For instance, if she should manifest displeasure because he bestowed an ardent caress upon one of his lovers, she would be regarded as having acted as insanely as if she had been displeased because he ate his dinner with relish. We do not have these conditions upon Venus, because all of our citizens have been so thoroughly instructed in the principles of mathematical equity. To show you how our lovers act, I will relate the method of a very delightful social custom. Notwithstanding the fact that the choice of consorts has been made, and the minds of the parties are regarded as settled, after a scientific and sensible method of choice, the fact is recognized, that the delight of the parties in each other can be greatly increased by the congratulations of their friends. So when a betrothal is announced, it is the custom for the lovers of both parties to arrange a series of receptions in their honor, and to write frequent letters of congratulation, in which some virtue of the consort is commented on. By the time the parties are ready for the final ceremony of the act of consorting, they are in the highest possible condition of mutual admiration and love, and the attachment is thus cemented and continued. It is considered a most elegant thing to suggest to a man some extraordinary virtue of his consort. If this custom prevailed on earth there would be fewer divorces, but your people lose all interest in the married man or woman, because they are regarded as the chattels of each other.

"It is this idea of ownership which is the curse of your social system and the cause of jealousy. Men and women will continue to be selfish until they learn the law of mathematical equity. While in ignorance of this law, and believing in the ownership of the marriage relation, an inferior man becomes the husband of a superior wife. As soon as she becomes his property he forbids her the natural association which it is her privilege to have with all good men. He is not agreeable himself, and he knows it. He knows that when she meets a superior man, he shows to a disadvantage, therefore he does not want her to meet any superior men. She craves a natural food which he cannot and will not provide her, and because she seeks the society of some good man he is torn with spasms of insane fury. He is jealous. Being jealous, he makes himself so disagreeable that it takes a saint to live with him. All women are not saints, and none should be required to be. All that should be required of any man or woman is to be natural. It is impossible to be natural in an unnatural state.

"I will state, in closing, that the social standing of a citizen of Venus is graded according to the number of fraternal and loving relations he has established. If he can make himself so agreeable that he can secure a brother he is credited with ten marks of merit. If he can secure a sister he has twenty marks placed to his credit. For every lover he receives one hundred marks, and for a consort five hundred. These credits are repeated for every year that the relationship continues. For every child, a maximum of one thousand marks is granted for perfection, and this number is proportionately reduced if there is any imperfection in the offspring. The citizen makes two records. A juvenile record, which marks his progress on a similar scale, until he is twenty years of age. At twenty he begins to make his life record. It usually happens that, on his twentieth birthday, all of the friends of his youth renew their covenants with him, so he starts with a very respectable record. It may interest you to know my record, of which I am proud. The juvenile record is composed entirely of fraternal relations, as a juvenile has no lovers or consorts. I closed my juvenile record with seven hundred and twenty brothers, and one thousand five hundred and ninety-six sisters, and as the relationships had continued on an average of nine years each, my social record was indicated by the number 352,080. All of my fraternal relations were renewed on my twentieth birthday, and at the close of the last year I had the following record, which has been slightly increased since. I am now thirty-five years of age:

I have brothers to the number of 2,960, with an average of eleven years of association, which entitles me to credit marks....................	325,600
Sisters, 4,320, average 12 years....................	1,036,800
Lovers, 276, average 14 years....................	386,400
I have had one consort, ten years.................	5,000
We have produced three perfect children...........	3,000
My social standing, therefore, last year was.....	1,756,800

Mrs. Bell, Myrtle and the doctor broke into applause. Loma, glowing with his exquisite magnetism, extended his arms to Myrtle, and said:

"Beloved, may I add you to the list of my lovers as my latest and sweetest accession?"

Myrtle, for an answer, sprang into his arms and covered his lips with kisses. "Oh! if I am only worthy!" was all she said.

Loma returned her caresses with fervor, and then, releasing her, extended his arms to Mrs. Bell. "May I claim you as my sister?" he said to her, and she responded with a warm and sisterly caress which left no doubt as to the sincerity with which she reciprocated his attachment.

Doctor Bell arose from his seat and extended his arms to Loma. "I offered you my resources and all my powers of assistance the second day of our acquaintance," he exclaimed. "May I now take the initiative and ask that you make the compact of Brotherhood with me, and that it may date from that happy moment?"

"With all my love!" said Loma. "In fact, I so considered it at that time, but it is delightful to renew it now," and so saying he embraced the doctor and kissed him affectionately. Then turning to the ladies he exclaimed:

"Beloved, if you were sufficiently clairvoyant, you would know that at this moment, in Venus, in one of the temples of my city, my exalted consort is presiding over a meeting of my lovers and most intimate brothers and sisters, who are able to be present, to the number of five thousand. Our entire proceedings of the last hour have been as well known to them as if they were in this conservatory. At this moment they are uniting in a grand anthem of love and friendship in honor of the birth on this earth of the true system of social fraternity. Let us unite with them, and for a brief period I will give you a glimpse into the regions of the blessed."

In a moment Loma glowed with an intensity of magnetism he had never before displayed. He stretched out his hands over his friends, and the conservatory seemed to change into a vast auditorium of such surpassing beauty that the senses were bewildered with the effect of its magnificence. The auditorium was filled with an audience of human forms, glowing with magnetism, and radiant with the perfection of their own superb loveliness. Upon a dias in the center of this auditorium was a woman, whose magnetism seemed to be more intense than any of her audience, and whose beauty was so surpassing that her image remained forever impressed upon the three beholders as a dream of never-to-be-forgotten loveliness. While they gazed entranced upon this vision, their ears were ravished with strains of music beyond the comprehension of earthly senses, but which they recognized as of the same type with which Loma had often delighted them. Then their receptive abilities were exhausted and they lost consciousness, and knew no more until they awoke in the conservatory and found Loma regarding them with his loving and exquisite smile.

CHAPTER XVII.

COMMERCE AND WEALTH.

"Give us this day our daily bread."
"We do not shatter for the sake of destruction. There is not one of the old doctrines for which we do not substitute what we believe to be better and more rational. We do not take down a single structure of the past, but that we seek to erect a more modern one and a better one in its stead. We have never taken away any belief, any cherished idea, without standing ready to put in its place something that to us, at least, seems nobler and more beautiful. To destroy for the sake of destruction is without excuse. To destroy for the sake of reconstruction is a work that is of God."

After the transcendent experience related in the last chapter, Loma allowed his pupil to rest for several days before he attempted any further instruction. He desired the impression he had made to sink deeply into her intelligence, and to create in her the ambition for her son to become the means of introducing upon the earth the conditions of happiness which she had been permitted to observe. In after years this ambition was to be her chief incentive to action, and the profound impression was also designed to be made upon her offspring, so that he would be filled with the loftiest desires of humanitarianism and philanthropy. Consequently, while the morning sessions in the conservatory continued without interruption, they were devoted to social intercourse, music, and such delightful conversation as would in no wise fatigue, while they gave Myrtle the opportunity to ask any question which occurred to her.

The day following the clairvoyant vision of the meeting of Loma's lovers upon Venus, she had, with his approval, entered into a compact of Love with Doctor Bell. As she expressed it, she considered that the compact of Brotherhood had existed ever since she had been an inmate of his home, and she certainly felt that he was entitled to a higher degree. Toward Mrs. Bell her relations were unchanged. Loma had pronounced the compact of Motherhood, which Mrs. Bell had extended to Myrtle upon their first meeting, as the highest and holiest that could exist, and as there were no national educators upon the earth who could assume the education of the future prophet and teacher who was to proceed from her womb, the compact of Motherhood was held to be peculiarly appropriate. Thus the social relations were organized, and for the first time in many centuries, the correct relationships of men and women were resumed on the earth. I say resumed, for Loma had explained that Jesus had established the same conditions, which he had designed as the permanent conditions of his associates, and which did continue until his admirable system was destroyed through the machinations of priests and politicians.

About one week after his last session, Loma announced that he was ready to resume, and at the next session in the conservatory Mrs. Bell began the conversation by saying:

"You have given us a masterly exposition of the origin of your civilization, and the organization of society upon a better basis. You have shown the superiority of your system of education and the regulation of the domestic relations, and after the marvelous vision of your consort and lovers, which we were permitted to enjoy, there is no doubt of the grandeur of your institutions remaining in my mind. But when we begin to teach your theories we will be met with the proposition, that it is all impracticable, and that the needs of the world cannot be met without the present commercial stimulus. I would like to be instructed as to the way that the necessities of life are produced and distributed, and what you use instead of the present system of merchandise and money. Our reformers all concede that the greatest obstacle we have to contend with is our present system of money and the measure and exchange of wealth, and the system in current use among all civilized nations is so unnatural, that, as you say, only those who have a superior development of the financial sense can succeed."

"I will cheerfully comply with your request," said Loma; "and all the more readily because the solution of the problem is comparatively simple. The only reason you have not solved it upon the earth is because your citizens are not working under the law of mathematical equity. As soon as you recognize the true character of wealth, you will have no trouble in obtaining it, and when your conduct is regulated by the law of mathematical equity, you will have no loss in its distribution. To begin with, then, wealth does not consist in the accumulation of property, nor in the possession of a medium of exchange which will purchase property. A man may have both and still be exceedingly poor, as an inspection of the true condition of your so-called wealthy citizens will immediately disclose.

"The whole trouble with your financial system grows out of the universal misconception which your citizens have of the object of existence. Your citizens may be divided into two classes. Those who are entirely absorbed in making money and accumulating property, and those who are indifferent to this world's goods, and who spend their time in comparative poverty, absorbed in religious or literary work, or perhaps in complete idleness. The first class consume the years of youth in a mad struggle for wealth, in the hope of reaching enjoyment in the later years of life. The majority of them die before these years are ever reached, and those who do live to an advanced age find that they have lost the capacity for enjoyment. The second class lose much of the development and enjoyment which rightfully belongs to them by not having the possession of the necessaries of life. Now these conditions are bound to remain until the citizens of this world learn the simple lesson, that the purpose of life is growth and enjoyment, and that the true definition of wealth is the power to gratify desire.

"Let me illustrate. A youth desires to visit a foreign country. He works at a trade and accumulates sufficient money to gratify his desire. In this case the money is wealth. A millionaire desires to take the same journey, but is prevented by poor health. In this case his money is not wealth, and he is not, in fact, as wealthy as the youth who, on arriving at his journey's end, finds himself without money but in the possession of enjoyment. The millionaire recovers and makes the journey. His money and his health constitute wealth. A chemist is anxious to try an experiment and make a new discovery. He is deficient in education, and for lack of information his experiment is a failure. He pursues a course of study, finds the missing information, makes a brilliant performance, and immortalizes himself. In this case the education, giving the information, is wealth. From these examples it is easy to see that the power to gratify desire is wealth. Now, on this planet, you have created conditions which deprive your citizens of all development, unless they can pay for it in money. Services are considered of little account, and poorly paid for when rendered, hence your people are under the universal misapprehension that money is wealth, or property which can be converted into money is wealth, because it is impossible to gratify desire without it. As a consequence of this misapprehension you are all miserably poor, and even your millionaires are not wealthy, for they have no healthy standards of desire, they do not cultivate enjoyment intelligently, and, as a consequence, they have a vast number of unnatural and evil desires which cannot be satisfied, and many of their best desires are unsatisfied, because the unnatural system under which you are working destroys the working capacity of those who would be able to satisfy the natural desires of all if they had the opportunity. I will give you a single example. We will suppose the case of a millionaire who desires to gratify his friends and himself with the finest class of music. Now the working of your unfortunate system has deprived a large number of your citizens who have musical talent of an education, and their talent has remained undeveloped. Your millionaire, therefore, finds that musicians are scarce, of the kind and quality he desires, and while a few exist, he finds to his mortification that they have all been engaged by one of his rivals, and he is obliged to postpone his entertainment until they can be had. Such instances are constantly occurring, and disappointment and dissatisfaction is the rule, even among your wealthy ones, and it is probably true that your working classes are the most wealthy after all, in one sense, because their desires are more natural and more usually satisfied.

"As soon as the law of mathematical equity was introduced into our civilization, as I have described to you, a better system was at once evolved. Our financiers discovered that the true essence of wealth did not consist in the accumulation of vast aggregations of property or money, but in having such a condition in society as would insure to every citizen the greatest possible facilities for the gratification of all natural desires. As soon as this was established in the intelligence of our financiers, they went about producing it. It naturally followed that they discovered that the only way to secure it for themselves was to make it the universal rule of society, and that the only way to secure it for all was by the introduction of a complete education for every citizen, and the application of the rule of absolute and universal justice, which secured for every citizen his share in the commonwealth, irrespective of his own financial ability.

"You will remember, that, by the operation of the new system, as I have already described, the actual labor required in society was reduced at least nine-tenths, and that the working hours of all of our citizens were reduced to four hours per day. This in itself made a vast difference in the condition of our citizens, and gave them a wealth of time, which is the first element in the gratification of any desire. I have also explained to you that there was an immense increase in the productive capacity of the workers by the improvements in machinery and every element of production, which was still further greatly increased by the extension of education to every citizen, and by the fact, that he had time to improve himself and his working capacity. You can readily understand, therefore, that every community soon found itself surcharged with everything that was necessary for the gratification of the desires of its citizens. As no one was interested in holding these productions for any market, they were, of course, at the disposal of any citizen who had a desire to be satisfied. All that was necessary to be done was to appoint an administrative force, which preserved the property and saw that it was given in good condition, and then every citizen was at liberty to help himself. You will observe, that the source of supply was the government, and that a citizen was not expected to appropriate the property of another citizen. There was no reason why he should do so, for he could obtain anything he wanted at the government bureaus. For instance, if a citizen of Venus decides that he wishes to establish a home, he goes to the government bureau of real estate and states his desire, and he selects whatever location he wishes that is not already occupied. He is not permitted to occupy any more ground than he can use to a good advantage and keep in excellent condition. He states in his application the kind of an establishment he desires to maintain, and if his request is in accord with equity and decency, he has everything furnished to him in short order. The house is built as he desires it, and he calls on the various bureaus for the furnishings. He is permitted to own these things and enjoy them as long as he lives and makes use of them. If he abandons them, or if he dies, the property reverts to the government, and such as is valuable is preserved, and everything which is not valuable is destroyed. The law of mathematical equity, which is

such an important part of every citizen's education,
regulates his desires, and he is not likely to ask for
anything which is unreasonable. In fact, this system
is its own great regulator, for as soon as a man finds
that he can gratify his desires at will, he does not
encumber himself with a great deal of property. Most
of our citizens live in the government hotels, which
are excellently conducted, and very few require more
than two rooms. There are some who prefer to reside
in one place nearly all of their lives, but the most of
us are migratory, especially after the years of professional service, and so there is not much demand for
permanent homes. The introduction of this system
completely destroyed the production of large cities.
The crowding together of so many persons, and the
inconvenience and misery which is so noticeable in all
of your large cities, was abolished. Instead, the population was distributed over a large area, and as we
soon developed the most excellent facilities for transportation, there was no necessity for anything of the
kind. The country was divided into townships, and in
each of these a government storehouse was established,
which supplied every article of merchandise, in the
very best quality, to every citizen upon demand. The
distribution of food and all of the necessities of life
being done without competition, there was no necessity for the multitudinous stores and trade shops
which cumber your cities and pollute the atmosphere
with decay. As a large majority of our citizens are
under the direct jurisdiction of the government dur-

ing the three first decades of education, and the fourth decade which is devoted to the professional employment, and the mothers and most of the fathers are quartered in the palaces of maternity, under the same jurisdiction, you see that the supply of necessities is carried on with the same perfection that your country would supply as many soldiers, only that the soldiers are provided with the best of everything, which is not the case in your army. Our people are not engaged in commerce, and the most that there is to do in the management of the problem of supply, is to provide food, education, house room and fine sanitary conditions for our people, and the rest of the problem is simply how to produce the most enjoyment, which is left to the intelligence of the people, after they are properly educated, and they have no difficulty in solving it."

"The trouble would be, on the earth, if such a system could be introduced, that the criminal classes would be rampant, and there would be no means of controlling them from appropriating the best of everything," said Doctor Bell. "The great majority of our citizens are only held to good conduct by the pressure of poverty, and if they could gratify their desires at will, as you say your citizens do, they would plunge into every form of dissipation. How do you prevent this on Venus?"

"Such a system cannot be introduced until the people are prepared for it by education," answered Loma. "You must remember that we did not reach our present liberties by a single bound, but that they are the natural consequence of the application of the great principles of Gallheim's code. You must first comprehend the nature of man, then you must study each individual and improve him, then the great principle of the improvement of the race must be made the patriotic duty of every citizen, and then, when you have produced a generation of good men and women by this obedience to natural law, they will be able to learn the law of mathematical equity and follow it. It would be impossible for you to take a collection of Chicago business men and teach them the law of mathematical equity. They might be able to comprehend the principle involved, but they would not live up to it, for their entire discipline up to this time has been against it. They have been taught to violate equity all the time, and the one who could violate it in the shrewdest way and make the most money by so doing, without laying himself liable to indictment for positive crime, has been the most applauded. But if the children of these same business men were educated to a full comprehension of the law, and were made to understand the practical application of it, and they were made to comprehend that the possession of wealth, social position, beauty and happiness depended upon the observation of the law, you would have an altogether different set of conditions, and there would be a marked improvement in the conduct of the young generation, as compared with the old.

"The vitality of our system, however, depends upon

the fact, that we constantly appeal to the strongest faculties of all of our citizens, to induce them to obey the law. Under your system, you appeal only to the fear of poverty and the sense of commercial value. Our citizens learn in early youth that all of their wants will be supplied, and all that is required of them is to reach the highest form of culture. Now, the desire for personal beauty and the love of applause are two of the strongest incentives to human action. There is hardly a young man or woman in the world who is indifferent to personal appearance, and the desire to be considered beautiful, and to stand well in society, is a ruling passion even on this earth, where the principles of right living are so little understood. Now, if you convince the young man or woman, that, by conforming to a certain law of propriety, they can achieve both of these desires, and they see the results of obedience in the beauty and acknowledged excellence of their associates, it is not unreasonable to believe that a strong effort will be made to obey the law. Now add to these strong motives the knowledge which is imparted by our complete system of education, and you will see, at once, that the attainment of the excellence which I have described is not only practicable but extremely easy."

"I can readily understand how, in each township, these regulations can be carried into effect, where every citizen is known and his right to an establishment in the commonwealth is proved. But I have not yet comprehended how you manage the matter with strangers. Suppose that this system were now in force here, and our citizens were advanced sufficiently in education to practice it, how can a citizen of Chicago go to New York, where he is not known, and be recognized as having a right to his entertainment? How do you prevent your different communities from being imposed upon?" asked Myrtle.

"The habitable portions of our globe are divided into states, about the size of the state of Illinois," said Loma, "and these states into counties and townships, very much as you have them here. This is only a matter of convenience for the administration of justice, for the whole world is governed in the same way, and we have adopted the same language and social customs. Until a citizen is forty years of age, his duties confine him necessarily to his own state, to a great extent, except when he goes upon an excursion on leave of absence. But the limitation of population, as practiced upon Venus, makes it possible for our officials to keep an accurate record of every citizen, and his stage of development and personal appearance. Every citizen is numbered, according to his class and place where he resides. In this way, the officials of every state are able to be responsible for the identity and standing of every citizen. Here, again, you have an example of the inestimable value of a complete education and the law of mathematical equity. We have no criminals, and we have no citizens who would be guilty of an attempt to defraud. Each citizen starts right when he leaves his mother's breast and becomes subject to the jurisdiction which is to educate and protect him through life. As a consequence, such a thing as a citizen attempting to defraud any sister community is unheard of. There is no necessity for it, for he can obtain everything he desires in a perfectly legitimate manner. To insure his protection, however, and for the identification of his body in case of accident or death, each citizen has his number and the place of his birth indelibly placed upon his body, under his right arm." And Loma lifted his right arm from his side and displayed a small tattoo mark of the figures 2—8—124—35.

"These figures I will translate as follows," said Loma. "The figure 2 stands for the state of my birth, the figure 8 for the township, 124 is my number, which means that my birth was the one hundred and twenty-fourth which had occurred in that township that year, which is indicated by the last number, as the thirty-fifth year of the present century, according to our calendar, which, of course, does not agree with yours. By these numbers and the careful record which has been kept of every important event in my career, it is easy enough to identify me at any place on the globe. The date of my birth being known, the officials of any community know about what stage of my development I represent, and my claims, of course, would have to correspond. If there was any attempt on my part to be absent from my duties at home, my absence would at once be noted, and my number would be advertised through the official gazettes throughout the world. In the absence of such a notice, the officials of the various states take no notice of the passage of a stranger through their jurisdictions, as the presumption is that he is entitled to all that he claims. Here we have a chance to cultivate hospitality as it is altogether unknown on the earth. The moment a stranger appears at one of the government hotels in any state, and registers as hailing from another, he is at once made the recipient of every possible social courtesy. Every state has a local pride in its hospitality, and the possibility of a stranger being snubbed or neglected is not to be thought of. As soon as he introduces himself, and indicates his desires, every facility is placed at his disposal. Of course, by consulting the official gazette, his social standing is at once known, and he is expected to maintain his reputation. Therefore, to answer your question, if a citizen of Chicago were to go to New York under the conditions which prevail upon Venus, he would be very likely to have such a delightful experience as one of your citizens at present could scarcely comprehend."

"This is great!" exclaimed Doctor Bell. "I attended the triennial conclave of the Knights Templar, with my commandery, at Boston, the month before you arrived on this earth, and I thought then we had a delightful experience in the hospitality of that cultured city, but I imagine that your civilization could teach us much we do not know in this direction."

"I took a similar excursion upon Venus, about the same time," said Loma, "and I will describe it to you and let you compare the entertainment. The occasion was the meeting of the Association of Scientists for the Promotion of Inter-Planetary Correspondence, of which I am a member, and which numbers something over thirty thousand members. We met at the city of Delicia, which is on the opposite side of the globe from the city of my residence. Our transportation was effected in air-ships, which are in common use on Venus, and which are sumptuously furnished beyond anything you have here. Of course, this was all furnished by the government of our respective states, but when we arrived at Delicia, we were royally entertained, for a whole month, by the citizens without any expense to us. Everything we could use was bountifully provided, and in the fullest sense we made ourselves at home. Now, if I am correctly informed, the people of Boston felt that they were giving you a splendid example of hospitality when they permitted you to come on their ground and exist without raising the hotel prices beyond the usual schedule, and it is hardly unjust to say that the chief reason which actuated their committee in securing the conclave for Boston was the large amount of money which would be spent by the knights during their sojourn in the city. Now, such an example as that would be regarded on Venus as anything but hospitality. Such a condition of things would not be tolerated for an instant in any of our states, and any city which would make an effort to secure visitors for the hope of pecuniary gain would be ostracised from the social compact, until such time as it reformed its methods, and the officials of such a city would be forever disgraced. Under our system, such a thing could not occur.

"But the grandeur and beauty of our institutions are shown in our treatment of those who have faithfully served their time and have reached the age of forty years. After that age, the citizen is master of his own time and he can gratify any of the desires of his nature. He is bound by no law but that of decency, and his education has been so complete that he is not only certain to behave himself, but he has developed the capacity for enjoyment. Wherever he goes, he is made the recipient of the most delightful social courtesies, and life becomes a poem of pleasure. He has earned his living and his honors, and the closing years of his life are absolutely free from care and anxiety. Under such conditions enjoyment is possible, and the young citizen who witnesses the delights of the old is stimulated constantly to the emulation of their virtues."

"There is one objection which is constantly urged by the opponents of socialism to this class of reform," said Mrs. Bell, "upon which I would like to have the benefit of your experience. It is urged that it will be impossible for any one to be persuaded to adopt that class of work which is now considered menial. It is conceded that, if there were nothing but the professional employments to be considered, the adjustment might be made. But under the new system, which contemplates a just division of labor, who is to perform the disagreeable tasks?"

"Most of the difficulty comes from the conception which has been implanted in the minds of your citizens by your social customs, that certain kinds of employment are degrading, because, being in a manner disagreeable, these occupations have been assigned to slaves and those who by poverty were obliged to serve as slaves. This is merely a product of human selfishness. Under our system all of this is changed. It is considered just as honorable to wait upon the table at a government hotel as it is to write the records in a government office. All labor is honorable, and if any task occurs which is disagreeable, it is considered all the more honorable on that account, because it involves a certain amount of self-sacrifice, and those persons who devote themselves to its performance are rewarded by a higher degree of social standing, on account of the nature of the work. Every citizen is credited with a certain number of marks of merit for his services, and if there is any work to be done which is specially disagreeable or dangerous, there is a higher credit allowed. The result is, that the government has no dearth of applications for that kind of employment, because it offers the shortest and quickest avenue to social preferment. To make this more plain, I will show you how I have added materially to my own standing. In my profession as a scientist, I receive one thousand marks annually for the faithful performance of my duties. I received this emolument ten years as an apprentice and five years as a professor, which would entitle me to fifteen thousand marks. But during my apprenticeship I also served as a volunteer laborer in the construction of one of our large ship canals. I did this partly for the physical development it gave me, in working in the excavations two hours per day, but during that time I earned in two years eight hundred additional marks. I was awarded seventeen hundred marks one day for saving the life of a fellow laborer under dangerous circumstances, and during my professional career of five years, I have increased my regular emolument to the extent of three thousand and four hundred marks. This gives me a present professional standing of twenty thousand and nine hundred marks, which is considered a highly creditable record, and if I pleased, when I reached the number of twenty thousand, which would represent the required earnings of two decades, I could have applied for a discharge and I would have been released, the same as I will be by operation of time when I reach the age of forty. But I preferred to remain in the professional ranks, as most of our citizens do, and if I am successful in my present undertaking, I will be enrolled among the members of the Academy of Heroes. Those who reach this distinction are no longer graded. The social number is lost in the brilliancy of the achievement, and it is the highest honor to which a citizen of Venus can attain, that no figures appear opposite his name in the official gazette."

"What special advantage is it, to have a high social standing, in a world where all the citizens have so many privileges?" asked Myrtle.

"The principal advantage is the satisfaction which comes from being the object of the admiration of our fellow citizens. This is always one of the strongest incentives to human activity, but while your citizens seek this admiration by accumulating wealth and by display in dress, our citizens have no means of obtaining it except by good conduct. Of course, the possession of a high degree of social standing entitles the citizen to special favor at all public functions, and at the theaters and places of amusement the matter of social position is important, if the occasion is a formal one. There is a marked difference in our formal and informal occasions. At the former, the utmost attention is paid to rendering great respect to those who are entitled to it by reason of a distinguished record. At the informal occasions, however, all of this is disregarded, and the genius who has been enrolled in the Academy of Heroes associates on the same level with the youngest member of the professional ranks. In this way the young receive the encouragement of those who have distinguished themselves, by intimate association, while due honor is rendered at the proper time. In the fullest sense, our people have learned to do everything decently and in order."

CHAPTER XVIII.

IMMORALITIES OF CHRISTIANITY.

"Woe unto you, scribes and Pharisees, hypocrites! for ye are like unto whited sepulchers, which indeed appear beautiful without, but are within full of dead men's bones, and of all uncleanness."

"What! Shall I call on that infinite love that has served us so well?
Infinite wickedness, rather, that made everlasting hell!
Made us, foreknew us, foredoomed us, and does what he will with his own?
Better our dead brute mother who never has heard us groan!
The god of love and hell together, they can not be thought.
If there be such a god may the great God curse him and bring him to naught.
Blasphemy? I have scared you pale with my scandalous talk;
But the blasphemy to my mind is all in the way you walk."

Since the reconciliation of Myrtle and her uncle, the latter had been a frequent visitor at the residence of the Bells. Myrtle had also been made happy by frequent visits from her aunt, his sister, and many tokens of their love were received by the young mother as the time for her approaching parturition drew near. Mr. McDonald, when stripped of the crust of phariseeism which had hitherto obscured his virtues, was in reality a most liberal and genial man. He became devotedly attached to Doctor Bell, but he regarded Loma with respectful awe, for he was sufficiently acute to know that the latter was the most extraordinary man he had ever met, and while he had not been taken into confidence as to the origin of the citizen of Venus, he was quite sure that he was not merely a cultivated and scholarly physician. He had a strong element of the superstitious in his nature, and was inclined to regard Loma as a genius gifted with supernatural power.

No attempt had been made by either Loma or Doctor Bell to engage him in conversation in regard to religion. He spent most of his time when calling in the parlor with the ladies, or in the library in friendly conversation with the doctor, who always encouraged him to make himself completely at home. Mr. McDonald was a gifted conversationalist, and being of pure Scotch blood, he was not wanting in wit and pungency in his remarks. He had been educated for the ministry of the Presbyterian church, but having a stronger taste for commerce, and having inherited a large fortune, which he had been shrewd enough to greatly increase, he had engaged in banking, and was at the time the president of one of the leading national banks of Chicago.

One day, when at the pressing invitation of Mrs. Bell he had remained to dine with the family, the conversation accidentally turned upon religion. When the subject was mentioned, he turned rather abruptly to Doctor Bell and remarked:

"I am anxious to be instructed in the elements of the religion you profess. When I first became acquainted with you, I was told you were all atheists, which was at that time sufficient to fill me with the greatest aversion, and I would not have considered you capable of any good action. But the peculiar circumstances which have resulted in compelling me to know you better have forced upon me the conviction that you are animated by a spirit of benevolence and goodness which is stronger than I have experienced elsewhere. Until I became acquainted with the members of this family, I did not believe that any person could be good who was not a Christian. With the people of my religious belief, Christianity and goodness are synonymous, and we have come to believe that all goodness has originated in Christianity."

"We believed even more than that, uncle," said Myrtle, smiling, "for in Sunday school I have often heard the teachers say, that all the goodness which was possessed by people who were not Christians was absorbed by them, in a manner, from those who were."

"True, my child," said her uncle, thoughtfully. "I, myself, have made statements to my class which amounted to the same thing. But more serious consideration has caused me to reconsider that decision. There have been good men in nations who have not heard of Christianity, and there must be some other source of human righteousness. At all events I am now liberal enough to hear both sides, and while I would be loth to surrender the inestimable benefits of the Christian religion, I am willing to learn. I am sure of one thing, and that is, the Christian churches of to-day are not doing their duty. We have relapsed into a formalism which destroys the spirit of the gospel to a great degree."

"I would be unwilling to force upon you a discussion which might be distasteful to you," said Doctor Bell; "but if you are inclined to listen to a complete exposition of what we regard as the immoralities of Christianity, I am quite sure that our brother Loma will take pleasure in considering them for the benefit of us all."

"Immoralities! Do you mean to say that Christianity is immoral? I have often heard it arraigned as lax and the churches criticised for their want of zeal, but I have never met any one who s so bold as to say that Christianity was immoral."

"I suggested that the discussion would possibly not be pleasing to you, and if you please, we will drop the subject, for it is a principle with us to allow every one to enjoy his religious convictions unmolested."

"I am not a bigot," said Mr. McDonald, with dignity; "and, as I said before, I am anxious to be informed. If you can show that Christianity is immoral, I would abandon Christianity at once. I do not think you can do so, and I will not be offended at you if you will speak freely and defend your remarkable doctrines to the utmost. You will, of course, allow me the freedom of questioning you?"

"Certainly," said Loma. "If we go into this discussion at all, I shall be pleased to have you propound any question you desire. I shall speak plainly, as I desire Myrtle to be impressed with what I shall say.

But I wish you to be clear as to my position. I shall not claim that the teachings of Jesus are immoral, for he derived his authority from the same school from which I claim mine. By 'Christianity' in this discussion we will understand the doctrines which are agreed upon by the so-called 'orthodox' churches, as constituting the plan of salvation, through the atonement of Jesus."

"That is well understood," said Mr. McDonald.

"Now, let us see if we can agree upon a substantial statement of those doctrines," said Loma. "I will formulate them into propositions, as follows:

"First—That there is one God, composed of three persons, a Father, Son and Holy Spirit, jointly constituting the Creator of the universe and originating all good, who is omnipotent and omniscient.

"Second—That there is an arch-fiend, called Satan, who originates all evil, and constantly wars with the triune God, besides vexing men to evil deeds.

"Third—That there is a place called heaven, the residence of the triune God, and a place called hell, the residence of Satan. That those persons who believe on the Son will eventually be taken to heaven to reside there eternally, enjoying eternal happiness, while those who do not believe will eventually be consigned to hell, to suffer endless torment. That the sole condition of salvation is belief on the Son, who is usually called the Lord Jesus Christ, and is identical with the man Jesus who was born of the Virgin Mary in Palestine, nearly nineteen hundred years ago.

"Fourth—That man, by reason of innate depravity, had become wholly alienated from God, and because of his natural tendency to sin, was guilty of a form of depravity which justified his eternal punishment in hell. That to appease the wrath of the Father, the Son came down to earth and was incarnate by the Holy Spirit of the Virgin Mary, proclaimed the doctrine of salvation through his death, and did actually suffer and die, to appease the wrath of his Father, and by his sufferings and death, made such a sacrifice, that the wrath of the Father was appeased toward all those persons who would thereafter believe on the Son.

"Fifth—That this sole condition of salvation, viz., belief on the Son, applies to all men that have been born since the atonement of Jesus was made, and will apply to all future generations. That the substantial requirements of this belief are, that Jesus died, rose again miraculously from the dead, that he returned to heaven, that he is God, and that this belief will, when conscientiously followed, secure for the believer a residence in heaven after death.

"Is this a fair statement of the essentials?"

"I do not see that you have omitted any important doctrine that is considered essential to salvation."

"Very well. Now I will state my reasons for considering the doctrines immoral. Before I do so, however, I will define immorality. That is moral which conduces to the understanding and practice of the truth. Whatever tends to teach untruth, or which will stupefy the intellect of man so that he will not be able to understand the truth when it is presented to him, is immoral. Immorality is therefore that quality of a doctrine, action or thing which causes it to work an injury instead of a benefit."

"I will agree to that definition," said Mr. McDonald, promptly.

"The first proof of the immorality of this creed," said Loma, "is found in its being contradictory in its statements. Passing over the doctrine of the trinity, and supposing that it is capable of being explained on the basis of a partnership, or some form of association of its members, the second and first positions are hopelessly irreconcilable, because if the triune God is omnipotent and omniscient, and he permits the existence of Satan, he thereby becomes *particeps criminis* in the origin of evil, and Satan becomes one of the quartette of gods, and by no means the least important member. Your omnipotent, all-wise Creator is thus shown to be the Arch-Conspirator against human happiness, and directly responsible for all the evil that exists. Now, this is an absurdity, and hence a doctrine which requires the intelligence of man to accept that which is logically absurd, trains his intellect against sound reason, and unfits him for the reception and understanding of the truth when it is presented to him."

"But may we not believe," interrupted Mr. McDonald, "that God permits the existence of evil for a purpose we may not be able to understand?"

"Not when our own salvation depends on the conditions here stated. We are required to believe on the

Son, who is presented to our comprehension as one form of this God, and whose mission is to lead us into a perfect state. We are required to believe that God is good. Now, if the creed presents him to us as a participant in evil, we are thereby led to believe that it is consistent with perfect righteousness to connive at evil, and we are encouraged to the same course ourselves, having God constantly before us as an example. It is perfectly consistent with good morals to believe in a supreme power who is all-wise, all-powerful and wholly good, but Christianity does not take that view of it. It insists upon the recognition of Satan, and thereby destroys the moral character of the triune God."

"But did not Jesus, himself, recognize the existence of the devil, and did he not cast out devils, and is not this proposition clearly founded on his teachings?"

"Most of the passages of the Bible in which this doctrine is ascribed to Jesus require a very strained construction to admit of such a belief. But even supposing that he did use the language which is attributed to him, and allowing nothing for the exaggeration of the writer of the history, interpolations and the lapse of time, you will not be able to find a passage where Jesus teaches that this belief is essential to salvation. The belief in devils of various kinds was practically universal in that superstitious period, and it is very reasonable that Jesus spoke in the language which his hearers were likely to understand, without entering into a controversy upon a nonessential which he knew must disappear before the expanding intelligence of mankind. You will not find that a belief in Satan is at all essential to the system of ethics which he inculcated. But whether he did or not, is not essential. The ultimate test of a doctrine is whether it accords with reason and truth, and not with the teachings of any philosopher. The greatest proof of the immorality of this doctrine is that it contradicts itself. If man is responsible for believing, and he is exposed to conditions which destroy his belief, with the consent of God, then God is responsible for the unbelief and not the man. This is another absurdity.

"A still greater proof of the immorality of this creed is found in the third proposition. According to this proposition, man is bribed to believe, by a promise of endless bliss in heaven. This destroys the moral sense of man by educating him to do right for the sake of reward, and not for the sake of righteousness. He is also urged to do the will of God, and to believe, through the fear of hell. Thus, hope of reward and fear of pain are the two principal motives appealed to, and these are set forth as the results of the relative powers of God and Satan. Because God is the most powerful, he is able to offer heaven to the believer, and to punish him in hell for his unbelief. The prominence given to these motives destroys all education of the other powers of man, and keeps him in slavery to his abject fear and his love of gain. The conception of God inculcated by these motives is that of an absolute tyrant, and this tends to make the man who serves and worships this conception a tyrant also. The sole condition of salvation is made a belief in something which is contrary to the usual order of things, and thus, while the curiosity of man is excited, he is forbidden to reason about it, because if he does, he will be in danger of disbelieving. This stupefies his intelligence and he is constrained to believe through his strongly excited fear and his hardly less strongly excited cupidity."

"Indeed, sir, I have never considered it in this light," exclaimed Mr. McDonald. "It has never occurred to me, that the hope of reward in heaven and the fear of punishment in hell are unworthy motives."

"They are not unworthy motives, except in so far as they are made paramount to all other motives. If the emotions of fear and the love of gain were only two of the incidents of this creed, there would be no criticism of it on that account. These emotions are made a part of man by the nature of his constitution, and are therefore not to be despised. But when they are appealed to as the chief motives of human conduct, to the exclusion and, in fact, destruction of the other motives which should form a part of the impulses to correct judgment, the result is stupefaction instead of enlightenment, and the agency which accomplishes this must be condemned as immoral. A still greater proof of immorality is found in the doctrine of eternal punishment, visited by God upon those who fail to accept the belief of the creed. The constant worship of a being of infinite cruelty tends to make men cruel themselves, and this belief is directly responsible for the fact that men in all ages have imprisoned and tortured their fellow men who would not believe as they did. The fact that this same conduct was one of the chief attributes of the God they had been taught from infancy to adore, justified them in following his example. Now we believe that goodness means justice and kindness, at all times and places, toward every creature, under all circumstances. We believe that Nature is altogether good, that there is no positive evil, and this conception fortifies us constantly in the exercise of kindness toward all creatures.

"The fourth proposition, on its bare statement, convicts your omnipotent God of imbecility or insanity, according to the way you look at it. If he was omnipotent, and he created man in such a condition that he is innately depraved, then man is merely as it pleased God to have him, and God has no right to feel wrath toward that which exists by reason of his own desire. If he is angry at man for being as he desired him to be, then he is insane. If, on the contrary, man has acquired his depravity by reason of his opposition to the will of God, then God is imbecile, or he would have prevented it. To allow man to become depraved when he could have prevented it, and then to punish him for it, is the act of an insane savage. The fact that his wrath was of that character that it could only be appeased by a bloody sacrifice, also convicts him of savagery, and the further fact, that he imposed or permitted the burden to be imposed upon his own son, shows that he was destitute of the most ordinary instincts of affection. The whole idea of the atonement is based upon the principle of retaliation, which is always brutal; it inculcates the principle of revenge, which is directly contrary to the teachings of Jesus, and it is directly responsible for neutralizing the effect of the greatest efforts made by Jesus toward placing the world upon a higher plane of action.

"The last proposition we have formulated, however, has still additional proofs of the immorality of the system. It inculcates the idea of a trial and a judgment before the accused has come into existence. This is the essence of injustice, and as immorality is always the result of injustice in some form, it creates the fundamental condition which produces all the immorality that exists. There can be no morality without fairness. The conception of a God who judges before the crime is committed, and who consigns endless myriads of human beings to torment in advance, has familiarized the human intelligence with infinite injustice, and made it a thing to be admired and followed as nearly as is practicable. It is not wonderful, in this view of the facts, that injustice prevails, and that the cultivation of the moral sense has not been known among Christian nations."

"Indeed, sir, you astonish me," said Mr. McDonald. "I had not supposed that such statements could be made with any degree of plausibility against a system of religion and morals that I have been taught to revere from my youth up. But I am far from being convinced that you are right, and it seems to me that you are judging the conduct of God by purely human standards."

"All standards are human that can be comprehended by human intellects. If your God will not stand the test when judged by human standards, we can hardly hope for a better result when standards of a higher degree are applied. We are required to believe with a human intelligence. In the very nature of things, what we are required to believe must be consistent with human reason. If it is contrary to reason, justice requires us to reject it. It has been well said that the man who will not reason is a bigot, the man who dares not reason is a coward, and the man who cannot reason is a fool."

"It seems to me," said Mr. McDonald, "that this conception of the wrath of God, and the fear of eternal punishment in hell, is necessary to hold the evil passions of men in check. If this fear was removed I do not discern what would prevent men from running riot in every form of crime and excess."

"You have entirely overlooked the strongest factor in human conduct, the natural impulse of every man to do right. Experience and observation have shown that even the worst criminals do right oftener than they do wrong, when the sum total of all their actions is taken into account. The ordinary citizen does right nearly all the time, or so nearly so that his obliquities are so trifling that they are not considered important. Think of the thousands of laborers in this city who will toil all day without committing any wrong, and whose work will be so perfect that the commerce of the world will glide along without friction. If it were not for the fact that humanity is naturally good, you would have anarchy at once, for the sense of fear is not strong enough in the majority of men to deter them from following the dictates of their wills. When we consider the efforts that have been made to stupefy men with fear, it is remarkable what good conduct is the rule. Fear is always brutalizing, whenever it gets the mastery of a man. It is true that most criminals are cowards. Therefore, if we wish to eliminate the criminal from society, we must commence by educating men to be brave."

"If there is no innate depravity in the nature of man, how do you account for the prevalence of crime? There is a desperate lot of wickedness in the world from some cause, and all the efforts of teachers, lawmakers, and philanthropists have not succeeded in eliminating it to any appreciable extent. On the contrary, the world seems to be growing worse every day."

"The world is not growing worse, but man is becoming more enlightened, and is therefore made to realize more and more the existence of discord, and the necessity for removing it. He therefore becomes more conscious of the conditions that surround him, and his moral sense is becoming awakened. As soon as he becomes sufficiently enlightened, and learns his own nature, and adopts a rational system of character study, he will progress very rapidly toward a better condition, and will ultimately reach it. But before he can do this, he must abandon the idea of his dependence upon supernatural agencies, and learn to regard himself as a natural product and subject to the same great laws which govern the growth of the objects which surround him. Man is now struggling with two serious misconceptions. The first is, that he is more highly favored of the gods than any other creature, and for that reason he trusts to the gods to do for him that which must come as the result of his own effort. The most conspicuous example of the pernicious working of this misconception is in the generation of his offspring, which he trusts wholly to the providence of his gods, instead of applying the well-known laws of reproduction, which he has so successfully applied to the generation of animals and vegetables. Because he regards animals and vegetables as under his own jurisdiction, he uses his intelligence with the happiest results. Because he regards his own offspring as under the jurisdiction of the gods, he neglects his duty in the study of human culture with disastrous results. The second misconception is, oddly enough, the antithesis of the first. It consists in regarding his own nature as wholly depraved. This doctrine has clothed humanity in one universal disgrace and destroyed the possibility of self-respect. As long as it is permitted to cloud the human intellect, it will render the world a penitentiary. Put a man in convict's clothing, and he will commit crimes of which he is incapable in the garb of a freeman. Until this misconception is removed, man will be a criminal in as much as he has allowed this idea to influence his conduct."

"If this view of the case is true, it seems to me that all men would be criminals. The strongest objection I can bring against your argument, and one which seems to me to be conclusive, is that those nations which have achieved the greatest advancement have been those in which Christianity has obtained the strongest foothold. If these doctrines have the effect which you ascribe to them, I do not see what has prevented the Christian nations from becoming the most barbarous. But we certainly compare favorably with the Mohammedan nations and with the civilization of the oriental nations where Christianity has been unknown," said Mr. McDonald, with spirit.

"Your argument is not conclusive, for two reasons," rejoined Loma. "In the first place, because the religions you name have features which are quite as objectionable as anything which can be found in modern Christianity, and I will not attempt to defend them or to make any comparison with them and Christianity. I am even willing to admit, that Christianity is superior to any of them. But supposing this to be true, the reason why Christian nations have advanced morally beyond their competitors is because there has been more scepticism among the Christians. The finest compliment that can be paid to the manhood of the Christian nations is that they have at all times refused to be bound by their religion, and constantly violating it, they have advanced. The Mohammedan and the oriental devotee is more devout. He accepts absolutely the precepts of his religion and lives and dies by it. Consequently it stupefies him and he has no moral sense. The Christian, on the contrary, is a natural disbeliever. This is shown by the great diversity of belief among Christians and the division into numerous sects. Even in any given church you are constantly dividing and disputing on points of doctrine, and of the great mass of church-going people, the majority are not believers. Thus while there has been, among what you call Christian nations, a formal recognition of the religion on the part of the state, there has been a constant repudiation of it on the part of the populace. You have at no time ever had a representative church membership in any nation, except in Catholic nations, where the members of the church in full sympathy with their creed constituted a majority of the citizens. The Catholic church is the only one which has ever succeeded in establishing a complete control of any nation, and wherever this has occurred you have witnessed the death of intelligence and the reign of superstition. So that we may safely assert, without fear of successful contradiction by historical facts, that the advancement of the so-called Christian nations has been entirely due to their rejection of the creeds, and that civilization has advanced, not because of Christianity but in spite of it. The fact that the organized church in every nation and under every set of circumstances has bitterly fought every scientific discovery and every important invention, as well as every advance in social science, is too well known to need repetition."

"I must confess that you have the best of me at present," said Mr. McDonald, "and I am unable to answer some of the arguments you have advanced. I am unaccustomed to the consideration of religion from this standpoint, and I see now that I have been looking at the subject wholly from one side. But I am far from being convinced, and I have this to say, at the present moment. Suppose you are right, am I not just as safe as you are?"

"You may be just as safe, with reference to the possibilities of a future state of existence in hell, but you are suffering a great deal of unnecessary anxiety, losing most of the pleasure of life through a false philosophy, committing a great many mistakes, and losing the development which comes from a correct life."

"That may be true, and it is a loss to be seriously considered, if it is true. But suppose I am right, what will become of you?"

Loma regarded the visitor fixedly for a moment and then inquired, "Mr. McDonald, is that line of questioning original with you?"

"No, sir," said Mr. McDonald, promptly; "but it is the usual line of questioning with which we are wont to silence the infidels we have to deal with."

"Then, without being impolite to you, I can answer,

that it is the argument of a coward, who dares not think. It is the privilege and the duty of every man who has the capacity to reason, to judge for himself what is right, and then live up to it, with the courage of his convictions. It is also the argument of the bigot, and I will force you to relinquish it or abandon your religion which you at present profess. The Catholic church says that no one can be saved outside of her pale. The Presbyterian church admits that a Catholic can be saved. Now, by the same logic you are bound to become a Catholic, for if you are right, he is reasonably safe, while if the Catholic church is right you are hopelessly damned."

"I give it up," said Mr. McDonald, laughing. "You are one of the best logicians I have ever met. But I am not yet satisfied. I will think this over a couple of days, and then come at you with some more questions."

CHAPTER XIX.

THE RELIGION OF LOVE.

"Jesus said unto him, Thou shalt love the Lord, thy God, with all thy heart and with all thy soul and with all thy mind. This is the first and great commandment. And the second is like unto it, Thou shalt love thy neighbor as thyself. On these two commandments hang all the law and the prophets."

A few days after the conversation narrated in the last chapter, Mr. McDonald was again the guest of Doctor Bell. He had expressed himself as anxious to continue the discussion, and on this occasion he presented himself armed with questions and a full stock of good humor. Myrtle and Mrs. Bell, to whom the conversation was intensely interesting, listened with great attention. Loma encouraged the guest to state his questions with the utmost candor.

"While you have impressed me very much with the arguments you stated in our last conversation," said Mr. McDonald, "I have this objection to offer to your whole philosophy. Suppose you succeed in destroying the entire plan of salvation, which has comforted so many aching hearts, what can you give us that is better? When you consider the misery that exists in the world, the sorrow over the death of those we love, the broken hearts, the blasted ambitions, the poverty, the crime, the degradation, and all of the misfortunes with which mankind has to contend, you must admit that this life is a failure. If there is nothing better than this world, then life is not worth living. Now Christianity holds out to the believer the hope of something better after this life, and opens to his view a vista beyond the grave, which is the only comfort and solace of the aged, as well as the chief stimulus to an observance of the laws of morality on the part of the young. If you take away the comforting assurances of the Christian religion, you destroy nearly everything which makes life endurable."

"Your statement is constructed upon a false theory of conditions," answered Loma. "You have assumed that the conditions which would obtain after the destruction of Christianity would be the same as now exist under it, which is contrary to the nature of things. As society is at present constructed, the laws and customs which have been made by those who proceeded upon the Christian theory are the chief forces which create conditions. The fact that life is a failure under Christian conditions is the principal reason why those conditions should be abolished and something else tried, if only for the sake of experiment. You admit, that after nearly two thousand years of trial, Christianity has not given us a world that offers many inducements to live in it. Now the fact that poverty, crime, degradation and misery abound under the dispensation of Christianity, and that many tribes of happy and contented savages have been completely destroyed by the advent of Christianity into their lives, is evidence that something is wrong, not with the world, nor with humanity, *per se*, but with the conditions which Christianity imposes and the education which it gives. I have already shown you, that the plan of Christianity appeals, principally, to only two of the faculties of the nature of man, viz., fear and the love of gain. Now, because, after the race has had nineteen centuries of riotous dominance of these two faculties, to the entire subordination of all the other good impulses of man's nature, you have conditions of degradation, misery and crime, you shrink from experimenting with any other form of education, because you are dominated by the fear of unknown consequences, and the love of gain prompts you to hold to the miserable comfort you get out of promises that have never in a single instance been verified. Your most devout Christian is always the most conservative man in the community. He is cautious and acquisitive, and the plan of salvation suits him. He can be reasonably consistent in its practice, because he loves gain, and he is always cautious and prudent, and he is happy in keeping on what he considers the safe side. He, therefore, orders his conduct reasonably well, according to Christian standards, yet the majority of men are not so constituted, and as the plan of Christianity does not appeal to them and does not fit their lives, they have no other system of moral or ethical culture, and they abandon themselves to wickedness. Thus, it appears, that the real reason why you have such unfortunate conditions in the world, is really because that religion which is to satisfy the nature of man has not yet been introduced. Jesus attempted to introduce such a religion, and to a great degree succeeded, and when the world accepts his teachings as they were intended by him, and not encrusted with the dogmas of politicians and superstitious priests, you will find, that while you have been acting in his name, you have been constantly violating his precepts, and you have accepted instead of the pure philosophy he taught, a mass of ridiculous contradictions which will not stand the test of reason. These incongruities and absurdities of the system have been exposed many times, but your people continue to cling to them, because the true teachings of Jesus are shrouded in doubt, and it is necessary that these principles should be presented again to the human race in the clear light of philosophy to enable them to grasp the truth. The extraordinary character and work of Jesus came very near demolishing the entire fabric of supernaturalism in his day, but the ingenuity of the priests, who saw their fabric tottering, saved it for a time. Instead of combating the new philosophy, after it had obtained a hold upon the people, they pretended to adopt it, and deified Jesus, so that the idea of the supernatural for a long time gained strength by the sheer popularity of his character. After the administration of the new philosophy had passed into the hands of the priests, it was an easy matter to falsify the records by interpolations, and to inculcate new doctrines which Jesus never taught. This process has been continued, with slight variations, down to the present day, when the true teachings of Jesus are being better understood than they ever were before, and, consequently, there is more scepticism against the received interpretation of his philosophy. The Christianity of the churches must fall, and Jesus must be restored to his original glory as the best of philosophers; the tawdry investments of godship must be torn from his figure, and it must be permitted to stand out in all of its pristine beauty of manhood. Then the absurd contradictions and untenable doctrines which have been attributed to him must be disregarded, and when a proper allowance has been made for the misunderstandings of his auditors and scribes, his original philosophy will be found to be substantially correct."

"I understood you to say, in our former conversation, that you derived your authority from the same school of philosophy in which Jesus was educated. Will you please explain?"

"Jesus was educated in the school of philosophy of which I am a pupil, and he represented a perfect type of a civilization which has existed for many centuries anterior to his extraordinary career on this earth. You will excuse me, when I say that I am not at liberty to give you the location of the cult to which he belonged, for confidential reasons. But if you will accept my statements for what truth they contain, and subject them to the tests of an impartial criticism, I will recite to you the essential articles of a creed which is substantially what he inculcated on this earth, and in which I have been educated from my youth, which may fully answer your question, when you asked what could be given in exchange for the accepted creed of Christianity which would meet the demands of man's nature."

"I shall be delighted to listen."

"The essential doctrines of Jesus are all summed up in his great proposition of supreme love to God and equal love to man. This is the sum total of all philosophy. But it is necessary to understand what he meant by the proposition, and we must not accept the interpretation which has been put upon his words by designing and prejudiced expounders.

"The first and great commandment, 'Thou shalt love the Lord, thy God,' does not mean that man shall bow down to any of the idols which man has made, whether they be of wood or stone or the savage ideals of ignorant and savage men. 'The Lord, thy God,' is that to which man owes his existence, his Creator, and the ruler of all the forces which surround and govern him. It is man's highest duty and privilege to question the universe and find what this force of creation is, and when he has reached the limit of his intelligence, to accept the demonstrated conditions of nature, and to love and obey them to the very best of his ability. When the limits of man's intelligence taught him that there was a power superior to his own in the flashing lightning and the rolling thunder, he was justified in falling down and worshiping it, but he was not justified in allowing that conception of God to remain fixed in his mind. Now, that man has progressed beyond the primitive savage state, and his intelligence enables him to comprehend reason, benevolence and justice, and he has solved many of the perplexing problems of the material universe which surrounds him, he is not justified in clinging to the savage conception of Jehovah, Jove, or any other ideal of a departed and darkened standard of intelligence. If he clings to these and loves them, he is not loving the Lord, his God. The highest duty of man is, to love the highest and best conception of the creative power of the universe which it is in his intelligence to comprehend. In the present degree of intelligence, we are able to prove that the creative power which is expressed in Nature, and which is manifested in the phenomena of growth and development, is the nearest and best revelation of the character of the Creator, and hence it is the imperative duty of man to abandon all of the supernatural conceptions which he has outgrown, and to devote himself to the study of Nature. The command, therefore, becomes translated into these words, 'Thou shalt love Nature.' Loving Nature means to study natural conditions and conform to them. When man does this he finds that every element in Nature is good. He finds that every condition of growth and development is the very best that could possibly exist. As soon as he conforms to the conditions of his environment he becomes happy and contented himself. Instead of cringing before a tyrannical and capricious deity, he stands erect in the presence of a universe which is altogether lovely, and in which there is no flaw. He learns that whatever is, is right. It is in accordance with the immutable laws of Nature, and he learns to accept these conditions and to conform to them. As long as he believes that his conditions are governed by the caprices of a supernatural deity to whom he can go with a petition, with the hope of having natural laws suspended for his selfish benefit, he will continually array himself against Nature and be punished accordingly. As soon as he learns that conception, birth, growth and death are natural and inevitable conditions, he will accept them as they are, and be satisfied with their consequences and not attempt to change them. He will learn that disease and pain are the natural results of disobedience of law, and he will develop his intelligence to the degree that he will be able to avoid them. Instead of neglecting every duty on this earth, that he may enjoy a hypothetical existence in an unknown sphere, he will enjoy his present life by conforming to his present duties. We may therefore say, that the sum total of man's highest duty is the rejection of the supernatural, the study of the natural,—which, of course, implies the study of himself, as well as the conditions of his environment,—and the adoption of such habits and customs as will promote his highest development."

"I must confess that this is a very extraordinary exposition of the first and great commandment," exclaimed Mr. McDonald. "I have heard it preached

from many times, but I am bound to acknowledge,
that, while the duty of loving God has always been
impressed upon me very forcibly, and I have been devoutly conscious that I was in a manner obeying the
command, my conception of God has always been that
of the stern and powerful Jehovah, who brought the
Israelites out of the land of Egypt. There is much in
the character of this deity as depicted in the Old Testament, that I have not been able to reconcile with my
conscience, but I have always bowed to the doctrine
that His ways were dark and inscrutable, and that it
was not given to finite minds to understand the workings of the Infinite."

"And by so doing you darkened the windows of your
own intelligence, and adopted the standard of the savage of four thousand years ago."

"I begin to believe that that is so, and in any event
I begin to be grateful to you for helping me to a better conception of the nature of the Creator. I know
that, whatever He is, He must be in harmony with His
creation, and I am willing to accept your statement,
that the development of intelligence and the study of
natural conditions is the highest form of worship."

"If you are willing to make this advance, you must
begin by removing from your mind the conception of
the deity which has heretofore existed," said Loma,
"and you must be honest with yourself. When you
think of God as the creator and designer of the universe, as its omnipotent, omniscient and eternal preserver, when you restore Jesus to his legitimate place

as the perfect type of man, and in that fact the revelation of God, and in the Holy Spirit you recognize and enthrone the spirit of universal Love, you will be ready to comprehend the importance of the second great commandment, which is like unto the first, 'Thou shalt love thy neighbor as thyself,' and you will indeed realize that on these two commandments hang all the law and the prophets."

"I am willing to be instructed," said Mr. McDonald, earnestly.

"Will you seriously claim that any form of Christianity expressed through any of the denominations makes any respectable pretense toward living up to the second great commandment?"

"No, I will not attempt to make such a claim. But I have always considered it impossible to do so, and have attributed the failure of Christians to fulfill the demand of this commandment to the inherent depravity of our nature and the evil constitution of man himself."

"By so doing, you impeach the judgment of Jesus, and accuse him of laying upon man a command to perform an impossible act. Now I think I shall be able to convince you that it is not impossible, and that, on the contrary, this command implies only a most reasonable and necessary duty, by which the happiness of man can be greatly increased. I will formulate the implications of this command into a number of propositions.

"First—This command implies, that man should love

himself. If he does not love himself, then an equal amount of love toward his neighbor will do that neighbor little good. Universal love includes self-love, and self-love, rightly directed, implies self-culture. Therefore, the first implication of this commandment is, that man should surround himself with the best possible conditions of growth, and that he should endeavor to obtain the highest possible education and use of his faculties. As long as he cringes in fear before a God who is ruled by the most despicable passions, this is impossible; but when he realizes that he himself is a part of the great and glorious cosmos, whose beauty delights him by day, and whose visions of rolling worlds inspire him by night, he may rise to a proper conception of his own value, and think of himself as a great and glorious personality, instead of as a crawling worm of the dust. You will agree with me that, instead of teaching this conception of manhood, Christianity has always emphasized humility, and enforced it with the doctrine of the utter unworthiness of man. With his unworthiness and depravity kept constantly before him, in a world which his own intelligence has taught him was filled with beauty and perfection, it is easy to see that all men who have conscientiously accepted Christianity and tried to live up to it have learned to hate themselves. A normal mind must always hate that which is depraved and unworthy. With this conception of himself, it has been the most natural thing on earth for man to regard his fellow man as unworthy and depraved, and hence he has made no rational effort to improve either himself or his neighbor. The first condition of obedience to this commandment is, that man shall learn his own value, that he shall develop self-respect, that he shall study himself in the light of science, and realizing his nature and destiny, that he shall love himself into the best possible conditions.

"Second—Man must realize the value of his neighbor. Until he adopts the plan of character study, he will never have a rational conception of human nature, or the nature of the other objects which surround him. Man does not understand the virtues, the possibilities or the destiny of those who surround him. He has yet to realize the value of human energy. He must comprehend the measure of human pain and human happiness. Until he does this, he will not awaken to the necessity of avoiding the one and increasing the other. The horrible mistake has been ground into the understanding of man, that he should not seek for happiness on this earth or in this life. If he is barred from this himself, what possible interest can he take in the happiness of others? When this pernicious doctrine shall have been destroyed, and man comprehends that he is placed in this world to enjoy it, and that his highest duty is to crowd into the brief period of his existence the greatest possible amount of happiness, and he learns that this is best accomplished by ministering to the enjoyment of others, then life will be for man what it is for every other creature which has conformed to natural conditions, a long, sweet symphony of pleasurable experiences.

"Third—It is necessary that man should learn who his neighbor is. The common conception applies only to those who have become intimately associated with us in some way. But the true definition of the term implies any being with whom we are brought into contact. In this broad acceptation, man must include, in the term 'neighbor,' not only the man who is near him but the animal also. It means that man shall apply the rule of universal justice, and that he must not only be filled with good will toward everything in nature, but he must study the rights and duties of things, and respect the rights of all the inhabitants of the planet, and perform his duty in all directions. Here, again, the value of a system of correct character study is disclosed. When man learns the character of those who surround him, he will learn to respect their rights and privileges. Man loves his liberty, and he desires the privilege of enjoying himself. He must learn to concede the liberty of every animal to enjoy life, and he must cease considering the animals as only created to serve his selfish purposes. He must also learn that those members of mankind who are not as fortunately endowed with resources as himself are not to be made his slaves, but that it is his highest privilege to bear to them a share in every blessing which he himself enjoys. There is not a Christian church in the land which inculcates this doctrine. Your rich church member continually aggregates to himself numberless blessings which he does not share with poorer members. He rolls in the luxury of his carriage, while his poor brother walks, and he usually makes him clean the stable into the bargain. He feeds on the fat of the land at all times, and occasionally throws a sop to his stifled conscience by sending a turkey to a poor family, or by giving money to some charity, where he will be sure to receive an equivalent in free advertising. The charity which builds a hospital for the poor, to gratify human vanity, while it makes no effort to change the conditions which produce poverty, is a stench in the nostrils of intelligent love. Christianity builds palaces for its imaginary gods, while it permits its neighbors to dwell in hovels. Your churches have degenerated into mere palaces of indulgence, where the majority of the men and women who attend go to gratify their passions. Some have a passion for display in dress, while others have a passion for religious emotions, which are only another form of self-indulgence. There is no moral difference in the status of the person who goes to church to indulge a passion, and that of one who goes to a brothel for the same purpose. The absence of a good motive in each case makes them equally sinful. Man must realize that his neighbor is every living thing with which he comes in contact, and he must learn to apply the law of universal kindness, justice and helpfulness.

"Fourth—Man must learn the doctrine of forgiveness. When he commits a wrong himself, and finds

that he is in the power of the one who has been
wronged, the first thing he does, is to sue for forgiveness. Man never becomes weary of being forgiven, and he invariably forgives himself, whenever
he can find the slightest excuse. To love one's neighbor as himself implies that man shall be as ready to
forgive his neighbor as to be forgiven. Jesus inculcated this doctrine when he announced the Golden
Rule, and also suggested that seventy times seven
would not be too often to forgive one offense. Even
supposing that he set a limit at four hundred and
ninety times, the practical effect would be the same,
for it is incredible that any one would commit the
same offense that number of times against the same
person, unless he were insane. Herein we find the
essence of a true system of criminal jurisprudence.
The proper treatment of the criminal is not to follow
him with vindictive punishments, nor to frighten him
into the path of morality by the suggestion of dire
penalties for wrongdoing. Both of these methods foster crime instead of abolishing it. The true application of this commandment is, for society to so regulate itself that those conditions which produce criminals shall be abolished, and then if a brother offend,
forgive him, and if he repeats the offense forgive him
again. If he shows such a disposition to commit
crime that he is really dangerous to society, he should
be regarded as insane, and he should be treated as
any other diseased member is treated, that is, as man
would wish to be treated himself, when he is sick,

with justice and kindness, and when he recovers, he should not be deprived of his liberty. Now the whole policy of Christian civilization is opposed to this commandment. Your code of criminal laws and punishments is all constructed upon the principle that I have condemned in your conception of God. You appeal only to the sense of fear, and you follow offenders with the same vindictiveness that your God is supposed to consign those to hell who offend him. You consign your neighbors to living hells for life, and if the poor wretches could be prevented from dying, your Christian civilization would extend the punishment indefinitely. It will not do for you to say that this is outside of the jurisdiction of the church, for your religion, having been on trial for these long centuries, is responsible for the civilization it has produced, if it has produced any, and if not, then it is responsible for the fact that it has not produced a better form than that which exists. But you cannot escape this indictment, for the same policy is pursued in your churches themselves. What forgiveness do you give to the brother who, through pressure of poverty, commits a defalcation? You expel him from the church, and turn him over to the bloodhounds of the law. What love do you show to the sister who commits an offense against your marriage customs? You degrade her below the level of the brute. You regard certain animals as unfit for association with man on account of their ferocity and violent disposition, but when you learn the truth, you will find that there is no ferocity so great as that which Christian man exhibits toward his neighbor man, no violence so wicked as that which Christian woman has at all ages displayed toward a neighbor woman who has erred in the violation of a social custom."

"Your arraignment of the system of religion which we have been taught to regard as the sum total of all that is good, is severe, but I am not prepared to say that it is not deserved," said Mr. McDonald. "You have certainly given me new light on the meaning of the two great commandments of Jesus. I am quite willing to accept your views on these commandments, but I still do not see why you should tear down the conception we have of heaven. Surely there is no harm in the belief in a future life, and the reunion of those we love on a blissful shore, from which the painful conditions of this life have been removed. This is a last, and as it now seems to me, a conclusive objection to your philosophy. Even if it were a delusion, it seems to me that its effect could only be good. I am willing to adopt all you have said, in regard to the duties of man to live naturally here, but I am unwilling to surrender the hope of a blessed immortality after death. I am anxious for you to discuss this topic."

"It is always wrong and injurious to believe what is untrue," replied Loma. "If you have any facts upon which to base a belief in the existence of a soul, or individual intelligence, which continues to exist after the death of the body, you are justified in believing what the facts seem to indicate. But the belief in the immortality of the soul is based, first, upon the bald assumption that man possesses a soul, which has never been shown to rest upon a single natural fact. The greatest proof of this is found in the fact that man has never seriously conceded that any animal possesses a soul, but he regards these creatures as simply products of growth, which is true. In fact, the principal distinction which your greatest mental philosophers have drawn between man and the animals is, that man possesses a soul, while animals do not. Now the science of character study discloses the fact, that man is subject to exactly the same conditions of growth as the animals; he comes into existence in the same way, and he leaves it by the same universal exit. The difference between man and other animals is simply this: Man has a greater complexity of organization, and a greater number of faculties united in him than any other animal possesses. But he does not possess a single faculty that is not found in some degree of development in some animal. He makes a higher use of some of them because he is able to form greater combinations. The almost universal belief of man is, that animals have no souls, but he is unwilling to consider himself in the same way, because he has been taught differently by his priests, and the belief has flattered his egotism. Man loves to believe that he is different from and more highly favored than any other product of growth. When these facts have been forcibly presented to some of your boldest and most liberal religious philosophers, notably such men as John Wesley, they have avoided the surrender of their cherished belief in the soul of man, by boldly accepting the conclusion, to which they are logically forced, that animals have souls as well as men, and are correspondingly immortal. This is the only course open to the consistent believer, for there is no argument which suggests the existence of a soul in man which does not apply with equal force to animals. But man does not generally consider this doctrine seriously with regard to animals, for the reason that all the observed facts of nature combine to teach him that it is false.

"The principal objection to the belief is, however, that it causes man to be indifferent to his duties in this life. He is constantly looking forward to the realization of his extravagant hopes for the good time in the future, and he neglects the enjoyment of the present. He is taught to have a contempt for the pleasures of this world, by the magnificence of the furnishings of his imaginary heaven, if he will conform to the teachings of the priest, and believe the system of theology which is furnished to him ready made. To compel him to accept the system without question, and to prevent him from reasoning upon its absurdities, he is instructed in early youth, that the church is infallible, or what amounts to the same thing, that the Bible from which it derives its authority is inspired beyond the possibility of a mistake. By this ingenious system of fraud and arrogance, your intelligence has been stupefied, until you are unable to reason with the same degree of perspicuity upon religion that you display upon other topics, where you are not dominated by fear. Under such a system it is impossible to develop moral character, for moral character depends upon the ability to reason without fear, and to decide upon a duty and its performance for moral reasons. The indifference to the discharge of moral duties is increased by the emphasis which is laid upon belief as the only condition of salvation. While your advanced theologians concede, that faith without works is dead, yet it is not to be expected that the mass of your ignorant and degraded classes will ever be able to draw a distinction upon these fine points. It is a common spectacle to see a criminal of the worst class executed in the presence of a priest of some denomination, and dying assured by him that he is saved at the eleventh hour by his confession of belief. This is logically correct, according to the plan of Christianity, and it cannot be abandoned without surrendering the whole theory of salvation. But the effect upon the popular mind is, that it places a premium upon wrongdoing, and comforts the criminal with the assurance that he may persist in his wickedness as long as he likes, and unless he dies too suddenly, he is always sure of the chance of heaven, if he has time and opportunity to call in any minister of an orthodox church and make a profession of penitence and belief. This is a miserable substitute for that education, which the state owes to every citizen, on the rights and duties of persons and things, which will cause him to deal with moral questions intelligently, according to the mathematical principles of equity. Your doctrine of the immortality of the soul, and the jurisdiction of the priest which has grown out of it, has crowded out of your education every form of instruction upon moral questions.

"A serious consequence of this belief is, that it creates so much anxiety about the future in the mind of the earnest and conscientious believer, that it consumes his energies. He is so busy preparing for the future life that he has no time to devote to the development of himself or his family here. It is pitiable to see what a destruction of happiness this doctrine has caused in the lives of Christians. Lest his imaginary God should be offended, and therefore his chances for heaven decreased, the Christian has forfeited every good which bountiful nature affords. The most fanatical have gone to the extent of torturing themselves. They have denied themselves food, raiment, sleep and every form of comfort; have withdrawn from the society of their fellows and lived in cells and caves; have suffered disease and tortures worse than death, to exalt the soul at the expense of the body. You may say that this is fanaticism. It is only the complete application of the logical consequences of the system. Men who are not considered fanatics have fought every form of human enjoyment for the same reason. The church goes into a spasm of wrath whenever any new form of pleasure appears. It has condemned dancing, many denominations have fought instrumental music;

it anathematized every form of the drama, and fulminated its curse upon roller skating and, more lately, upon the pleasures of the bicycle. Women have been expelled from churches because they ornamented their bodies with appropriate colors of ribbons and with jewelry. There has never been a development in art, science, or the study of morals itself, which has not received the fiery opposition of those who were thoroughly indoctrinated with Christianity, and the force of the opposition has always been in exact proportion to the sincerity and zeal of the Christian representative."

"It seems to me," said Mr. McDonald, "that you hold Christianity responsible for the eccentricities of Christians, which is unjust. Any system is likely to have adherents who will go to the extent of fanaticism. And you have not made clear to me yet, why immortality may not be contemplated with satisfaction by those who have lived according to their profession. Suppose a man does live according to the principles of eternal justice and righteousness, why should he not have a prolongation of his life in eternity?"

"The eccentricities of the Christians which I have described," said Loma, "were the legitimate outcome of the system. If the principles of Christian theology are true, these men did right. Their actions were approved in their day by the highest concensus of opinion in their respective denominations. And these actions were not modified until the prevailing spirit of scepticism produced a force which compelled the

Christian authorities to revise their judgment. And when this revision took place, it was not according to Christian standards of right and wrong, but in accordance with the enlightened demands of science and public sentiment. The answer to your last question is as follows: When an organization has completed the purpose for which it was created, it is a waste of material to keep it in existence. Nature demands that all bodies shall live, die and decompose into original elements. In the sense that all matter is indestructible, so everything is immortal. But in the constant mutations of matter organizations change. As the intelligence of man changes with the changes in his organization, so his individuality must be lost with the loss of the individuality of his organization. This is in accordance with the facts which Nature lays before us, and there is nothing which seems to indicate the contrary. The acceptance of this doctrine relieves all anxiety as to the future, which is the bane of man's existence. With the fading of his vision of a palace in an imaginary heaven, which he would not know how to use and enjoy if he had, there is also an extinction of the nightmare of a dungeon in hell. Accepting the command of Nature to live and enjoy her bounties, he thrills with the pleasure of the present, and when he has finished the use of the faculties with which he has been endowed, he surrenders them back to her keeping, and slumbers peacefully in the broad receptivity of the universe, of which his substance was always, and ever will be, a component part."

"The true doctrine of immortality is this," continued Loma, after a pause: "The amount or measure of magnetism which a person is capable of generating and expressing through the machinery of his body, constitutes his intelligence or mind, and the character of that mind will be determined by the form which the body takes. In other words, the amount of mind of any given individual is determined by his state of health, quality, temperament and magnitude. The kind of mind is determined by the form of his body and head, and this is proved by Phrenology to be as true of animals as of man. The character of the mind is constantly changing, as the form of the body changes, by growth and the influences brought to bear upon it. The volume of mind varies constantly with conditions of health or disease, depletion, exhaustion, recuperation, etc. If you wish to use the terms 'soul' and 'spirit,' the following are the only definitions that would accord with reason, human experience and observed facts:

"The 'soul' of man may be properly considered as the capacity he possesses to generate mental power. Considered as a measure and not as an entity, the word 'soul' is useful.

"The 'spirit' of man is his influence derived from the exhibition of his mentality. In the highest and best sense this 'spirit' never dies, but preserves its individuality and progresses in an ever-widening circle. The spirit of Moses as a lawgiver and political leader is more powerful to-day than when he gave the Decalogue to the children of Israel. The Christ spirit is present whenever any good deed is performed in obedience to his influence, and this is probably the most powerful spirit in existence to-day. The spirit of every man, animal, tree, flower or crystal is in this sense forever immortal. But it survives as an influence and not as a personality.

"Now, it is true that every good influence continues indefinitely as well as every evil one. Good is positive, evil is negative, and all of these influences return at last to the center of Creative Energy, which we recognize as God. In figurative language God is said to 'put on His right hand' all good things and on 'His left hand' everything that is evil. This is only another way of saying that He is the great ungenerated source of all goodness, and the ultimate end of all goodness also, and that, as all good impulses originally proceed from Him, to Him also will they ultimately return. All evil He 'puts on His left hand;' that is to say, renders it negative. The spirit of Jesus Christ, set in motion by him during the performance of his glorious mission on this earth, not only encompassed this globe but our planet also, and made itself felt throughout the universe. How it has affected other spheres it does not concern you to know, even if I had the power to tell you, which I do not claim. But this we know as a matter of philosophy, that any disturbance in any part of the universe, for good or evil, affects the whole. It is a grandly inspiring thought that any good action performed by the humblest individual swells the volume of goodness throughout the universe, and makes conditions upon the most distant star better because it has been performed. Because Jesus was perfect in his goodness, it follows that his whole spirit has been placed at the right hand of God, because it was wholly and completely good. May we so conduct our high and holy mission that the offspring of our beloved Myrtle may reach an equally high destiny!"

"Oh, is it possible!" exclaimed Myrtle, with rapture.

"Certainly," replied Loma. "Human perfection has been attained once and it can be attained again. Volumes have been written and great energies have been expended in trying to induce men and women to be like Jesus, when from their faulty organization it was manifestly impossible. But if the same effort had been put forth to regenerate the parents before the unregenerate sinners were born, and they had been instructed in the true philosophy of complete generation so as to produce men and women capable of comprehending and expressing goodness, better results would have been reached. The only way that men and women can be brought to truly resemble Jesus, is to conceive them in pure love, as he was conceived, and educate them, as he was educated, from the beginning of life in the womb of the mother, in all goodness. If the true facts in relation to the conception and education of Jesus had been taught to the world, instead of the absurd and pernicious mystery with which priestcraft has veiled them, there would be more men and women in the world to-day Christ-like in character, beautiful in appearance, worthy to be placed at the right hand of God with the 'spirits of just men made perfect.'"

CHAPTER XX.

THE REIGN OF JUSTICE.

"Therefore all things whatsoever ye would that men should do to you, do ye even so to them, for this is the law and the prophets."

"Your exposition of the conditions of civilization upon the planet of Venus has been exceedingly interesting to me in all of its phases," said Doctor Bell to Loma at the next session; "but there are still some economic matters of great value upon which I am anxious to be enlightened. For instance, I have understood you to say, that cremation is the usual method of disposing of the dead. Is this the universal practice?"

"It is not only the universal practice in the disposal of the dead, but also of all other decomposing and offensive accumulations," said Loma. "The universal principle is recognized, that after a body has served its purpose, and it has passed from the state of life to that of death, the best way to dispose of it is to reduce it to its original elements as quickly as possible. Fire is the greatest and most effective purifier of all things, and it is a mistaken and morbid love which would cling to the lifeless body after the animating and magnetic condition has departed. We do not recognize the desirability of perpetuating the organization after Nature has begun the work of final disintegration. Nearly all of our citizens live to advanced ages, and after their social standing has been registered in the national gazettes, they are sure of a just recognition of whatever services they have rendered to humanity after they have ceased to exist, hence there is no occasion for expensive monuments. When a citizen dies, his lovers and associates assemble and witness his cremation, and listen to a recital of his history by competent orators. Music of the most cheerful character is rendered, and there is no grief, no weeping or wailing or any of the uncanny performances which form so much of the stock in trade of your undertakers and those who conduct religious services on this planet. As the citizen has lived during his life for the benefit of those who surround him, so in death every precaution is taken to avoid contaminating and unhealthy influences. The burial of bodies pollutes the ground and causes a long train of diseases and calamities, of which your citizens are ignorant, while they constantly suffer from them. Your cemeteries are usually placed on elevated grounds, so that the monuments may make a display, and the decomposing bodies pollute the water for miles in all directions. You drain your cities into your streams, and after a river has flowed through one such city as Chicago it becomes a river of death. Even in the country where healthier conditions should prevail, and where there is plenty of room, this universal blunder continues. You discharge your excreta and refuse into pits dug in the ground, and in a majority of cases these are so near to the dwellings and wells that the poison is continually reabsorbed by living bodies. Now, in Venus we have a much better system. All of our garbage is collected and burned, the product converted into fertilizing material and returned to the earth in purity, and every stream on the planet flows with living water, so pure that under all circumstances it is acceptable for drinking purposes without filtering. The perfect system with which the food supply is administered prevents waste, and as we use only fruits and vegetables for food, and we have only such domestic animals as are companionable, we have no great amount of garbage to dispose of. The principal burden in your garbage problem arises from the large herds of domestic animals that are kept in unnatural confinement, in close proximity to man, and the use you make of animal food, which causes a great percentage of the diseases with which you are afflicted."

"What became of the herds of domestic animals which existed on Venus, after your present system was inaugurated and you found that you had no further use for them? Were they slaughtered?" asked Myrtle.

"By no means," replied Loma. "The law of universal justice forbade any such brutality. While they remained in confinement the reproduction of domestic animals was discontinued, but as soon as the new society decided upon what portions of the globe were best suited to human habitation, the remaining territory was abandoned, and as soon as it became evident that certain animals had ceased to be useful to man, and that man was not essential to their existence, they were transported to those portions of the globe which were not required for man's use, and set at liberty. The consequence was, that many species which had served their usefulness became extinct, while others, according to the survival of the fittest, occupied the territory, where they live in happiness and development, according to their standing in the scale of creation."

"Another question in which I am greatly interested," said the doctor, "is this—What uses do you make of gold and silver and diamonds? From what you have already said, I infer that you use no currency or money of any kind, and as you do not use clothing, I do not see what use you would have for these articles as ornaments."

"We have no use for money," said Loma, "hence we are never troubled with such economic problems as you have on the questions of money and values. It is the duty of the state to produce all the commodities needed by its citizens, and the citizen having performed his duty, is entitled to have all of his legitimate desires satisfied. He has no desires that are not legitimate, for he is too well educated to desire anything that is not according to the law of mathematical equity. We use gold and silver as we use all other metals, in manufacturing desirable articles, but there is no special value set upon these metals. In fact, aluminum, which is much more common, but which is subject to a great many more uses, is much more esteemed. Diamonds are worn as ornaments, in rings and necklaces, on formal occasions. They are all the property of the state, and at the death of a citizen all of his ornaments revert to the state, to be again disposed, where worthy services have been performed. Thus every woman who becomes pregnant is invested with a diamond ring at the middle day of her pregnancy, and at parturition she is presented with a diamond necklace, which at first bears a large single stone. For every citizen she bears for the state, a diamond is added to her necklace, and so it is easy to tell by the jewels worn by a woman how many jewels she has given to the state in the form of good citizens. The same decorations are worn by fathers, and other precious stones are used to denote other services. I did not wear my decorations to the earth, for the reason that in the transit they would have been destroyed. Only those bodies capable of developing a high degree of magnetism can pass from one planet to another."

"You have said a great deal about rewards that are given to your citizens for good conduct, both in this matter of decorations and in the system of credit marks in social standing," said Myrtle, "and the question of punishment naturally suggests itself. How do you correct delinquents, and what method do you pursue in establishing guilt?"

"The system of complete education practically eliminates delinquency, and all lapses are treated as mistakes. There is no occasion for punishment, for the mortification of a bad performance is, in itself, sufficient to the educated person. Take your own case, for instance. We do not have to threaten you with punishment, to cause you to speak your language correctly. I have known you many weeks, and you have not, as yet, been guilty of a single blunder in this department of conduct. You speak correctly because you have been educated to do so, and it has become habitual. If you should make a mistake, you would be mortified, and all that would be necessary to cause you to correct it would be to call your attention to it. The credit marks and ornaments we use are not given as rewards, but simply as evidences of achievement, to suggest to the young the desirability of reaching a similarly high grade. Complete education, as practiced on Venus, completely destroys the possibility of crime, and as the principal incentives to crime which exist here are removed, there is no unnatural pressure upon our citizens to cause the various forms of insanity which produce all the crimes with which you are afflicted."

"Is crime always the result of insanity?" asked Mrs. Bell.

"Always," replied Loma. "There are only two conditions which can result in a criminal action, viz., idiocy and mania. Idiocy is of two kinds, congenital, where there is some portion of the brain which is imperfectly formed, and acquired, where there is originally a complete brain, but where some parts are permitted to become paralyzed through disuse. Now, the science of Phrenology, even in the crude form in which it is practiced on this planet, discloses the fact that the great majority of your citizens come into existence partially idiotic. They have, in most cases, sufficient brain to learn all of the subjects which are taught in your schools, but as these subjects are very limited in scope, and successive generations are educated in the same general channel, where considerable culture is given to a few faculties, and no culture whatever to others, the deficiencies are not usually noticed, and you have a great many citizens who are considered well educated, and mentally responsible, who are nevertheless incapable of correct judgment and moral action. A man may read in all languages, be capable of excellent mechanical skill, be a skillful musician, and show great shrewdness in business, and still be morally idiotic, because he has no development in certain other portions of his brain, which enable him when properly educated, to reason correctly on the rights and duties of persons. It is even possible, that, when questioned, he might be able to answer correctly on the abstract moral question involved, when he is free from excitement, and yet, when he is confronted with a temptation, he yields to an irresistible impulse, because the faculties which should restrain him from the commission of a wrong act have never been educated, and are therefore powerless to act. The unfortunate offender is arraigned before a court and jury who know nothing of these psychological problems or principles; the commission of the offense is fairly proved, but the psychological condition of the accused is never considered, unless he presents such evidences of insanity as amount to complete stupidity or actual mania. Even in the first case, he is usually condemned and hustled off to a stupid punishment, because such unfortunates are, as a general thing, without money or friends. In cases of mania, your courts are inclined to administer justice, but the people frequently defeat justice by clamoring for condign punishment, because they are inflamed with the spirit of revenge, which is such a conspicuous feature of your religious education. Complete congenital idiocy and mania are recognized in your courts, but the large class of unfortunates who are rendered incapable of correct action by congenital deformity and insufficient education will continue to be afflicted with inhuman punishments until your people adopt the code of Gallheim, as it will be proclaimed by Myrtle's offspring, and learn to study character correctly and apply the law of mathematical equity in all classes of actions. Then they will learn the value of human culture and apply it in its complete form, and there will be no congenital idiocy or deformity, and the adoption of correct habits of living will prevent mania, as well as all other forms of disease. Then the law of love will be recognized, and revenge will cease to be the ruling motive in the enactment and enforcement of law."

"Then it is a true principle, that all corrective measures should be remedial and reformatory and never vindictive," said Doctor Bell.

"That is strictly true. It is a monstrous injustice for the state to punish a citizen, when it has denied to that citizen the conditions which make it possible for him to have a complete organization and a complete education. A government which cannot protect its citizens in growth and development, and which permits some of the members of society to absorb all of its benefits to the impoverishment of the majority, is worse than no government at all. What, then, shall we say of a government which derives a large part of its revenues from fostering and putting in motion forces which destroy its citizens by wholesale? Your government is the principal partner in every distillery, brewery and saloon in the country, as well as every manufactory of tobacco, opium and every other product which ministers to the vices of your citizens and destroys virtue. Your government, for a pecuniary consideration in the form of a tax, grants to an army of unscrupulous persons the right to manufacture and sell products which will destroy the health and moral character of every citizen who is brought under their influence. By this system of taxation and the monopoly which is thereby created, the destruction of humanity has become the most profitable business in the catalogue of your industries. It is the lasting disgrace of your civilization that the saloon is more profitable than the provision house, and that a man can become rich more rapidly by manufacturing criminals than by any other industry known to your commerce. The same system has been extended indirectly to the brothel, and among the most profitable industries pursued by your citizens is that of recruiting and selling into a form of slavery worse than death, thousands of young girls annually to supply the ranks of prostitution. It is estimated that two hundred and forty thousand young girls are now being annually sacrificed in the United States. With the saloon on the corner, the brothel in the rear, the tobacco stand on the sidewalk and the courthouse and jail across the street, all of them managed in partnership by your government, the wonder is, that any citizen can walk the street without falling into crime, and experiencing some form of the vicious penalties which disgrace your statute books."

"Our reformers recognize the truthfulness of your observations," said Mrs. Bell, "and many experiments have been tried to reduce the evil of intemperance, but so far these efforts have not been successful. I should like very much to have your views on the subjects of prohibition, license, moral suasion and such other remedies as we have tried, and also what you consider to be the correct remedy for the evil. We are generally agreed that until the curse of intemperance is banished, we cannot have any substantial or lasting reform in any direction."

"Prohibition is wrong in principle, whether it be directed against intemperance or any other crime. It is folly to prohibit any wrong action, as long as the state is engaged in producing conditions which impel its citizens to the commission of the acts prohibited. But in this respect, your state follows the example of your God, who is represented as prohibiting certain actions, and then creating men and women in such a condition as insures the commission of the prohibited actions. This is your conception of justice, and until you learn better, both in religion and statecraft, you will continue to suffer the consequences of injustice. You cannot legislate away the inherited or acquired propensities of the citizen. The only way in which these propensities can be changed, is by education, and this must be commenced in the youth of the citizen. Now, your government stands in the position of a national educator in vice. It licenses the saloon, the tobacco stand, and practically licenses the brothel, and the youth of your land are instructed, by the very presence of the sumptuous palaces of sin, which are constantly frequented by those who hold high places among you, that it is elegant, respectable and correct to patronize them. The feeble efforts which are put forth by your churches are, as a rule, only advertisements of these evils by attracting attention to them. While a very small contingent of your youth is kept from temptation by good influences, the majority is constantly drawn into the meshes of evil, and if it were not for the inherent goodness of your young manhood and womanhood, the results would be frightfully worse. It is not the result of your laws, your system of morals or your religious training that your citizens are not wholly given over to indulgence, for all of these are hopelessly inefficient and are working on a wrong principle. It is the natural good sense of a large number of your young people which keeps them out of evil practices, and their natural susceptibility to education causes them to observe and avoid evil. But as long as men are paid princely salaries in breweries to drug the liquor, so as to enslave the appetites of the consumer, and as long as men are governed by the acquisitive instinct in its uneducated form, which prompts them to trade in human flesh and blood for pecuniary gain, it is useless to attempt to stem the tide of evil by prohibitory measures. The only form of prohibition which can be effective is that which comes to the individual citizen by the action of an enlightened conscience. Before you can have an enlightened public conscience, there must be a general and complete education of your citizens. As long as the education of your citizens on moral questions is left to the feeble and ridiculous methods of your churches, you will have no development of the sense of justice."

"What immediate policy would you recommend to our reformers as the best to pursue in relation to the liquor traffic?" inquired Mrs. Bell.

"Instead of advocating prohibition, or merely confining your efforts to moral suasion, which latter policy is well enough as an educating force as far as it goes, the temperance advocates should make a vigorous war on the partnership of the government in the saloons. License is simply the compounding of the crime. High license makes the manufacture and sale of liquor profitable, by creating a monopoly, and this results in the making of tippling a luxury, which it is fashionable and popular to cultivate. It is entirely to this fact that the practice of treating owes its popularity. Now, if the government would withdraw its protection, and the manufacture and sale of liquor were free to every citizen, large quantities of pure and unadulterated stimulants would be produced and for a while the consumption would be greater among those upon whom the habit is firmly fixed, but the consequences would not be as serious as they are now, for the liquor would not be poisoned. The universal cheapening of the product, and the freedom with which it could be obtained, would destroy the saloon, and the practice of treating would disappear. When it became common, it would cease to be fashionable, and then your efforts in the line of moral suasion and education would become effective. It would take one generation to reduce the consumption, another to develop the educational influences required, and the third generation would be entirely free from the vice, and would have concurrently advanced to the same high plane along other lines, in which the same rational policy had been pursued. That was the history of the movement upon our planet, after the code of Gallheim began to be generally adopted by the barbarians. The followers of that distinguished philosopher, however, reached a much more immediate result, by the formation of their society, in which the laws of correct living were studied and applied, and as soon as they were established they were at once adopted and practiced by the entire membership. It was easy for them to adopt reforms, because they had ceased to struggle for riches, and the society guaranteed to every member everything that he needed. The trouble with reforms on this planet is, that your citizens are so wholly given to the consideration of money getting, that you have sold your consciences, your self-respect and your entire moral character to the forces of evil. The destruction of the saloon and similar institutions means that your so-called respectable citizens will have to pay higher taxes, temporarily. I say temporarily, for it would only be a short time before the reduction in crime and misery would more than compensate for the increase in the tax rate. But your citizens are not interested in the suppression of crime and misery as much as they are in the accumulation of wealth. If a citizen finds that his taxes are being increased to a small degree, he is seized with a spasm, and the administration which increases the comfort of the great mass of citizens at the expense of the taxpayer is doomed. It is a melancholy commentary on your civilization, that any form of vice can flourish if it is able to pay a heavy tax, and your cities vie with each other in offering premiums to demoralizing enterprises and brutal exhibitions, whenever it can be shown that they will bring with them a large crowd of persons, no matter how vicious, who will spend money. Until your citizens learn the law of mathematical equity, and become convinced that every evil act brings its own punishment, and that the law of ethics cannot be violated without disaster, you will have these conditions. The state must learn that it cannot suppress crime until it ceases to be criminal itself in its policy."

"I should infer from the principles that you have announced in this lesson, that capital punishment, imprisonment for life, and, in fact, every punishment which is inflicted in the spirit of retribution, is radically wrong." said Myrtle.

"That is exactly the impression that I wish to convey," said Loma. "These punishments are all in the nature of prohibitory measures, directed against conditions that cannot be successfully prohibited until society ceases to foster them. The nature of the punishment is a natural outgrowth of the doctrine of eternal and unmerciful cruelty which is preached as one of the attributes of the God which your people are instructed to worship. The ideas of retribution, revenge and atonement must be eliminated from the public mind, before you can form an adequate idea of justice. I will analyze some of your most brutal expressions of retributive punishment and see in what they originate, and what consequences are inevitable.

"The worst form of retributive punishment which has become common in this country, is the burning and torturing of negroes in the South for the crime of rape. It has occurred so frequently of late, that even your sluggish public conscience is becoming awakened to the enormity of the crime, by the side of which the original crime of the rapist pales into insignificance. The negro who commits the rape is usually a low brutalized type, frequently crazed by liquor which is sold to him by the community without protest, and his condition is the natural outgrowth of the brutalizing and degrading institution of slavery, which was so long practiced in this country. The community in which he resides has given him little chance for improvement. He is not encouraged to rise above the condition of the slave by education or social intercourse. The community permits him to be surrounded by every form of education in vice, and discourages his elevation, while it grants him the opportunity to commit the crime. In this condition he commits the crime of rape, perhaps under circumstances of great atrocity, which are in themselves the best evidences of his insanity, and this insanity is the direct result of his environment, for which the community is responsible. If the law of justice were strictly applied, the community would be found responsible for the rape and not the negro. However, he is caught by an infuriated mob, and we will admit that the proof of his commission of the act is clear. The sentiment of the community is in favor of retributive punishment. They worship a God who deals largely in that commodity. He is paraded around the public square, before assembled thousands. Men, women and children witness the spectacle, and he is tortured and burned under the mistaken impression that the example will deter others from the commission of similar offenses. But it produces an entirely opposite effect. While it may deter a few timid negroes from the commission of crimes of a similar nature, for a short period of time, immediately following the outrage, the subsequent consequences are disastrous. An entire community has been educated in brutality. Pregnant women by the score have been impressed with horrible conditions. A monstrous object lesson in injustice has been given to the young who witnessed the spectacle. The instincts of kindness, forbearance, friendship and love have been blunted in the organizations of hundreds, if not thousands of citizens, who have, on the other hand, been stimulated to deeds of violence, hatred, vindictiveness and cruelty. Veneration for law and established forms of judicial procedure is destroyed and a premium set upon lawlessness. The result is a long train of calamities to the community, which is never fully appreciated, for the full effect of the reaction is not felt for years, and the series of crimes and evils that result are not attributed to the true cause. Let me illustrate with a single example. A pregnant woman witnesses such an outrage and rejoices in the cruelty which is inflicted on what she considers a human monster. She impresses her offspring with the spirit of vindictiveness. In childhood he manifests it by burning and torturing animals and playmates. He has an ungovernable and disagreeable temper which embitters his whole life. He reaches manhood and becomes a seducer of women and a violent, quarrelsome man. His whole career is marked by violence and crime, and his history is infinitely worse than that of the unfortunate and brutalized negro whose execution and torture is responsible for his own unhappy condition. He leaves a progeny of five daughters, who are, like himself, violent, unchaste and ungovernable, and who lead criminal lives and become the mothers of criminals. He finally terminates his career on the gallows, after the commission of some horrible atrocity which is worse than that of which the negro was guilty. Now, if you will consider, that this is only one of the results which may flow from such an outrage, and consider further that instead of one witness, there are usually not less than ten or twenty thousand, all of whom are exposed to consequences as awful as those I have described, it is possible to form a remote conception of the fearful injustice and inexpediency of retributive punishment."

"What is the proper procedure in such a case?" said Doctor Bell.

"Kindness and restraint. The state must recognize that whenever a crime is committed, the state and not the individual is responsible. There has been a defect, either in the generation or the education of the criminal. If the defect can be remedied, he is entitled to a cure, and if not, he must be gently and kindly restrained from the commission of future offenses. It is a true principle that the exhibition of love and forbearance generates goodness, exactly as the exhibition of hatred and violence generates evil. The state is the worst criminal in society, and until it is reformed there is little hope for the citizen. The practice of capital punishment, when performed legally, is open to all the objections that I have stated as applying to the practice of burning and torture, except as it is modified in the brutality of the exhibition. Public hangings are nearly as bad as public burnings. Private executions are only less evil, as they are witnessed by a smaller audience. Electrocution is merely a modification of the same evil. Imprisonment for life is a monstrous exhibition of cruelty and injustice, the legitimate offspring of the detestable doctrine of eternal imprisonment in hell. Imprisonment for long terms of years for trivial offenses against property or person is a constant lesson in injustice, and it is a wonder that the moral sense of your citizens is not wholly obliterated by the constant appeal that is made to fear, while no appeal is made or education given to the sense of justice."

CHAPTER XXI.

FOUR GREAT MISTAKES CORRECTED.

"It is inconceivable that inanimate brute matter should, without the mediation of something else which is not material, operate upon and affect other matter, without mutual contact, as it must do if gravitation, in the sense of Epicurus, be essential and inherent in it. And this is the reason why I desire you would not ascribe innate gravity to me. That gravity should be innate, inherent and essential in matter, so that one body may act upon another at a distance, through a vacuum, without the mediation of anything else by and through which their action may be conveyed from one to another, is to me so great an absurdity that I believe no man who has in philosophical matters a competent faculty of thinking can ever fall into it. Gravity must be caused by an agent acting according to certain laws; but, whether this agent be material or immaterial, I have left to the consideration of my readers." —NEWTON.

At various times during his tuition of Myrtle, Loma had unfolded to her the mysteries of astronomy, in which he was an expert. His great abilities as a teacher, and the interest with which his delightful personality invested every subject upon which he conversed, made the contemplation of the heavens under his guidance a pleasure more than a task, and filled the mind of Myrtle with sublime raptures. He did not burden her with mathematical problems, but rather directed her intelligence to the comprehension of the true theory of the creation of the universe, and the contemplation of its simplicity and grandeur. In this way her appreciation of the beautiful and the sublime was increased, and her worship of the good, the true and the beautiful in Nature impressed her offspring with those faculties which would enable him to comprehend the same subjects and give him power to speak and write in the loftiest strains. In the course of his instruction, Loma had imparted to her all of the knowledge of the sublime philosophy of the genesis of worlds, the nature of space and matter and their sexual affinities, as expressed in electricity and magnetism, together with the causes of heat and light, which he had so graphically explained to Doctor Bell on the second day of his sojourn on the earth. Myrtle was an apt pupil, and while she received each startling disclosure with girlish delight and wonder, her practical intellect absorbed the information, and she soon became able to converse on these grand topics with brilliancy and effect.

Doctor Bell was no less enthusiastic than Myrtle in this part of Loma's instructions. Shortly after the arrival of Loma upon the earth he had caused a small observatory to be constructed upon the roof of his residence and had equipped it with all the necessary instruments for elementary studies, such as Loma designed to impart. A fine six-inch equatorial telescope had been purchased and mounted in this observatory, and many delightful evenings were spent under Loma's direction in the practical observation of the wonders of the heavens. This telescope, as may be supposed, was most frequently turned upon Venus, which planet Myrtle, as well as the rest of the family, had invested with more than affectionate interest.

Doctor Bell had also set apart one of the commodious rooms of his residence as a physical laboratory and had equipped it with all the apparatus necessary for the practical study of physics and chemistry. He found the tutorship of Loma invaluable to himself in his professional work, and he became as enthusiastic in the study of the advanced problems of these sciences as Myrtle was in the more elementary work. Loma had explained that the elementary studies pursued by Myrtle at this time would serve the purpose of impressing her offspring with the necessary capacity for the comprehension of the subjects, while the advanced studies pursued by Doctor Bell would fit him to become the instructor of the coming prodigy when he arrived at the proper age to pursue these branches.

Loma illustrated his instructions with brilliant experiments which fascinated his pupils and kept them in a constant state of wonder and admiration. His perfect powers of analysis and description, added to his wonderful stock of knowledge, which represented the advanced stage of development upon Venus, no less than his loving and genial companionship, made the experience of his pupils a never-failing source of entertainment, instruction and happiness.

It happened that while Myrtle was deeply engaged in these studies Doctor Bell received a visit from one of his intimate friends, a former classmate in the

University of Michigan, and at present one of the expert astronomers of the Washburn Observatory at Madison, Wisconsin, connected with the University of that state. This gentleman, Professor George Hamilton, became at once greatly interested in Loma, whom he immediately recognized as a person of superior attainments, and as he remained several days as the guest of Doctor Bell, the acquaintance soon ripened into warm friendship. Toward Myrtle the professor was genial and polite, but like many scientific students, he had allowed his scientific proclivities to develop at the expense of his social faculties, and he was not inclined to spend a great deal of time in the society of ladies if he could avoid it. He found, however, that the best time to get Loma to expound his remarkable philosophy was when the ladies were present, and he submitted to the conditions with a good grace. But one day at dinner, he laughingly remarked:

"I see that Doctor Loma is attracted to the society of you ladies, as inevitably as matter is attracted to matter."

"I fear if such were the case that I should be deprived of the delights of their association," said Loma, "for the principle you have used as a comparison is incorrect."

"Do you mean that matter does not attract matter?" inquired the professor.

"Precisely. Matter never attracts matter, and to assert that it does is to violate the universal principle that likes never attract each other but always repel.

Consequently matter always repels matter instead of attracting it."

"You astonish me. I have supposed that the principle that matter attracts matter was as well established as the fact that the earth revolves on its axis."

"Both are equally incorrect," said Loma with a smile, while the professor regarded him with amazement.

"This is getting interesting," said the professor, at last. "If I did not know you to be a philosopher of no mean merit, I would be inclined to regard you as a crank, for you are denying the two principles upon which astronomy has based its greatest triumphs. But knowing your character, I cannot afford to let your statements pass unchallenged, and I ask you to be explicit. If matter does not attract matter, then Sir Isaac Newton was wrong in his theory of the law of gravitation, and the foundation of our philosophy is destroyed. In view of the fact, that our profession, resting upon the correctness of his theory, has reached out into space and discovered a planet which eluded the telescope until it was located with mathematical certainty by the application of the Newtonian philosophy, I feel secure in the statement that you have committed yourself to a doctrine you cannot maintain."

"Sir Isaac Newton is merely the example of an astute philosopher, who is right in his practice, while he is wrong in his theory and explanation," answered Loma. "He did not comprehend the nature of matter and space, nor of magnetism and electricity, and hence

in observing the operation of these forces, he was led
into a wrong statement. But he never taught the
doctrine which has been ascribed to him, that matter
has an innate attraction for other matter, at a distance
without contact, or the intervention of some other
medium. Before you can understand the true theory,
you must be informed as to these matters yourself,
or my explanations would be futile. I will therefore begin at the foundation of things, by remarking that all worlds are the product of growth, the offspring of the two grand, prime, genitive potencies,
space and matter, which have always existed, and
will always exist, in precisely the same quantity
in which they now exist, but in constantly changing
conditions. Space is the eternal, omnipresent, persistent and continuous female parent of all that is.
Matter is the eternal, limited, consistent and divisible
male element which occupies only a part of space, and
is continually striving to fill it, but never succeeds.
There is a genitive passion in matter for space, and a
genitive passion in space for matter. Space continually
generates this passion in the form of electricity, which
is manifested by the states of receptivity, gravity and
coldness. Matter continually generates this passion
in the form of magnetism, which is manifested by the
states of radiation, vibration and warmth. If you
will recognize the fact that each planet or star is a
body of matter contained in space, but not filling it,
and acting as a center of magnetic radiation, and that
among these centers of radiation are great volumes

of matterless space, which furnish corresponding centers of electrical receptivity, and that each subjective center of magnetic radiation has a special objective center of electrical receptivity, toward which it is impelled by the eternal affinity of matter for space, as expressed in these passional attributes, and that for this reason these centers are constantly changing their positions in space, you will have comprehended the fundamental principle which lies at the base of philosophy, and accounts for the constant mutations of matter as expressed in motions of all kinds. This leads to the statement of the true law of gravitation, which is that *matter is always attracted toward the center of electrical receptivity which is the center of its own sphere of organization.*"

"In the absence of some restraining force, matter always organizes itself into spheres. This absence of a restraining force can only exist where there is an equilibrium between magnetism and electricity, because where either preponderates there would be a controlling and hence a restraining force. When this equilibrium exists, we have the fluid state of matter; when electricity preponderates it becomes solid, when magnetism dominates it becomes gaseous. But in the state of electro-magnetic equilibrium matter always assumes a spherical shape, because the particles of matter instantly arrange themselves around a center of electrical receptivity. As soon as this organization is perfected, the sphere moves toward another center of electrical receptivity which is the center of the next higher form of organization and so *ad infinitum.*"

"Assuming, as the atomical theory does, that the atom is the smallest possible division of matter, the molecule is the first arrangement of atoms around a center of electrical receptivity. In the case of a substance of matter in a state of electro-magnetic equilibrium, as water in the fluid state, you will find that these molecules arrange themselves into another sphere in the form of the drop. Small drops will coalesce into another superior sphere and form a large drop, and this organization will go on indefinitely until a restraining force is encountered. It is in this way that star germs are produced at last, and it is by continued accretions and crystallization that they grow. As soon as electricity dominates over magnetism, the process of crystallization occurs, and the matter becomes hard.

"Now, right here occurs a truism, which your philosophers have recognized, but have not accounted for, and that is, that the atoms of matter do not touch each other, but are separated by spaces, inconceivably small, but still sufficient to keep the atoms apart. If this were not true, there could be no motion among the atoms, and the theory depends on this fact for its explanation of phenomena. Now if the atoms attract each other, this could not possibly be true, for they would cohere eternally and compactly, and there could be no mutation. The truth is that *every atom is sur-*

rounded by an aura of magnetism, which repels and separates it from every other atom.

"The pressure of other atoms surrounding it, which are seeking the same center of electrical receptivity, causes cohesion, and the process of crystallization produces solidity. Now, if sufficient heat is applied to cause magnetism to equal electricity, the fluid state will be restored, and if the heat is increased until magnetism dominates over electricity, the matter will be restored to its previous gaseous condition, which is simply the expansion of the magnetic auras of the atoms until spheres are disorganized. In neither case is there any attraction of matter for matter, but always a repulsion. However, as there is always, in any organized body of matter, a center of electrical receptivity, there is an apparent attraction of other particles of matter, because these particles seek the same center. As a matter of fact, however, they can only approach within a limited distance of each other, when their magnetic auras hold them apart. As the force with which two bodies of matter will approach a common center of electrical receptivity and organize themselves into the same sphere varies directly as the separate spheres of the bodies under consideration, which corresponds to their respective masses and inversely as the square of the distance between the centers of their separate spheres, you see that the law of gravitation as practiced by your astronomers has been correct as to its mathematical practice while it has been ascribed to incorrect causes.

In other words, you have ignored the true relation of particles of matter toward each other, while you have calculated correctly their behavior toward their respective centers of electrical receptivity."

"Well, I declare," exclaimed Professor Hamilton, "you have certainly put forth a most plausible explanation of a theory which I was at first inclined to regard as merely visionary. But how do you explain the fact that if a piece of sealing wax is electrified by rubbing it with a piece of flannel and then presented to two small balls of pith, the balls will first be attracted to the electrified sealing wax and afterward repelled both from it and from each other? This certainly seems to prove that under certain conditions matter attracts matter, and also that when electrified, matter repels matter."

"You should say that the sealing wax and the pith balls are 'magnetized,' instead of 'electrified,'" said Loma. "All of your nomenclature is incorrect on electrical subjects, because you do not recognize the true nature of electricity and magnetism, and consequently you are constantly putting forth false explanations of the phenomena. The exceedingly mobile force which is developed when matter is subjected to friction, as in the case of the sealing wax, and as is the case with electrical machines, so called, or when it is developed by chemical action, as in a battery, is the magnetism of matter. The corresponding degree of genitive passion which exists in space is electricity. When sealing wax or glass is subjected to friction by certain kinds of material, notably flannel or silk, a high degree of this passion is generated, and the radiation of magnetism is increased by the friction which produces vibration. The pith balls are in a state of gravity, coldness and receptivity, and when the excited substance is brought near them a mutual attraction exists as it always does in bodies that are in opposite conditions. The magnetism from the excited substance passes into the pith balls, and they are changed from a state in which electricity dominated over magnetism to a state in which magnetism dominates over electricity. As soon as this condition is reached they are in a state of repulsion from the originally excited substance, and from each other, according to the law that bodies in a similar condition universally repel each other, while those which are in an opposite condition invariably attract."

"You astonish me," said Professor Hamilton with great interest. "Your theory seems to be consistent as far as we have gone, but it is so new and so radically different from the accepted teachings of the schools that I am obliged to press you further. I shall be under obligations to you if you will enlighten me fully as to your remarkable doctrines. I am always willing to learn, and if I can obtain any information from you which will aid me in my professional employment or shed new light on any of the problems in which my profession is interested, I shall forever consider myself your debtor."

"If you investigate my theories," said Loma, "you will reconstruct nearly your entire professional equipment, for nearly all the accepted theories respecting physical astronomy are radically erroneous. To be brief, and at the same time astonish you, I will remark that the results to which this investigation will lead you are as follows:

"First—That the law of gravitation as stated by Newton is entirely wrong, upon the grounds I have already stated.

"Second—That the sun does not attract, but constantly repels the planets that surround him, and that the earth does not attract the moon, nor does any body of matter ever attract any other body.

"Third—That the earth does not revolve upon its axis.

"Fourth—That the sun does not radiate light or heat.

"Bold as these propositions are, and flatly contradictory to everything taught in the schools, I am confident that I will be able to make you acknowledge their truth within two hours."

At this point in the conversation dinner was concluded, and the friends adjourned to the library, where Loma resumed his instruction. Professor Hamilton was incredulous and curious, Doctor Bell and the ladies intensely interested, but confident that Loma would be able to fully maintain his position, however radical it might seem.

"Before you begin your demonstration, Doctor Loma," said the professor, "I wish to be fully informed as to the precise meaning of the terms you use. I understood you to say, a few minutes ago, that our nomenclature is incorrect on electrical subjects. Now, to avoid confusion, let us understand each other. What is electricity?"

"Electricity is the emptiness of space," replied Loma. "As the term is usually employed, it signifies the force which is generated by the passage of magnetism from matter into the receptivity of space, which is incorrect. The expressions 'electric current,' 'electric fluid,' etc., are all incorrect. To understand this, let me explain:

"If you can imagine any quantity of space divested of every atom of matter, you would have absolute emptiness, a complete vacuum. It would be absolutely dark, cold and composed; for without matter in some form, there can be no manifestation of light, heat or vibration."

"Certainly," assented the professor.

"Now, if you will conceive such a vacuum to exist, and conceive that in close proximity to it there is a body of matter, you will have in the matter the antithesis of the conditions of space, for matter is always vibratory, in some degree, and heat and light are the natural results of this vibration. Now, matter is always disintegrating and throwing off in vibratory radiation an essence which we call magnetism. This magnetism is the finest essence of matter, moving in straight lines in all directions from the body of matter from which it is radiated. This radiation of magnetism is the universal property of matter. The phenomena of light, heat, sound, odor, and all other sensations which assail our senses are simply different degrees of vibration."

"That is generally admitted as to light and heat," said the professor, "but not as to odor. But proceed with your explanation."

"Now," continued Loma, "it is this antithesis of conditions between space and matter which gives us the solution of all the problems to which I have referred. Space is empty and receptive, matter is vibratory and radiant, and this property of radiation results in a continued effort on the part of matter to fill space. You say that Nature abhors a vacuum. The true statement is that Matter loves Space, and Space loves Matter, and this eternal affinity results in a constant energy which is in some form responsible for every phenomenon of growth and mutation which we witness. When this force is gathered into a channel by reason of some restraining conditions operating to form the channel, it is currentized to such an extent that we recognize it in some special form, as in the lightning of the clouds or the current of a telegraph apparatus. Then you erroneously call it electricity when you should call it magnetism. The performances of a dynamo, an electrical machine, a chemical battery, or any other form of generator, is in obedience to this law. In either case matter is decomposed by vibration, radiation results, and you have magnetism expressed in some form which is capable of being recognized by one or more of the seven senses of man."

"Seven senses!" exclaimed Professor Hamilton. "Do

you claim that man has seven senses? Please enumerate them."

"With pleasure," replied Loma. "Man is only able to recognize the vibration and radiation of magnetism according to the scale of his senses, and the degree of vibrations to which each sense is attuned. The lowest vibrations are those which are cognizable by his sense of gender. For the recognition of these vibrations he is provided with sexual organs, which are just as much organs of sense as his eyes or ears. The sexual organs take cognizance of gender, and you will discover as you study life that the lowest forms of life recognize gender, and reproduce themselves intelligently before they develop feeling. The vibrations which relate to the sense of touch are next in order. Just one stage finer are the vibrations experienced in the sensations of taste. Increase the rapidity of the vibrations another stage, and you have the sense of hearing; next comes sight, then the finer vibrations of smell, and above that the exquisite perception which is exercised in clairvoyance."

"I am obliged to confess again that you astonish me," exclaimed the professor, "and yet your statements seem to be in accordance with observed facts. We have been a long time reaching the conclusion that heat and light are simply different degrees of the same energy, but it is now generally conceded. I see no reason why your explanation of the cause of other sensations should not be correct. But I am anxious to hear you. Proceed."

"We have now reached a substantial foundation for a philosophy," resumed Loma. "If we are correct about this radiation of magnetism from all forms of matter, then every particle of matter is repelled by every other particle of matter, and not attracted by it, as erroneously stated by Newton. But matter is attracted by the receptivity of space, and it is the drawing power of the vacuum which attracts. The presence of centers of electrical receptivity in space is all that is necessary to cause particles of matter to arrange themselves around these centers and form spheres. While every particle of matter is repelled by every other particle, yet as they are drawn to a common center of receptivity they seem to be attracting each other. But this is not in fact true, as I have clearly shown. Now, this philosophy is in exact accord with the universal law that likes repel each other while opposites attract. You cannot find a single exception to this law in all nature, and yet in the face of it your profession has gone on, since the time of Sir Isaac Newton, asserting that matter attracts matter."

"If you have any lingering doubt about the correctness of this theory," continued Loma, after pausing to give the professor time to think, "consider the difference between ice, water and steam. In ice, electricity dominates to such a degree that crystallization has occurred, and heat is at a minimum. Increase the degree of heat and you have fluidity as a result, or the equilibrium between electric and magnetic conditions. Increase the heat and the increased radiation of magnetism will separate the molecules and you will have steam. You will, of course, admit that all the elements are subject to these conditions according to the degree of heat existing.

"The experiment with the pith balls simply proves the same fact. While the sealing wax and the pith balls remain at the same temperature as the surrounding atmosphere, there is no special exhibition of phenomena, because the electro-magnetic conditions are not disturbed. But friction applied to the sealing wax causes vibration and radiation, a change in the temperature and a disturbance of the electro-magnetic equilibrium occurs. Then the balls being dominated by electricity really attract the sealing wax, but the balls approach the sealing wax because they are light and suspended, while the sealing wax is heavy and fixed, but the attraction is mutual whenever a sphere of receptivity is organized with radiant matter to fill it. But if this sphere is occupied by a radiant body of matter and the balls are also radiant with magnetism, they will be repelled, both from the radiant body and from each other."

"I can readily understand from these facts," said Professor Hamilton, "that all that you claimed in your second proposition must be true. The sun as a radiant body of matter must repel the planets that surround him, and, obeying the same law, the moon must be repelled by the earth. Now, this repulsion of the planets by the solar center clearly explains the centrifugal force which we have always recognized as existing, but which I must confess I never before comprehended. And, if I understand you, the universal tendency of matter to organize itself into spheres explains the organization of the planets themselves, and furnishes the centripetal force by the universal tendency toward centers of electrical receptivity. Now, if we carry this to its fullest extent, the particles of matter composing the moon are drawn to its center; the moon and the matter composing the earth are organized into a larger sphere, represented by the orbit of the moon around the earth; this sphere is included in a still larger one represented by the orbits of the planets around the sun, and the sun and all of these spheres are moving together through space toward another center of electrical receptivity, and so on *ad infinitum*. Am I right in this statement?"

"Precisely," said Loma, "and you may continue the process indefinitely as long as the intellect of man can comprehend it, for there is no limit to space. Matter is limited and divisible, but space is unlimited, persistent and continuous. You have gone as far as it is possible for man to go in comprehending the unlimited."

"I believe you are right in your theory of gravitation," said the professor, after a pause, "but I reserve the right to find objections to it if I can. But you said that the earth does not revolve on its axis. I am curious to know why you should entertain that theory. If the earth does not revolve on its axis, what causes day and night?"

"The earth revolves, but not on its axis. The question of the production of day and night is not involved, for we are agreed that these conditions follow from the revolution of the earth in some way. But instead of revolving on an axis, as a top spins on the floor, it rolls on the periphery of its magnetic aura, as a wheel revolves on the ground."

"Please explain."

"First, let me ask you some questions," said Loma, with his most winning and diplomatic smile. "In round numbers, what is the circumference of the earth?"

"Nearly twenty-five thousand miles," replied the professor.

"The earth is progressing through space in the direction in which it revolves, is it not?"

"Certainly."

"At what rate of speed?"

"About eighteen miles per second."

"And that would be per day?"

"About one million five hundred and fifty-five thousand two hundred miles."

"Good. Now, how do you explain this discrepancy? A ball rolling along and progressing in the direction of its rotary motion will only progress the length of its circumference during each revolution. According to this the earth should only progress about twenty-five thousand miles in twenty-four hours, when we know it progresses more than a million and a half."

The professor was nonplused for a moment, but instantly rallied.

"Why, it does not follow that the earth is confined to the progression given by its circumference. That would be true of a ball rolling on a solid surface, but the earth is not rolling on a solid surface. It is revolving through space, and its progress is due to some other force."

"What is this other force, when did it originate, and what causes it to continue?"

"I don't know."

"There you are, and that is where you all land, until you comprehend the true facts. You understand from our previous conversation that the earth and sun are both bodies of matter radiating magnetism and repelling each other, but drawn together by a common center of electrical receptivity which attracts them both. Now, both the earth and sun are surrounded by their respective auras of repellant magnetism. These magnetisms collide at some distance between the earth and sun, and the smaller sphere of the earth's magnetism rolls around the larger sphere of the sun's magnetism, as a small wheel may be made to roll around the rim or periphery of a larger one. According to the figures you have just named, representing the progression of the earth, the diameter of the earth's sphere of magnetism is something less than five hundred thousand miles; hence the line of equilibrium upon which the sphere of the earth travels must be about two hundred and fifty thousand miles

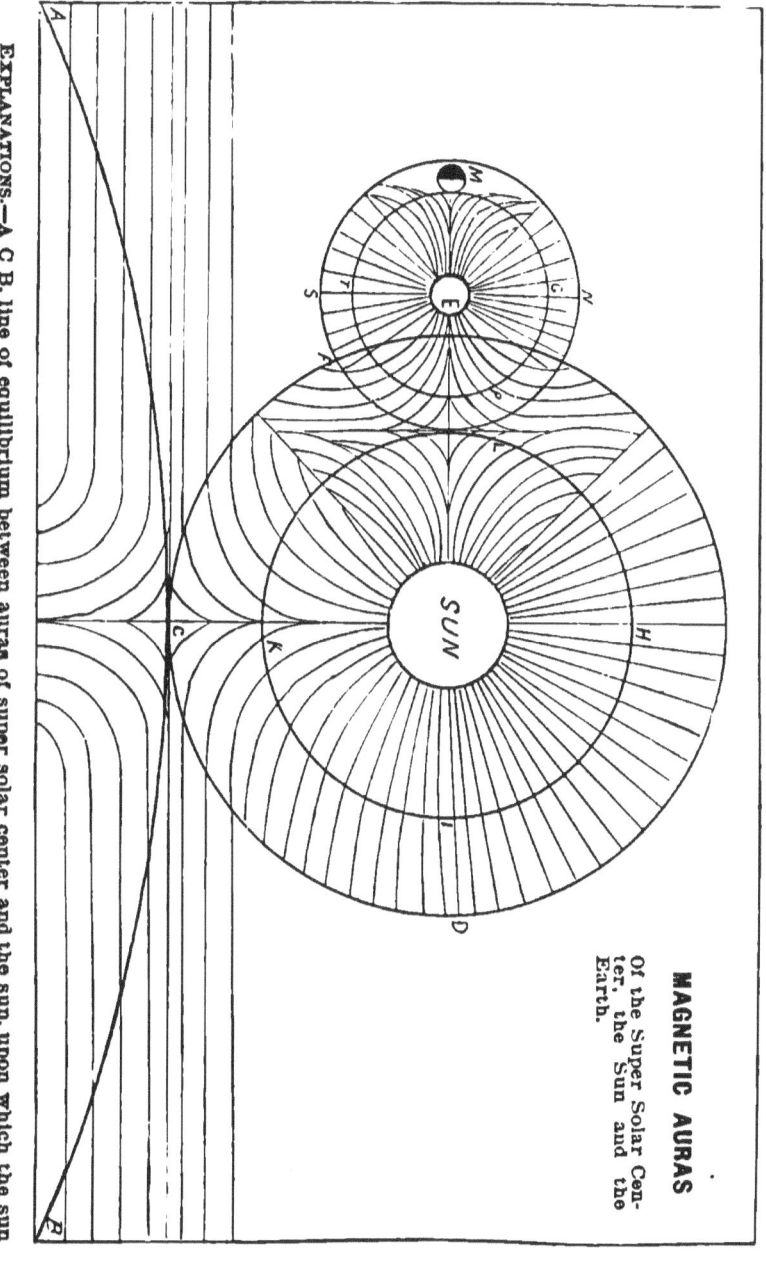

MAGNETIC AURAS
Of the Super Solar Center, the Sun and the Earth.

EXPLANATIONS.—A C B, line of equilibrium between auras of super solar center and the sun, upon which the sun revolves. H I K L, same between sun and earth, upon which earth revolves. G P T, same between earth and moon, upon which the moon will revolve when mature. C D F, aura of sun. F N S, aura of earth. E, the earth. M, the moon.

from the earth's center, in the direction of the sun. This theory accounts not only for the progression of the earth through space, but for its revolution also, as the constant mutation of the centers of electrical receptivity in space produces a constant gravity, and this line of equilibrium being established by the collision of the earth's magnetism with that of the sun there is nothing more inevitable than that the earth should revolve and progress in obedience to it. Every other star, planet and satellite revolves and progresses in the same way in obedience to the same great law."

"Your theory certainly seems plausible," said the professor admiringly, "and I will take it under consideration. At the first blush it certainly seems reasonable, but I must subject it to careful scrutiny before I adopt it. But I am curious to know why you believe that the sun does not radiate light or heat. You have commanded my respect and admiration by what you have already explained, and I am anxious to hear your discussion of the last proposition."

In a few brief but comprehensive sentences Loma explained the causes of heat and light as he had explained them to Doctor Bell on the first morning of their acquaintance, showing that heat and light are the result of the vibration of the magnetism of the sun in the atmosphere of the earth. The professor plied him with searching questions, all of which Loma answered with his usual graciousness and perspicuity. Finally, the professor said:

"You have certainly defended your remarkable doctrines with great ability. I shall give them the most searching investigation and criticism, and shall hope to meet you again for a more complete discussion."

"I shall be delighted to meet you at any time," said Loma, "but my stay in Chicago will be short, and I may not have the pleasure. But while you are studying these doctrines, there is just one more problem I would like to leave with you for the exercise of your mentality. We have seen that the earth revolves about the sun at a mean distance of 91,328,000 miles, consequently the amount of heat given off by the sun must be sufficient to heat a sphere of double that distance in diameter surrounding his center, to the same degree that he heats the earth."

"Certainly," said the professor again.

"Now, we also know that the sun is progressing through space in the direction of the constellation Hercules, carrying the earth with him, at a rate variously estimated from 150,000,000 miles to 1,051,200,000 miles per annum, of which the latter figures are probably the most correct, and during this process the orbit of the earth moves through a cylinder of space 182,656,000 miles in diameter, and in one year 1,051,200,000 miles in length, which the sun must heat in his passage to the same degree according to the accepted theory. Now, it is one thing to heat a given quantity of space with a heater that is stationary, but quite another thing to heat new space with it when it is moving through the new space at the rate at which the sun travels. I would like to have you figure on the amount of matter the sun contains and then estimate how much fuel it would take to warm up that much space with a heater of the sun's magnitude moving at that rate. You will find it about as absurd to ascribe the warming of this space to the sun as to propose to raise Lake Michigan to the boiling point by the heat from the furnaces of one of the steamers on its bosom.

"Magnetism, however, travels with greater velocity than light, and it is not difficult to conceive of a much larger space being filled with the light developed by the magnetism of the sun during his passage, if there was an atmosphere to develop it, so that there is nothing unreasonable in supposing that he fills the space of this stupendous cylinder with his magnetism, and this magnetism passing to the planets around him produces all the phenomena I have described as it encounters the resistance of the atmospheres of the planets."

"There is only one thing in your sublime explanation of astronomy that I have not fully comprehended," said Doctor Bell, who, up to this point, had remained a silent but absorbed listener, "and that is, how star germs are produced by parent stars."

"Every star, including the earth, is a hollow sphere," replied Loma, "and is a living organ of the male gender, having an outer crust with which we are familiar, an inner crust lining the interior cavity, and between these two crusts a bed of molten lava, which is the product of the restrained magnetism of the star, which produces internal heat. The inner cavity of every ma-

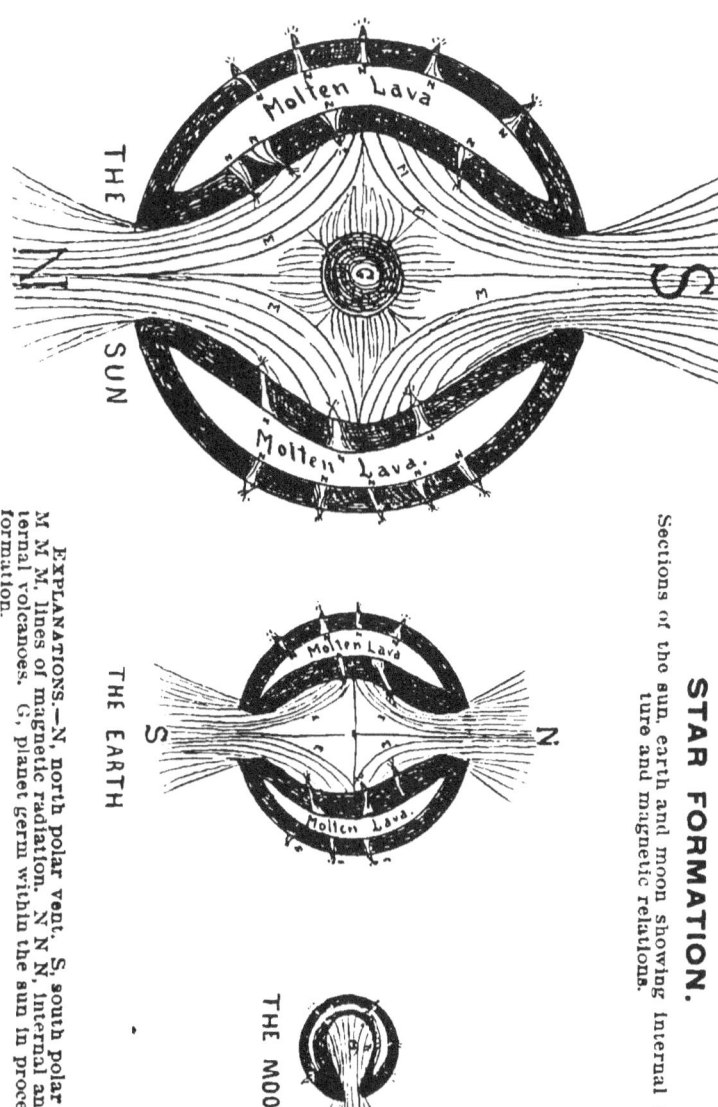

STAR FORMATION.

Sections of the sun, earth and moon showing internal structure and magnetic relations.

EXPLANATIONS.—N, north polar vent. S, south polar vent. M M, lines of magnetic radiation. N N, Internal and external volcanoes. G, planet germ within the sun in process of formation.

ture star is provided with two vents, one at each pole, from which there is a constant escape of magnetism which produces the phenomena known as the *aurora borealis*. The restrained magnetism of the star breaks through the crust in both directions, on the inner and outer surfaces in volcanic eruptions. The matter which is thrown out upon the outer surface in obedience to the law of gravitation falls back upon the star and is incorporated into its sphere. But the constant discharge of matter from the inner surface is collected in the cavity and formed into small spheres, just as pills are formed in the pill box of an apothecary. When one of these spheres collects sufficient material to radiate magnetism strongly repellant to the magnetism of the parent star, it is discharged by the force of these repellant magnetisms through one of the polar vents into outer space, and these discharges are accompanied with great seismic disturbances. You can understand that it takes ages to form one of these germs of sufficient magnitude to produce a discharge. But at intervals these discharges take place, and the germ thus originated in the 'loins of its father' (to use a figurative expression) is deposited by its father, the parent star, in the broad womb of space, where it passes through the stage of incubation. Our moon is a planet germ in the stage of incubation. It has progressed so far that it has a hollow interior and one polar vent which is on the side opposite the earth, as it would naturally be, as the discharge of magnetism from the vent antagonizes the magnetism of the earth and forces the moon into that position; hence we see only one side of the moon, which is the side opposite the vent. When it progresses far enough to form another vent, which will occur opposite the first, in the side now turned toward the earth, the moon will pass from incubation to complete life, turn sideways to the earth and begin a diurnal motion similar to that displayed by the earth, or any other completely incubated planet. It will also form an atmosphere, and then will occur upon the moon the same succession of growths that have already occurred upon the earth.

"The principal reason why these scientific facts have escaped the comprehension of modern scientists is this," said Loma, in conclusion: "The human race has become so saturated with a theology which teaches that all things have their origin in the decree of a lone masculine god, and which ignores completely the motherhood of God which is just as essential as the fatherhood, and human sociology has so degraded woman to the level of a chattel of man, so that she is held in contempt and all things feminine are despised, that your scientists are incapable of comprehending the passional relations of space and matter. As long as they ignore the prime, ungenerated, infinite all-mother, space, in their calculations, their conclusions will be erroneous, their efforts vain, their attempts to solve the problems of nature puerile, and their own advancement impossible."

CHAPTER XXII.

THE NATIVITY.

"And the angel said unto them, 'Fear not; for behold I bring you good tidings of great joy which shall be to all people.' * * *
"And suddenly there was with the angel a multitude of the heavenly host, praising God and saying:
" 'Glory to God in the highest, and on earth peace, good will toward men.' "

The time for Myrtle's parturition arrived at last, and the young mother, prepared by every precaution and assistance which science could suggest, and sustained by the loving ministrations of her devoted friends, passed through the ordeal in perfect safety and with no pain. The careful attention which had been given to her diet and regimen had resulted in the most favorable bodily conditions, and instead of the distressing circumstances usually attendant upon childbirth, Myrtle experienced only delightful sensations. In this she was greatly assisted by Loma, who, being a master of hypnotism, placed her under control at the proper season, and not only protected her from unpleasant effects, but by the power of suggestion, regulated the precise moment of her delivery and its attendant consequences. So perfectly did Myrtle yield to the masterful influence of her protector and lover that on the second day after her delivery her normal condition was completely regained.

The first signs of parturition manifested themselves at eleven o'clock in the forenoon of the day upon which Loma had suggested her delivery, and the birth occurred precisely at noon. Loma explained that this was arranged in accordance with Myrtle's temperament and constitution, and that she reached the highest point of her daily vitality at that hour. Consequently he had suggested the delivery at the precise moment when her delicate and impressionable constitution was at its most favorable condition for the display of resistance and strength.

At the moment of parturition Loma stood at the foot of the couch upon which Myrtle reclined, and, extending his arms, poured forth his incomparable magnetism in a flood of glory. Myrtle, bathed in this sustaining and life-giving emanation, felt no pain, but simply relaxed her nerves in a succession of happy impressions. Doctor and Mrs. Bell, administering the professional details of the accouchement, performed their duties with consummate skill. In a few moments Myrtle, radiant with joy, clasped to her breast the beautiful fruit of her first maternity.

When the last details of the delivery had been accomplished, Loma spoke:

"Beloved, as I once gave you a glimpse into the regions of the blessed, when the first compact of our love was sealed, so now if you will join hands and become receptive, I will show you how the advent of the fifth member of our sacred circle is celebrated in Venus," and as Myrtle extended her hands to the doctor and Mrs. Bell, Loma raised his hands and extended them, as he had done on a former occasion, while the intensity of his magnetism increased to its dazzling degree.

A vision of enchanting loveliness overwhelmed the senses of the young mother and her devoted friends. Again the strains of heavenly music ravished their ears, but this time their senses were sufficiently developed to comprehend its import. Human forms of surpassing beauty encompassed them, while the very air they breathed was surcharged with the magnetism radiated by these forms in waves of glory. Delicious sensations assailed every avenue of intelligence, and all seemed to unite in one grand crescendo into the expression:

"Glory to God in the highest,
On earth peace, good will toward men."

Loma permitted his proteges to thrill in the joy of this experience for several minutes. Then as their receptivities became exhausted, and they were unable to comprehend more, he lowered his magnetism, and they fell into the deep sleep which had before followed the manifestation of his power. For several hours they continued to sleep while Loma maintained his vigil over all. Doctor Bell and his mother regained consciousness before Myrtle, whom Loma continued to impress with loving and solicitous affection until the last vestige of fatigue and weakness from her recent experience had passed away.

Beautiful indeed was Myrtle's offspring. Perfect in every feature, strong in every element of vitality, instead of coming into the world crying, as is the case with nearly every child born to the human race, as it was received by the motherly hands of Mrs. Bell it instantly began its respiration, and as it did so *smiled*. And as the deft hands of the experienced matron assisted it to increase the power of its lungs, soft cooing notes of inexpressible sweetness came from its infant lips. And thus began the life which was destined to bless the world with the unfolding germs of the new civilization.

When Myrtle had in some measure regained her composure after the first thrilling sensations of motherhood, Loma approached her, and, clasping about her neck a beautiful gold necklace, bearing upon its front a magnificent solitaire diamond, weighing over six carats, kissed her affectionately, and said:

"Exalted one, receive the badge of motherhood as it is worn in Venus. You have brought a jewel to the state. The state salutes you with its congratulations, and every citizen acknowledges an obligation to you. Henceforth your place is with the honored matrons, to whom the state is indebted for its life and perpetuity."

Myrtle received her new honor with becoming dignity. Doctor and Mrs. Bell congratulated her affectionately, and each presented her with a beautiful jewel. Faithful Nora headed the servants of the household in a brief but happy interview, and then the young mother again sank into blissful repose.

On the day following her delivery, Myrtle, with her full strength completely regained, held a levee of congratulation. Mr. McDonald and his sister were among the early callers, and the small circle of devoted friends to whom Myrtle had been introduced by the doctor and Mrs. Bell made the young mother supremely happy by their delicate attentions.

On the third day after her delivery a remarkable event occurred. At about eleven o'clock a visitor was announced, who was met in the parlor by Doctor Bell. As the doctor entered the parlor he was greeted by a man of commanding appearance and scholarly demeanor, who said:

"Doctor Bell, my mission may seem strange to you, but I am the representative of a scientific association which is unknown to the world, because its members live on a plane so exalted that we do not court notoriety. But among the privileges we enjoy by reason of our superior knowledge is the power of discerning from astrological data and clairvoyant perception when an extraordinary event takes place in any part of the world. We have discovered by means which I may not take time to explain, what I am sure must be known to you, that within the past three days a child has been born in this house which we are informed will bless the world with his greatness and virtue. There are within a few hundred miles of Chicago, thirty members of our cult, who have been summoned to meet in this city for the purpose of suitably recognizing and celebrating the happy event. I have been delegated by my associates to come to you and ask for the privilege of congratulating the mother of the coming prodigy, and of feasting our eyes on what we know to be the only perfect human child which has been born upon this planet for nearly nineteen hundred years."

Doctor Bell was at first considerably surprised at this message, but he was too polite and self-possessed to betray it. With his usual courtly grace he requested his visitor to be seated, while he made some inquiries of his colleagues.

In the library he found Loma, to whom he communicated the request of the visitor.

"I have been expecting this," said Loma, with one of his peculiar smiles, "although it is not a necessary part of my experience. I have known of the existence of the cult to which he belongs, and I have been curious to see whether they would be able to locate Myrtle's offspring. They are proceeding upon correct lines and developing some very interesting powers, and it will be our happy privilege to extend them every courtesy. Mary and Joseph were visited by a similar delegation at the time of the birth of Jesus, and they are referred to in the Bible as the 'wise men from the East.' I shall be pleased to meet the gentleman myself."

Doctor Bell and Loma proceeded to the parlor, where they both extended distinguished courtesies to the stranger, who introduced himself as Professor

James Gannon. When the doctor asked his residence, he replied:

"I am not a resident of any city or country, neither are any of my colleagues. We are so thoroughly convinced that the present organization of society is wrong that we cannot consistently allow ourselves to become identified with any of its permanent organizations. We live natural lives as far as possible without offending those with whom we come in contact, but while we are organized for purposes of communication and mutual study, we are practically independent of organized society. We are simply known to each other as the 'Associated Philosophers.'"

It was arranged that the Associated Philosophers should have a reception at noon on the following day, and Professor Gannon took his leave.

Precisely at twelve o'clock on the next day the delegation arrived. They were at first received in the parlor by Doctor and Mrs. Bell, and by them conducted in a body to the conservatory, where Loma and Myrtle, with her beautiful babe, awaited them.

The Associated Philosophers consisted of fifteen handsome, dignified and scholarly men and an equal number of beautiful, attractive and cultivated women. Myrtle received them with her accustomed grace, and while she delighted her visitors with her own beauty and sweet womanliness, she was also herself overwhelmed with their expressions of devotion and kindness. Every one of the delegation caressed her and her baby boy, and each one presented her with some beautiful token of friendship.

Two hours were spent in delightful conversation and music, when the philosophers departed, leaving Myrtle enriched with a magnificent collection of presents, and what she valued more highly, substantial pledges of personal devotion to her and her highly favored offspring.

Doctor Bell was unremitting in his loyalty and devotion to Myrtle. Every possible provision had been made for her comfort and protection by him during her six months' sojourn under his roof. Now that the ordeal was safely passed by Myrtle, and she was a happy mother, in the complete possession of normal health, which had never for one moment been disturbed by her experience, his professional gratification was only exceeded by his personal joy in her happiness. Myrtle was deeply conscious of his devotion and love, and reciprocated it in a complete degree.

In one of their delightful interviews in the conservatory, when she and the doctor were bending over her beautiful babe in transports of affectionate admiration, Myrtle entwined her arms about his neck and kissed him affectionately, saying:

"Oh, I owe so much to you for all this happiness. Without your love and protection I would have been dead and disgraced, instead of being the happiest and most honored woman in the world. How can I ever reward you and show my gratitude and love?"

"My reward has come already, in being permitted to

share in this happiness," said the doctor, as he returned her caress. "Gratitude I do not require, for the consciousness of duty well performed is always the reward of correct action. But," he continued, as he stood before Myrtle and clasped both of her hands in his, while his manly voice trembled with deep emotion and his eyes gazed into hers with an expression which thrilled her with happiness, "if you wish to show your love, and you love me well enough, you can make me the happiest man in the world, by becoming my adored, my incomparable consort."

Myrtle buried her face on his shoulder while her slight frame trembled with the highest sensations of joy.

"Oh, Edward," she exclaimed, "I thought I was supremely happy in my glorious motherhood, but this is transcendent joy. I have loved you from the first day I knew you, and you have filled my life with every sweet experience of which it is capable."

Just at this moment Loma entered the conservatory, and seeing the expressions of the faces of the doctor and Myrtle, both of whom were radiant with their new happiness, he comprehended the situation at once. He advanced and embraced them both, glowing with his richest expression of magnetism.

"My blessed lovers!" he exclaimed, as he caressed them, "I have been wondering how long it would take you to realize how necessary you are to each other and to consummate your happiness. You will accept my loving congratulations and my highest blessing."

At this point Loma was interrupted by the entrance of Mrs. Bell into the conservatory, and when the situation was explained to her, she overwhelmed the lovers with her maternal benediction.

"I have been praying for this," she exclaimed with rapture, "and my prayer being answered, my joy is complete."

As Mrs. Bell ceased speaking the babe awakened from a deep slumber, and, opening its eyes, looked into the face of Doctor Bell, and smiled, at the same time raising its tiny hands and voicing the sweet and cooing sounds which were peculiar to it.

"See," said Loma, "the babe extends its congratulations also, and welcomes the protection of its devoted foster-father."

Doctor Bell pressed his bearded lips to the forehead of the beautiful child, while he murmured:

"May nature deal with me as I am faithful to the high trust imposed upon me, and as my love is devoted to this child and its royal mother."

"Amen!" said Loma fervently, while Myrtle embraced her betrothed lover and Mrs. Bell smiled upon both.

After the transports of this new experience had subsided in part, Doctor Bell addressed Loma affectionately and seriously, while he said:

"There is a subject which lies nearest to my heart at the present moment upon which I wish to be instructed, and I think Myrtle and my mother will also be grateful for an expression from you. Now, that Myrtle and myself are betrothed as consorts, the subject of marriage is before us. Hitherto I have never considered marriage at all, because I was absorbed in my profession, and I did not expect to ever assume the relationship, which I have always considered degrading to both woman and man, and I never expected to meet any woman who could cause me to consider it. But recent events have changed all of these considerations, and now that I have met and loved Myrtle, I am anxious to do what is exactly right. I do not wish that either she or myself should be subjected to the degrading conditions of marriage if I can avoid it. Yet I fully realize that unless we enter into some form of a legal marriage our social and my professional standing will be imperiled, and we will be subject to many inconveniences which will fall more heavily upon her than upon myself. At the same time we owe a duty to society to set an example of a correct life, and it seems impossible to do this in marriage. I appeal to you in this dilemma for complete instruction as to what should be done for the benefit of Myrtle, her offspring, myself and society at large."

"I have already considered this problem," replied Loma, "and am ready with its solution. The degradation of marriage consists, not in the fact that men and women marry, and call the contract by that name, but in the fact that they violate nature by promising to do impossible things, by assuming ownership over each other, and by regarding the relationship as only determinable by the death or the criminal action of one or the other of the parties. To enable Myrtle to enjoy the privileges of society, and to enable you to give her boy the advantages he should have, it is desirable that you should occupy a position giving the largest freedom of action without unnecessarily antagonizing the society in which you move. You will enjoy greater privileges in society, and greater immunity from persecution during the boyhood and adolescence of your charge if you apparently conform to the usages of society in this respect, while you may at the same time introduce a radical reform into the marriage ceremony itself. By so doing you will accomplish greater good for society and perform a higher duty than you will by antagonizing your associates and suffering martyrdom. This was the plan pursued by the followers of Gallheim upon our planet, who practiced a reformed style of marriage for several generations. This is the next natural step towards complete freedom, and you should conscientiously conform to it instead of overstepping the plans of natural development and attempting to force the growth of institutions which take time to mature. I therefore suggest, that as my time with you is necessarily short, and I am anxious to consummate my mission as speedily as possible, that you allow me to celebrate your ceremony of consorting as we practice it in Venus, and that you publish it as a marriage according to the reformed method proclaimed by Gallheim, while, in fact, you repudiate all the degrading implications of the conventional marriage, and that the ceremony take place in a public manner so as to create the greatest possible impression."

To this the doctor and Myrtle eagerly consented, and, after consulting with Mrs. Bell, it was aranged that the ceremony should take place on the following Wednesday, at noon, and invitations were immediately issued to five hundred guests, among whom were included Myrtle's relatives, the friends and associates of Doctor and Mrs. Bell, the Associated Philosophers and representatives of the press. As the immediate associates of Doctor and Mrs. Bell had for some time been incorporated as a religious society under the laws of the State of Illinois, and as Loma had been shortly after his arrival upon the earth admitted to the society and made one of its leaders and teachers, it was arranged that the ceremony should be conducted under the auspices of the society, and the invitations were so worded.

CHAPTER XXIII.

MARRIAGE UNDER THE NEW CIVILIZATION.

"For always in thine eyes, O Liberty!
Shines that high light whereby the world is saved."

"Self-abnegation, subservience to man, whether he be father, lover or husband, is the most dangerous theory that can be taught to or forced upon a woman. She has no right to transmit a nature that is subservient and a slavish character, either blindly obedient or blindly rebellious, and therefore set, as is a time lock, to prey or to be preyed upon by the society of the future. If woman is not brave enough personally to demand and obtain absolute personal liberty of action, equality of status, entire control of her great and race-endowing function, maternity, she has no right to dare to stamp upon a child and to curse a race with the descendants of such a servile, a dwarfed, time and master serving character."

The day which had been set for the celebration of the ceremony of consorting of Doctor Bell and Myrtle dawned auspiciously. The wedding ceremony was arranged to take place at noon, and some time before that hour the invited guests began to arrive in large numbers. The conservatory and music room, together with the two large bedrooms usually occupied by Loma and Myrtle, which connected, as the reader knows, with the conservatory, had been arranged into a charming auditorium capable of accommodating all of the invited guests, and had been beautifully decorated.

The devoted circle of young people who had taken such great interest in Myrtle from the first, were now much in evidence. Loma had taken enough of them into his confidence to make most elaborate arrangements for the use of their services to produce desirable effects, and as the doctor, Myrtle and Mrs. Bell were to sustain principal parts in the ceremony, with himself, he had arranged that the social and hospitable courtesies of the occasion should be performed by committees of these friends as he was able to make them available.

The guests were received in the parlors below, and escorted to the conservatory as they arrived by a committee of young ladies and gentlemen selected for this service. Another band of ushers received them at the conservatory, and provided them with seats. As each guest took the position assigned, one of the ushers presented a beautiful souvenir containing superb portraits of the doctor and Myrtle, and a copy of the ceremony ritual, printed in gold upon the finest quality of white silk.

The music room adjoining the conservatory had been beautifully decorated and made to resemble the chancel of a cathedral, being covered with white silk throughout, embellished with white roses. The fountain in the conservatory was transformed into a bank of white roses and calla lilies. Throughout the improvised auditorium the decorations had been carried out on a similar scale, white being the only color of the flowers and decorations used. The organ in the music room was concealed beneath a mass of white roses, and at the keys presided Miss Carrie Williamson, one of the most accomplished organists of the city, arrayed in a costume of pure white, with a single white rose in her hair.

Professor Hamilton, who had returned from Madison, Wisconsin, was among the invited guests, but not being a man of social tastes, he took no conspicuous part in the ceremony. Mr. McDonald and his sister were expected, but when he arrived, to the astonishment of the friends who formed the reception committee, he was accompanied not only by his sister, but by his wife. The latter had been entirely overcome by the accounts her husband gave of the munificent hospitality of the Bells, and by his description of the remarkable character of Loma. As soon as she realized that Myrtle had indeed been adopted by rich and powerful friends, her selfish and narrow nature had secretly craved for an opportunity to resume friendly relations with the girl whom she had so shamelessly cast out of her own home, but pride and the apparent lack of a suitable opportunity had prevented her from making the attempt. But when she heard that Myrtle was about to be married, and found herself included in an invitation to attend the ceremony, her curiosity to see Loma and Myrtle's prosperity found a ready excuse in the statement that she was glad Myrtle was about to return to the ranks of "respectability." And so she appeared among the invited guests, with her pharisaical crust a little thicker than usual over her thin veneer of intelligence, too ignorant to comprehend the hospitality which made it possible for her to be present, too narrow to appreciate the loving and forgiving spirit in which the invitation had been sent, and too much absorbed in the gratification of her own selfish desires and curiosity to realize the import of the event or the meaning of the ceremony with which it was celebrated.

And as she sat in the auditorium watching the progress of events, herself in fact, the least respectable person in the bright assemblage, she represented the current of modern society and public opinion, of which Loma had said to Doctor Bell:

"Society will look upon your ceremony of consorting with Myrtle as simply an ordinary marriage with perhaps some extraordinary features, of which they will take but little notice. But the thoughtful and the profound will see in this celebration a complete revolution of the institution of marriage, because the principles declared and the words spoken will be, in effect, a complete contradiction of the usual form. So while you will comply with the law in taking Myrtle as your wife, you will inaugurate an entirely new view of the relationship, and accomplish more for the reform of marriage than could be done in any other way. This was the course pursued by the followers of Gallheim, and as soon as the intelligent portion of the community are educated in this way to a rational relationship between man and woman, they will be prepared for the next great step which will consist in the abolition of all pledges and the simple recognition of the relationship, in which pledges will be unnecessary, because they will be implied by every principle of good behavior."

The Associated Philosophers were early among the guests, and were assigned to places of special honor near the improvised chancel. It was noticed that they were attired in striking costumes of white satin, the peculiar habit of their order on formal occasions.

Nora and the other devoted servants of the household had been given good seats in the auditorium, together with a number of other persons who were in some measure the recipients of the splendid philanthropy of Doctor and Mrs. Bell. Representatives of all the daily papers were on hand, prepared to report the details of what they had already been given to understand would be an interesting departure from conventional methods.

Precisely as the clock struck twelve, the organ filled the conservatory with the sublime strains of a new wedding march, which had been arranged by Loma for the organist, and which he had stated was first used in Venus on the occasion of the marriage of Gallheim's only daughter. At the same moment, amid a flutter of excitement, the ceremonial procession entered the rear of the conservatory and proceeded to the chancel, while the audience rose and remained standing.

First came seven beautiful little girls and an equal number of handsome little boys, arrayed in costumes of pure white, scattering white roses and delicious perfume over the aisle which led from the entrance to the chancel. Following these came Mr. McDonald, with Myrtle leaning upon his arm. Mr. McDonald was arrayed in a conventional dress suit of black, with a single white rose upon the lapel of his coat. Myrtle was dressed in a simple white gown, of the most delicate silk, beautifully embroidered, but wearing no ornaments save the ring and necklace which she had received from Loma, which were the badges of her glorious maternity. Her neck and shoulders were bare, and her golden hair, left without restriction, fell in beautiful waves to her waist. As she walked up the aisle leaning upon the arm of her uncle, her face was radiant with serene joy, and she presented a picture of classic loveliness and grace.

Immediately following Myrtle and her uncle came Doctor Bell, leaning upon the arm of his mother. Both were arrayed in garments of immaculate white satin, and wore no ornaments, save that Mrs. Bell wore a necklace bearing a large solitaire diamond, similar to that worn by Myrtle. Doctor Bell was a conspicuous example of manly dignity and self-possession as he advanced to the chancel with his mother and took his position on the right, while Myrtle and her uncle stood at the left of the chancel. The fourteen attending cherubs ranged themselves in a semi-circle behind the contracting parties, just as Loma, who had been concealed behind a bank of roses in the chancel, advanced and met the procession. Loma was attired in a simple toga of white silk, with bare arms and shoulders, and wore as ornaments a necklace bearing three magnificent diamonds, and four superb solitaire diamond rings, besides three smaller ones ornamented with clusters of sapphires and rubies. These had been manufactured at Doctor Bell's order for the occasion, and were exact duplicates, according to descriptions furnished by Loma, of the ornaments he wore in Venus as emoluments of his distinguished services. His body was pervaded with a mellow glow of his magnetism, which shone most conspicuously in a halo of glory around his head. His appearance was the signal for a complete silence, and hush of awe which fell upon the assemblage as they contemplated his glorious personality. Facing the audience in his commanding dignity and in tones which thrilled his hearers with new and overwhelming emotions, he said:

"Dearly beloved, the event which is about to occur is one of transcendent importance, not only to the high contracting parties, who have chosen in this manner to call you to witness the compact of their love, but to the entire human race, which has heretofore been impeded in its advancement and development by false conceptions of the duties of men and women to each other and to society. Marriage is honorable in all, if the motives and intentions of the parties are honorable, and those intentions are carried out in the spirit of love and devotion. But humanity is of more value than any ceremonial observance, and any compact which degrades humanity or any member of society is contrary to the laws of Nature, which are higher than any which are the result of the opinions or the enactment of any body of men.

"The laws of your commonwealth are almost sufficiently liberal and rational to allow the correct association of man and woman at this stage of the progress of the world. They merely require that the contracting parties should acknowledge in the presence of witnesses that they take each other as man and wife. Your civil law is in advance of your social customs, for in the usual ceremony performed in your churches and often by the civil magistrate, pledges of a degrading and stultifying nature are required of the parties, in addition to the simple declaration of marriage in which the law wisely leaves pledges of conduct to the implications of good sense and morality. As soon as your public sentiment is sufficiently educated, and your laws are so amended as to permit the correction of matrimonial mistakes, without the scandal of divorce, or the commission of crime by either party to secure liberty, your conditions will be favorable for the development of perfect morality.

"The only association of man and woman in marriage which can possibly result in good to society is that which is founded upon mutual love, respect and admiration, which associates persons who are adapted to make each other happy by the possession of those attributes of character which are conducive to each other's well being and which meet the demands of each other's natures, where love has been tested by sufficient association and experiment, and is known to exist, and where there is a mutual, sincere and reasonable desire for its continued exercise. In such cases we believe that, as far as the parties themselves are concerned, there is no necessity for any ceremonial declaration or mutual pledge. But for the edification of society, for the proper register of the relationship, and for an example for the emulation of those who have not progressed to a similar state of felicity, we believe in and practice the ceremony which follows."

While the organ vibrated the perfumed air with a solemn but exceedingly sweet refrain, Loma, glowing to a somewhat higher degree of magnetism, raised his hands toward the sun, which at that moment flooded the conservatory with light, and pronounced the following invocation:

"Infinite Source of Creation! Thou who revealest Thyself to us in the warming rays of the sun, in the perfume of the flowers, and in every progression of Thy handiwork, including our own intelligence and advancement, we invoke Thy blessing upon this compact of love which we are about to celebrate between two of Thy children. May the occasion be the beginning of a new epoch in the advancement of humanity upon the earth, and may the declarations now uttered inspire all hearers to grander conceptions of love and devotion, to a higher expression of morality and to a closer communion with Thyself as expressed in all of the beneficent processes of Nature."

As Loma ceased his invocation, the organ strains closed in a thrilling tremolo, and the audience waited in silent awe for the rest of the ceremony. At a signal from Loma, Mr. McDonald and Mrs. Bell turned and faced the audience. Loma addressed the assemblage as follows:

"Dearly beloved, you see before you the representatives of the present and the coming civilization, attired in colors which fittingly portray the conditions existing in each. The civilization of the present is wholly represented by man, and in it woman has no part. In this civilization she is regarded as the chattel and slave of man; by him degraded to the lowest uses, and ministering to his passions to the destruction of herself and the race. Blackness and darkness, the suggestive conditions of this unhappy state of death, are considered by you appropriate for your highest festivities. Behold in woman, attired in garments of brightness and purity, the harbinger of the exalted state toward which you are advancing and which you will ultimately reach. In this sublime ceremonial the civilization of the present must deliver to woman her freedom, that she may stand erect in her independence and strength to dispose of her favors of love according to the dictates of her own volition."

As Loma spoke the last sentence of this address, Mr. McDonald, who had been standing near Myrtle with his hand clasping hers, while she leaned upon his shoulder, released his hold and stepped back three paces, Myrtle remained standing facing Loma, who resumed:

"In the new type of civilization the sweet influences of woman must have an equal value with those of man. She will impress her sons with her goodness as man will impress his daughters with his strength, and the combined excellencies of both uniting in improved offspring will fill the earth with a humanity which will be complete."

At this point Mrs. Bell, who had been standing with her hand clasping that of her son, led him three paces forward where he stood opposite Myrtle, released his hand, and stepped back to her original position, where she remained standing in calm but regal dignity. Doctor Bell faced Loma on a line with Myrtle, standing about three feet from her on the right.

Loma, glowing with an exquisite emanation of magnetism, addressed Myrtle first:

"Beloved daughter, hast thou in the exercise of thy intelligence, without undue influence, coercion or fear, and in the full possession of knowledge of what is implied in the sacred relationship of consorts, discovered the one who is able to satisfy the yearnings of thy nature, and to whom thou art drawn in ties of complete respect, admiration and love?"

To which Myrtle responded in a clear, sweet voice, "I have."

"Art thou conscious of intense emotions of love and devoted affection toward this man, and art thou fully persuaded that the close and intimate association of the higher expressions of love will be a source of perpetual enjoyment, satisfaction and profit to thee, so that thou wilt be sure to desire its continuance?"

"I am."

"Hast thou tested thyself and him to a sufficient degree that thou art satisfied that ye are both sincere in your professions of love, and dost thou believe that ye are adapted to each other in the possession of those elements of character that are necessary to each other's happiness and the perfection of offspring?"

"I have tested both myself and him, and I believe that we are not only capable of promoting each other's happiness, but are essential to it, and that the elements of complete parentage will be represented in our union," responded Myrtle.

Loma addressed the same questions to Doctor Bell, and received the same answers in a clear, firm voice. He then took the doctor's right hand in his left and Myrtle's right hand in his right, and joining them, propounded the following question:

"Do you, in obedience to the laws of the state, declare in the presence of these witnesses, that you take each other as husband and wife; and in obedience to the higher laws of Nature, that you take each other into the higher, holier and grander relationship of consorts, for mutual love, protection and enjoyment; and for the advancement of the interests of humanity."

To which both of the contracting parties responded simultaneously:

"I do."

"Then," said Loma, "by virtue of the authority of the laws of the State of Illinois, I pronounce you husband and wife. And in the name of humanity and its most sacred interests I require of each of you, your declaration of the relationship of consorts and its higher and holier implications."

As Loma concluded the last sentence the organ began a sweet, low strain, which blended with the music of Myrtle's voice as she clasped the doctor's right hand in her own and recited the following declaration with faultless elocution:

"I, Myrtle Burnham, take thee, Edward Bell, as my exalted and holy consort. I declare that I love thee, that I admire and respect thee, that thou dost satisfy the yearnings of my nature, and that I will, in consideration of thy love and devotion expressed toward me, present myself to thee daily in the most lovable and companionable aspect of which I am capable. I declare that, to the utmost of my ability, I will promote and protect thy happiness, thy welfare and thy health. I concede to thee full liberty of thought, speech and action. I will render unto thee honor and love as thou deservest both, and in every reasonable and correct manner endeavor to develop, to win and to keep thy love and respect. I declare that I will live with thee according to the laws of Nature, and should it appear at any time that my companionship is injurious to thy welfare, thy health or thy advancement to a higher plane of life, I will voluntarily remove myself from thee, and giving thee complete liberty, will endeavor still to promote thy welfare by every means in my power."

As Myrtle finished this declaration she raised her face toward the doctor, who encircled her with his arm and imprinted a loving kiss upon her lips. Then clasping her right hand in his own, the doctor addressed her in a similar manner:

"*I, Edward Bell, take thee, Myrtle Burnham, as my exalted and holy consort. I declare that I love thee, that I admire and respect thee, that thou dost satisfy the yearnings of my nature, and that I will, in consideration of thy love and devotion expressed toward me, present myself to thee daily in the most lovable and companionable aspect of which I am capable. I declare that, to the utmost of my ability, I will promote and protect thy happiness, thy welfare and thy health. I concede to thee full liberty of thought, speech and action. I will render unto thee honor and love as thou deservest both, and in every reasonable and correct manner endeavor to develop, to win and to keep thy love and respect. I declare that I will live with thee according to the laws of Nature, and should it appear at any time that my companionship is injurious to thy welfare, thy health or thy advancement to a higher plane of life, I will voluntarily remove myself from thee, and giving thee complete liberty, will endeavor still to promote thy welfare by every means in my power.*"

As the doctor finished his declaration Myrtle embraced and kissed him, while Loma advancing placed upon the third finger of the left hand of each a magnificent diamond ring, each bearing a device enclosing two beautiful gems, encircled by a golden band, saying:

"Beloved children of Nature, receive the insignia of the exalted and holy state of loving, devoted and natural consorts."

Then raising his hands above them in benediction, he exclaimed:

"May all good influences surround and bless you. May Nature's highest, sweetest and holiest pleasures be yours, and may the fruit of your union be the beginning of a new race of exalted types of humanity who shall bless the world they inhabit and minister constantly to their own happiness and advancement. In the name of the higher civilization, I pronounce you accepted and devoted consorts in purity and love."

Loma concluded this sublime ceremony by imprinting a paternal kiss upon the brow of each. He was followed by Mrs. Bell, who embraced first Myrtle and then the doctor in her maternal congratulations. Mr. McDonald followed, and then the Associated Philosophers. While the organ pealed sublime and inspiring strains the invited guests, who had all been deeply affected by the splendid exhibition of Loma's powers and not less by the sublime implications of the declarations of the consorts, pressed forward to overwhelm the happy couple with every demonstration of affection and enthusiasm. Even Mrs. McDonald, narrow and bigoted as she was, shared the enthusiasm of the moment, and shed tears as she received from Myrtle's lips a kiss which expressed so much of forgiveness and goodness that she could not be insensible to its angelic sweetness.

The reception continued for three hours, during which time an excellent orchestra discoursed sweet music. A superb menu was served in the dining room, in which function the doctor's steward distinguished himself, and every guest was made to feel the genuineness and excellence of the hospitality dispensed.

When the last guest had departed, and Myrtle and the doctor were once more at ease with Loma and Mrs. Bell, Loma said, as he bent over the cradle and impressed a kiss upon the brow of the sleeping babe, which during the exciting events of the afternoon had been under the faithful guardianship of the devoted Nora:

"Beloved, it is now time for you to congratulate me. My mission to earth is finished, and all that remains is for me to return to my native planet, where my beloved consort is anxiously awaiting the successful consummation of my journey, to enjoy the felicity of seeing me enrolled in the Academy of Heroes."

This announcement would have been received by the friends with sorrow had it not been for two facts which prevented it. In the time he had associated with them Loma had succeeded in instilling into their minds so much of the principles of equity that selfishness was destroyed, and they rejoiced exceedingly in what they knew to be a source of supreme joy to their instructor and lover. Moreover, Loma had assured them that the perfection of their clairvoyant sense would enable them to hold communication with him occasionally, and he explained that Jesus had taught the same art to his disciples, and that it was the first exercise of this power which produced the remarkable occurrences of the day of Pentecost, as recorded in the second chapter of the Acts of the Apostles. The knowledge of this fact was a great comfort to the friends as the time of Loma's departure drew near; but even if the prospect of this sweet privilege had been denied them they could not have exhibited selfishness enough to have desired to detain him longer from the joys that awaited him on his return to Venus.

Loma had instructed them partially as to the requirements of his preparation for the journey, and it was therefore no surprise when he announced that he would take the train for Denver, Colorado, on the following morning, and that he desired the doctor and Myrtle as well as Mrs. Bell to accompany him. Preparations were immediately made for the journey, and Nora was included in the party, as it was impossible to separate Myrtle from her offspring at this time, and no one was deemed to be as capable of filling the duties of maid and nurse as she. Nora was delighted with the prospect of the journey when it was announced to her, and after the simple preparations were made for the trip and tickets and berths were secured, the family retired to rest, to gain strength for the responsibilities of the morrow.

The relations of Doctor Bell and Myrtle remained practically unchanged. Both were aware that at least ninety days must elapse between the birth of Myrtle's offspring and the beginning of any sexual relations.

Their previous association had been as intimate as it could be short of this degree, and the ceremony of consorting had simply made their relations permanent. Loma had imparted to them in a special instruction a complete knowledge of the exalted and perfect way in which the sexual relations were performed upon Venus, and they awaited the arrival of the proper time with calmness and the full consciousness that when it did arrive they would experience the highest joys of which their natures were capable. They were especially interested in the instruction imparted by Loma as to the manner in which the number and sex of offspring were regulated, and the uses of sexual intercourse in the strengthening and fortifying of every part of the brain. The doctor had, long before Loma's advent upon the earth, taught his patients that the prevailing habit of man and wife occupying the same bed was injurious to health and destructive of connubial happiness. Consequently, upon this wedding night, the beginning of a new civilization, fraught with tremendous consequences of good to the human race, the bride and groom retired to separate apartments, and rested in the negative recuperation of their energies, in the simple consciousness of complete happiness in the present and the hope of an exquisite realization of joy in the future.

CHAPTER XXIV.

THE ASCENSION.

"And when he had spoken these things, while they beheld, He was taken up and a cloud received Him out of their sight."

The journey of Loma and his devoted friends from Chicago to Denver was accomplished without special incident. The party enjoyed the trip as they did everything else, in the association of congenial personalities, and, as Loma remarked, so perfect was their harmony that he would have frequently forgotten that he was not already in Venus, if the incongruities of the strangers with whom he came in contact did not forcibly remind him that he was still on earth.

"But," he exclaimed enthusiastically, as he caressed the baby to which he was as much devoted as its mother, "this glorious boy will soon teach the world a better way. These plebeian crowds who throng the stations we pass, burdened with afflictions which they are deluded into regarding as natural, little realize the nature or the potentialities of this sweet babe who has come to lead them into a higher civilization. But it will come to pass, and future generations will bless the work we have inaugurated."

When the party arrived in Denver they proceeded at once to the Brown Palace Hotel, where elegant apartments had been engaged. Loma had explained that the preparations which were being made for his transit to Venus were about perfected, but that the distinguished electricians having the matter in charge were desirous of making several tests, so as to insure his safety, and it was probable that they might be delayed several days, in order to secure the exact conditions required for so long a transit.

Doctor Bell was much interested in the scientific nature of the process of translation, and begged Loma to impart to him as much of the process as would be consistent with his professional and scientific ethics. Loma smilingly assented.

"There is nothing mysterious about the process of translation, and nothing that I am required to conceal from you now, since you have been instructed in the principles of complete education. The ability to sustain such a translation is merely a question of the power of a complete and educated brain to generate a sufficient quantity of magnetism to sustain itself against the drawing power of the electrical receptivity of the earth's sphere. How to overcome the attraction of gravitation has been the greatest problem with which your scientists have grappled, but they will not solve it until they develop complete brains. Then they will find it very easy to walk on the water as Jesus did, and as Peter could have done if he had had a better brain. You will remember that when Peter began to sink, Jesus caught him by the hand, after which he had no difficulty because the magnetism developed by the complete brain of Jesus was sufficient for both when the connection was established.

"Now, the repulsion of magnetism being sufficient to sustain Jesus and Peter upon the water, you can readily understand that if the power of repulsion can be sufficiently increased it would sustain them in the air, or in interstellar space. It is this repulsion of magnetism which enables your spiritualistic mediums to develop the weak phenomena of table tipping, etc. Now, it is simply this principle we use in translation from Venus to the earth or from the earth to Venus. The body translated must have sufficient power to generate magnetism at will sufficient to repel it from the earth and other planets, and to decrease this magnetism as it approaches its destination so as to permit the force of electrical receptivity to draw it, and yet retain sufficient magnetism to exert resistance enough to prevent a violent fall. This requires education and training, as does every other form of athletic exercise.

"To initiate a transit it is best to start from a high altitude, as the rarer the atmosphere the less resistance we encounter, and we are also aided by the earth's magnetism, which is constantly being radiated from the summits of mountains. This is why Jesus took the disciples who were privileged to witness his ascension upon a mountain, as related in the Bible, and we have come to Colorado for the same reason. To finish a transit it is best to choose a location having a low altitude, a dense atmosphere and a large body of fresh water, into which the body can finally land, as these conditions furnish a natural cushion, and aid us in establishing resistance sufficient to prevent a violent concussion. These conditions were admirably met in Lake Michigan, as you know. I have chosen Pike's Peak, near this city, as the place of my exit from the earth because it is easily accessible, and the terminus of my transit will be in Lake Marieno in Venus, which is only one hundred and fifty miles from my residence, and where my exalted consort and nearly all of my lovers, sisters and brothers are already assembled, together with some twenty-five thousand other interested persons."

Loma's fine countenance glowed with enthusiasm as he spoke of the welcome awaiting him, and his ardor was not dampened when Myrtle threw her arms around his neck and imprinted a passionate kiss upon his lips, saying:

"Take that kiss to your glorious consort from the daughter of earth whom you have so greatly blessed by your mission. Tell her that next to you I love and honor her, and I know that what inconvenience she has suffered through your absence will be more than compensated by the magnificent honors which await your return."

"She has hardly suffered inconvenience," said Loma, smiling, "for each night I have held communication with her by means of clairvoyance in which we are both adepts. In fact, much of the success of my mission has been due to her splendid sustaining influences, and when I return to Venus she will be duly honored for her share in the work, as will also a large number of persons who have assisted me; two of whom I hope to have the pleasure of introducing to you before many hours."

As Loma finished this statement a telegram was handed to him by a bell boy. He opened it and read:

                          Manitou, Colorado, March 13, 1896.
Preparations complete. All ready for you to-morrow. Weather indications perfect.   Davenol.

"Good!" exclaimed Loma. "This is from Professor Davenol, the finest electrician in Venus. He awaits us at Manitou. We will depart at once and sleep to-night in Manitou."

A telegram was sent to Professor Davenol announcing the time the party would arrive in Manitou, and in a few hours the Denver & Rio Grande train bore Loma and his friends to that celebrated watering place. At that time of the year most of the hotels were closed, and the cog-wheel railway made few trips to the summit of Pike's Peak, but when Loma and his party arrived they were met at the depot by Professor Davenol in person, who explained that he had perfected all arrangements, and that after a good night's rest the party would be taken to the summit on a special train.

Professor Davenol was, like Loma, a magnificent specimen of manhood, and an example of complete education. He differed from Loma in the fact that he was of somewhat darker complexion and did not speak the English language as fluently. There was a peculiar accent in his pronunciation which was distinctly different from that of any foreigner Doctor Bell had ever met, but he was, like Loma, a prince of gentlemen in his social manners and general deportment.

After a delicious night's rest and an excellent breakfast the party took seats in the special train which was waiting to convey them to the summit, and in a short time found themselves at the door of the old signal station, where they were provided with excellent shelter from the intense cold which prevailed at that altitude at that season of the year.

Professor Davenol had arranged that the special should return to Manitou and that the party should be alone on the summit when the transit was initiated. He had explained to the officials of the railway that Doctor Bell and the two ladies would return without himself and Loma, as he desired to avoid any suspicion that might be caused by their absence on the return trip. As the transaction was not expected to consume more than a few hours, Nora and the baby had been left at the hotel in Manitou. The special was to return to the summit for Doctor Bell and the ladies precisely at noon.

At precisely 10 o'clock A. M. on the 14th day of March, the party arrived at the summit. At 10:30 the special was returning to Manitou, and the friends were in possession of the situation.

Then occurred a succession of the most remarkable phenomena ever exhibited upon the earth.

Professor Davenol and Loma divested themselves of clothing as soon as the special disappeared around the curve of the mountain. Then the professor marked a large granite boulder, about one hundred yards from the signal station, and drew around this boulder a circle one hundred yards in diameter, leaving the boulder in the center. A rope was tightly stretched around this circle, and the professor warned the members of the little group not to come within it for twenty minutes after his departure, as the results of a violation of this caution would probably be fatal.

When these preparations were completed Loma took an affectionate leave of his friends, holding Myrtle last, in a long, loving embrace. Then he stepped lightly inside the circle, and joined the professor.

Just at this moment a third actor appeared upon the scene. This was another man, evidently a citizen of Venus, from his likeness to the others, but who appeared, in a halo of magnetism, descending from space above the summit. As he approached, Loma and the professor began to glow with great fervor of magnetism, evidently for the purpose of aiding the approaching person to resist the force of gravitation. In this they were perfectly successful, as the new comer gracefully approached the summit and alighted without any greater shock than would be experienced in stepping out of a carriage.

Loma and Professor Davenol decreased their magnetism for a moment, and, approaching the edge of the circle, Loma said:

"Allow me to introduce my devoted brother, Professor Loyalice. He is Professor Davenol's assistant, and has just completed a transit over the route to insure my safety and perfect working conditions. He does not speak the language of earth, but he assures me that everything is auspicious for my transit."

Doctor Bell and the ladies bowed, and Professor Loyalice acknowledged this introduction with a graceful gesture, after which Loma said:

"Farewell, beloved; but remember that I am always with you in the sweet communion of the highest sense."

Then, as his body and those of his two associates began to glow with incomparable brightness, he made one of his exquisite gestures of gracious dignity and love, smiled sweetly upon his three friends, who clung to each other outside the circle in an ecstasy of intense expectation, and *began to rise.*

His progress was rapid and with gradually accelerating velocity until he was lost to sight. Professor Davenol and his assistant remained motionless, but continued to glow with the greatest fervor for several minutes. Then they relaxed the intensity of their radiation, but remained immovable for several minutes longer. Suddenly from the space above the summit, with startling distinctness, came the sound of Loma's voice, pure and musical as when he was upon the earth, but having a peculiar quality in the tone which betrayed the fact that it was sounding through some form of telephone constructed upon a stupendous scale:

"BELOVED, BE OF GOOD CHEER. I HAVE SAFELY ARRIVED AT HOME AND AM IN THE SWEET EMBRACES OF MY PRECIOUS CONSORT."

Professor Davenol smiled and looked relieved. In a moment he and Professor Loyalice began to glow again with great intensity of magnetism, and Professor Loyalice began to rise, and in a few moments disappeared as Loma had done. Again a moment of suspense, and once more the telephonic sound was heard, but this time it was a strange voice and in a language unknown to Doctor Bell and the ladies. But Professor Davenol seemed to be perfectly satisfied with results, for he bowed and smiled, and, beginning once more to glow with extraordinary fervor, rose majestically, waving his hands to the three absorbed spectators. In a moment he also had disappeared in the blue vault of the heavens; but although the doctor and the two ladies gazed and listened for several minutes in spellbound attention, no sound occurred. With the departure of the last citizen of Venus the telephonic connection had ceased to exist.

Doctor Bell, looking at the spot from which Professor Davenol had departed, noticed that the boulder which the professor had marked had disappeared, and in its place was a pool of molten lava, and the air was permeated with the odor of granite in a state of fusion.

Mrs. Bell and Myrtle, overcome with emotion, sobbed upon the doctor's shoulders. The latter, however, had been so absorbed in the contemplation of the majestic scientific phenomena presented to his senses that he could think of little else. But the emotions of the ladies recalled him to the duties of the hour, and, as he placed one arm around his queenly mother and the other around his lovely consort and led them toward the special train, which at that moment appeared upon the side of the mountain, he felt that he was indeed upon the mountain top physically, intellectually and socially.

THE END.

SCIENTIFIC PHRENOLOGY.

The author of this work sincerely believes that the code of Gallheim announced by Loma, if conscientiously followed, would result in a complete revolution of social conditions and a realization of the felicity which he depicts as actually existing upon Venus. The first, third, and fourth articles of the code will be readily understood by advanced thinkers. But the success of the code depends no less upon the second article, which enforces the doctrine that by the adoption of a correct system of character study, *i. e.*, mental philosophy, human nature can be understood and estimated at its correct value.

The system of mental philosophy inaugurated by Francis Joseph Gall, M. D., in Vienna, in 1786-7, elaborated by his pupil John Gasper Spurzheim, and later students, including the author, presents the foundation for such a system. It is still in its infancy, but it furnishes a more practical method for the study and determination of the elements of human character than any system of mental philosophy ever promulgated. The pure doctrines taught by Gall and Spurzheim have suffered much at the hands of charlatans, quacks, and pseudo-scientists, so much as to be the subject of great ridicule by the misinformed. It has suffered hardly less at the hands of its ignorant and bigoted friends, who have sought to make the doctrine of the new science conform to existing standards of morals and religion.

Believing that the present work would arouse an interest in the science, the author has considered it wise to append a brief statement of its leading principles and doctrines, as much for the purpose of educating the reader to a comprehension that Phrenology is not what it is usually represented to be, as for the additional purpose of creating an interest for its more comprehensive and exhaustive study. At best, such a treatise can only consist of brief statements of principles and definitions. These are given as they are applied by the author in his professional practice.

DEFINITIONS.

Phrenology is the science of *Intelligence*. It is a system of mental philosophy based upon accurate observation and comparison of the origin, structure, and manifestations of intelligent organisms.

As a *science*, Phrenology deals with the causes and effects of Intelligence. As an *art*, it consists in estimating the kind and amount of Intelligence manifested by any organism.

Intelligence is the power or capacity of any living organism to take cognizance of the facts of its environment. The amount and kind of Intelligence depends on the structure and development of the organism, and these are always the product of the environment of the organism and that of its ancestors.

All things whatsoever are included in *existence*.

Existence is composed of two prime, ungenerated potentialities, *Space* and *Matter*.

Space is unlimited, continuous, persistent, and immovable. It is the prime, ungenerated negative female parent of all that is.

Matter is limited, divisible, consistent, and movable. It is the prime, ungenerated, positive male parent of all that is.

By virtue of the inherent genderic degrees of state with which Space and Matter are endowed, like degrees of genitive passion are continuously generated between them.

Electricity is the genitive passion of Space. It is manifested by the states of gravity, receptivity, coldness, and darkness.

Magnetism is the genitive passion of Matter. It is manifested by the states of vibration, radiation, heat, and light.

The eternal affinities which exist between these conditions produce all the phenomena of *growth*.

Growth is the change which takes place in a structure in obedience to the law of conformity to the changes which take place in its environment.

All objects are the product of Growth. This is as true of stars and planets, mountains and rivers, as it is of vegetables and animals. All things originate from ancestors, increase by nourishment, and disintegrate by depletion.

All substances are composed of molecules, which are the smallest possible divisions of substances. All molecules are composed of atoms, which are the smallest possible divisions of matter. The difference in substances is due to the difference in the composition of the molecules. The difference in molecules is due to the different forms of association of which atoms are capable.

Every individual atom is capable of conforming to its environment in states of electricity and magnetism. When magnetism dominates in the environment, the atom vibrates and radiates its own magnetism. When electricity dominates in the environment the atom becomes composed and contracts its magnetism. Associated atoms repel each other when vibratory and radiant, and cohere when composed and receptive.

These principles explain the expansion and contraction of matter in different states of temperature, *i. e.*, of electricity and magnetism.

All changes in the conditions of space and matter are due to changes in conditions of electricity and magnetism. Therefore all changes in the environment of any object are attributable to the same great causes. The inherent property of atoms to conform to conditions of environment as to states of electricity and magnetism causes all associated atoms to behave according to the needs of the association, whatever it may be. Therefore every body changes according to the movements of the atoms composing it, and these changes are always in conformity to the changing nature of the environment.

Organisms are therefore simple or complex, according to the simple or complex nature of their structure and the simple or complex conditions of the environment with which they are brought into contact.

Man is the most complex organism known to this planet. He stands at the end of a long line of development, extending from the simplest form of mineral, through the vegetable and animal kingdoms, to his own position in the cosmos, and embracing and including in his own structure a representation of every form below him. But when this exceedingly complex structure is analyzed it is found to consist wholly of combinations of the simpler forms which existed before him.

In the light of a rational philosophy, therefore, we are forced to consider man as a creature of growth, and subject to exactly the same natural laws as the objects which surround him. Any attempt to regard him as an exception results in the calamities which must always attend presumption and ignorance.

The Intelligence of Man is his power to comprehend the conditions of his environment. The relative degree of this intelligence which any individual will possess depends upon the completeness and the complexity of his structure. The intelligence of the man is the aggregation of the power of his associated atoms. If there is any part of his organization incomplete, in its perfect relation to his environment, his structure lacks the requisite complexity of parts and a loss of intelligence is the result.

The Conditions of Environment can only be impressed upon an organism by the impacts of the various magnetisms of the surrounding objects constituting the environment. These impacts will make themselves felt by a variety of radiations and vibrations of magnetism, differing in intensity and rapidity, corresponding to the conditions of the bodies from which they emanate. If the organism upon which these radiations and vibrations impinge is susceptible to corresponding receptivity and similar vibrations, the conditions of the surrounding bodies will be communicated to it and it will respond to each with a corresponding state of vibration. This corresponding state of receptivity and vibration constitutes *sensibility*.

An organism develops degrees of intelligence according to its sensibility to some or all of the conditions of its environment. As these conditions are manifested by vibrations of lower and higher rapidity, organisms are provided with *Organs of Sense*, and corresponding *Senses*, according to the degree of intelligence developed. Each organ of sense comprehends a different stage of receptivity and vibration, and each stage is susceptible to different degrees. The stages correspond to the different senses and the degrees correspond to the different sensations experienced within the domain of each sense.

Man has Seven Senses, to-wit, Gender, Touch, Taste, Hearing, Sight, Smell, and Clairvoyance. He is provided with corresponding organs of sense, but the sexual organs of gender have been ignored, and the organs of Clairvoyance within the brain are not visible externally and have not been located, but we know they exist.

The Sense of Gender corresponds to the lowest stage of radiation and vibration. The sexual organs are attuned to these radiations and vibrations with a corresponding stage of receptivity and susceptibility to vibration, and communicate their sensations to corresponding organs of the brain.

The Sense of Touch takes cognizance of the next higher stage of radiation and vibration, and communicates its sensations to the brain in a similar manner, through the skin, and especially that of the hands and feet.

The Sense of Taste takes cognizance of the third stage of radiation and vibration, through the lips, tongue, and palate.

The Sense of Hearing enables the individual to comprehend the radiations and vibrations which exist in the fourth stage, and ears are provided for this purpose attuned only to the vibrations of this stage.

The Sense of Sight receives the radiations and vibrations of the fifth stage, and the exquisitely sensitive machinery of the eyes is beautifully adapted to the purpose.

The Sense of Smell, through the nostrils, receives impressions pertaining to the sixth stage which are more delicate than those of sight.

The Sense of Clairvoyance receives impressions of radiations and vibrations so intensely penetrating and exquisitely refined that they pass through all known substances, and for this reason the organs of this sense are contained within the skull, which forms no barrier to its operation. This is the highest form of sensibility, and completes the octave. Any sense beyond this must needs be the beginning of a new organization, and would be a repetition of the sense of gender as the foundation of a new octave, precisely as musical tones are repeated in the chromatic scale. This law applies throughout nature.

It will be noticed that the arrangement of the senses in this order corresponds to the position of the relative arrangement of the organs of sense on the body.

The olfactory nerves enter the skull at a point above the eyes and communicate their impressions to a higher point of the brain than the optic nerves. Hence although the external orifices of the nostrils are below the eyes, the real arrangement of the organs of sense is in the order above stated.

An organization may be perfectly adapted to its environment by growth, but if violently removed to another situation it may be very incompletely adapted to its new environment, in which case it will either perish, or become slowly adapted to it by growth, possibly extending through many generations.

Experience teaches us that the greatest happiness is secured by comprehending the nature of the individual and by placing him where he can have the most favorable environment for the largest possible growth.

Recognizing the foregoing definitions and principles, the analysis of the character of man considered abstractly, or the analysis of the character of the concrete individual, proceeds upon strictly scientific lines, as follows: As man is a complex organism, consisting of bones, muscles, respiratory, digestive, and circulatory organs, brain and nerves, all of which are subject to varying conditions, the practical phrenologist in his estimate of the character must consider carefully the Physiological Condition, Temperament, Organic Quality, and Size and Development of Brain. These subjects will be considered in their order.

PHYSIOLOGICAL CONDITION.

If the individual is supplied with strong vital organs, supported by an adequate frame of bone and muscle, and these are all in good working order, he is said to be in a condition of health. Under this head the phrenologist makes a careful note of the conditions of general health, personal appearance, breathing power, circulation, and digestion. The eccentricities of disease are carefully noted and allowance made therefor in the estimate of mental power. The use of tobacco, alcoholic liquors, narcotics, tea, coffee, or other stimulants or poisons, in any degree, is incompatible with normal intelligence. If normal health exists and the individual is supplied with a good equipment in all of the physiological conditions of organization, the foundation is established for the display of intelligence. The amount of intelligence depends upon the general magnitude of the organization and the perfect correlation of its parts. The particular kind of intelligence manifested will be greatly modified by the form of the body and brain as expressed in Temperament, Organic Quality and Size and Development of Brain.

THE TEMPERAMENTS.

Temperament is that peculiar state of the body, expressed in color, temperature, form, and proportion, which results from the preponderance of some element in the constitution, over some other element or elements. The Temperaments are classified with reference to electro-magnetic, anatomical, and chemical conditions.

ELECTRO-MAGNETIC TEMPERAMENTS.

The Electric Temperament exists when electricity dominates over magnetism in the organization. Its characteristics are Gravity, Receptivity, Darkness, and Coldness. This temperament was formerly called the Bilious or Brunette Temperament. It is distinguished by dark, hard, dry skin, dark, strong hair, dark eyes, olive complexion, and usually by a long, athletic form of body. It is remarkable for concentrativeness of design and affections, strong gravity, drawing power and cohesiveness, strong will, resolution, dignity, serious disposition and expression, moderate circulation and coolness of temperature. It is produced by a dry, hot climate, common in southern latitudes and almost universal in tropical natives. Persons of this temperament are better adapted to hot climates because electricity dominates over magnetism, and they do not antagonize the climate by the radiation of magnetism, but rather thrive on the magnetism which they absorb. This temperament is closely analogous to the condition of tropical animals and birds.

The Magnetic Temperament exists when magnetism dominates over electricity in the organization. Its characteristics are Vibration, Radiation, Heat, and Light. This temperament was formerly called the Sanguine or Blonde Temperament. It is distinguished by a light colored, warm, moist skin, light colored or red hair, fresh ruddy or florid complexion, light colored or blue eyes, rounded form of body, often plump or corpulent, large chest, square shoulders, indicating a very active heart and vital organs. It is remarkable for versatility of character, jovial disposition, fond of good living and great variety, changeableness, activity, and vivaciousness. The temperature of the body is warm and the circulation very strong. This temperament vibrates between great extremes of disposition, develops great force of radiation and driving power, and is universally characterized by warmth, enthusiasm, and high color. It is produced by the climates of northern and temperate latitudes, and is almost universal in the natives of extreme northern countries. Persons of this temperament are better adapted to cold climates, because magnetism dominates over electricity, consequently they produce more animal heat, and are better able to endure the rigors of a cold climate. The same general conditions are found to exist in birds and animals inhabiting northern latitudes.

ANATOMICAL TEMPERAMENTS.

The Temperaments are also classed anatomically as:

Motive, where the bones are large and strong and the muscular development is stronger than the nutritive or mental system. Persons of this temperament are active, energetic, and best adapted to outdoor pursuits and vigorous employment.

Vital, in which the nutritive or vital system is most active, large lungs, stomach and blood vessels, and corpulent and plump figure. Persons possessing this temperament are inclined to sedentary occupations, and if the brain is large and of good quality, are able to do an immense amount of mental labor without breaking down. They should take systematic exercise and avoid fats and stimulating foods and drinks to obtain the best results.

Mental, in which the brain and nerves are most active. The body is not adapted to hard muscular labor, and there is not enough vitality or nutritive power to nourish the brain in the heavy demands made upon it. Such persons incline to mental effort and literary work, and for a time display great brilliancy, but sooner or later collapse, unless this condition is corrected, by regular hours, plenty of sleep, the absence of stimulants and the cultivation of muscular and vital force. This temperament is distinguished by a relatively large head and small body, pyriform face, high wide forehead, and usually sharp features.

CHEMICAL TEMPERAMENTS.

There are three principal fluids which circulate through the body, viz., arterial blood, venous blood, and lymph. As the blood passes out from the heart through the arteries it is strongly charged with magnetism and is very strongly acid in quality. As it returns to the heart through the veins it has expended its magnetism and its acidity has been very much neutralized. The lymph is an alkali fluid, and it circulates through the lymphatic vessels as a reserve force of vital food. The predominance of either of these fluids in the constitution greatly modifies the character and gives rise to the classification of the chemical temperaments. As every cell in the body comes in contact with an acid and an alkali fluid, we may, by estimating the relative quantities of each fluid, arrive at a very accurate judgment of the chemical condition of the body, and these elements are also valuable in estimating the amount of magnetism that will be produced by the organization through chemical action, as every cell by its contact with these fluids is constituted a magnetic battery.

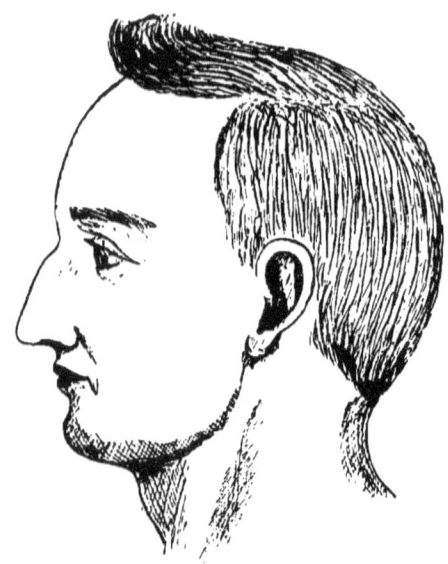

THE ACID TEMPERAMENT.

The Acid Temperament exists where arterial blood predominates. It is distinguished by convexity of features and sharpness of angles. The face is usually round in general outline and convex in profile, the forehead prominent at the eyebrows and retreating as it rises, the nose Roman, the mouth prominent, the teeth convex in form and arrangement and sharp, the chin round and sometimes retreating. The body is angular and generally convex in outline, with sharpness at all angles. This temperament is usually accompanied with great activity of mind and vivaciousness of disposition, and sometimes develops great energy and asperity. It is very likely to exhaust itself prematurely.

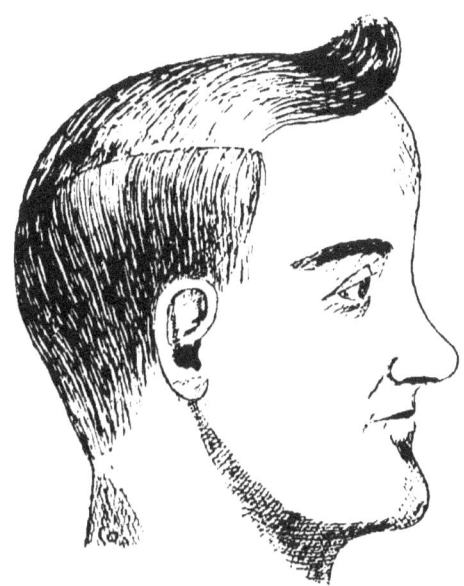

THE ALKALI TEMPERAMENT.

The Alkali Temperament exists where lymph is in excess over arterial blood. It is distinguished by concavity of features and obliquity of angles, or rather the absence of angles. The face is usually broad in general outline, and concave in profile, the forehead prominent and wide at the upper part, and medium in development at the eyebrows, the nose concave, the mouth retreating, the teeth flat in form and arrangement, the chin concave and prominent at the point. The body is round and inclined to corpulency, without angles. This temperament is usually well stocked with vitality, but unless actively employed is likely to become dull and overloaded with adipose tissue and lymph.

From the foregoing observations it is evident that the temperaments combine in each individual according to whichever temperament is found to predominate in these three divisions. Thus one man will have an electric-motive-acid temperament, another a magnetic-mental-acid temperament, another a magnetic-vital-alkali, and so on through all the combinations which can be made from the seven elementary temperaments. This blending when finally estimated constitutes the temperament of the individual. The ideal condition would, of course, be a perfect equilibrium of the elements of each division, in which case the individual would be said to have a perfectly balanced temperament.

III. ORGANIC QUALITY.

Organic Quality is the inherent, constitutional texture of the organization. It is analogous to the *grain* of wood, the *temper* of mental, etc., and is considered with reference to the attributes of *Strength, Delicacy,* and *Responsiveness.*

Strength signifies great capacity to undertake and successfully complete enterprises of great magnitude, requiring comprehensive thought and executive power. It also signifies great power of endurance and fortitude. When strength is marked low, on the phrenological chart, the individual has no surplus strength to waste and should carefully enconomize force and direct his power within the scope of his phrenological adaptation.

Delicacy indicates great refinement and sensitiveness of organization. Such persons are able to appreciate nice shades of thought and to cultivate the graces in an eminent degree. They are adapted to pursuits requiring delicacy of the senses and acute perception, such as music, painting, manufacturing of delicate articles, etc. In literature they display refined taste, and the head is symmetrical and generally well developed. Those who are low in delicacy lack refinement and grace and should carefully cultivate these qualities.

Responsiveness signifies that peculiar quality of organization which takes impressions readily and responds quickly to outside influences. It implies ability to learn readily and to adopt one's self to circumstances. Persons high in this quality are easily elated and correspondingly depressed, and should cultivate self-control. Persons low in responsiveness incline toward stupidity.

SIZE AND DEVELOPMENT OF BRAIN.

The Physiological Condition, Temperament and Quality of the individual being established, the size of his brain becomes the measure of power. Concerning the brain, the doctrines of Phrenology may be briefly stated.

I. The brain is the keyboard of Intelligence. The Intelligence of man manifests itself through many faculties, and each faculty is a result of some condition pertaining to his environment. Each faculty has a special organ in the brain.

II. Size of brain is the measure of power, temperament, quality and physiological condition being similar. Size of brain depends upon length of brain fiber. The brains of different individuals vary much in size and also in the direction of development, from which fact diversity of character arises, in brains of the same size and quality.

III. Forty-three organs of the brain, by careful observation and comparison, have been located and classified. The brain is divided into two hemispheres, and one organ pertaining to each faculty of the mind located in each hemisphere. Thus all organs are double, and there is one organ of each pair on each side of the head. The Phrenologist estimates the size of each organ by measuring the length of brain fiber from the surface of the brain to the Medulla Oblongata, which is at the base of the brain, at the head of the spinal column and opposite the opening of the ears.

We have reason to believe that there are sixty-four organs altogether, and that when all are discovered and classified that man will be found to possess sixty-four distinct faculties and be capable of acquiring sixty-four different kinds of knowledge and manifesting sixty-four kinds of intelligence. This is not stated as a demonstrated fact, but as a proposition believed to be true.

The following are the names and definitions of the faculties of Intelligence that are known to be possessed by man. For the location of the corresponding organs on the cranium the reader is referred to the accompanying Symbolical Phrenological Head. On this head the faculties are symbolized by a picture engraved within the territory ascribed to each organ representing some action of the corresponding faculty. Thus Constructiveness is represented by a suspension bridge, Combativeness by a fire scene in which the splendid energies of the firemen and the apparatus are opposed to the destructive element, etc.

For convenience in classification the organs are arranged in the six groups of Physical Love, Physical Energy, Dignity, Sympathy, Objective Intellect, and Subjective Intellect, but these divisions are purely arbitrary.

Each of the faculties of Intelligence is capable of manifesting four distinct powers, Attraction, Repulsion, Satisfaction, and Memory, depending upon corresponding electro-magnetic states of the atoms composing the organ of the brain representing that faculty.

When electricity dominates the atoms cohere, the brain cells become empty and Attraction results.

When magnetism dominates, the atoms repel, the cells become filled with magnetism and Repulsion results.

When electro-magnetic equilibrium is established, the faculty is said to be in a state of Satisfaction, and the organ is at rest.

The ability to rearrange the atoms and to repeat formerly existing states, constitutes Memory.

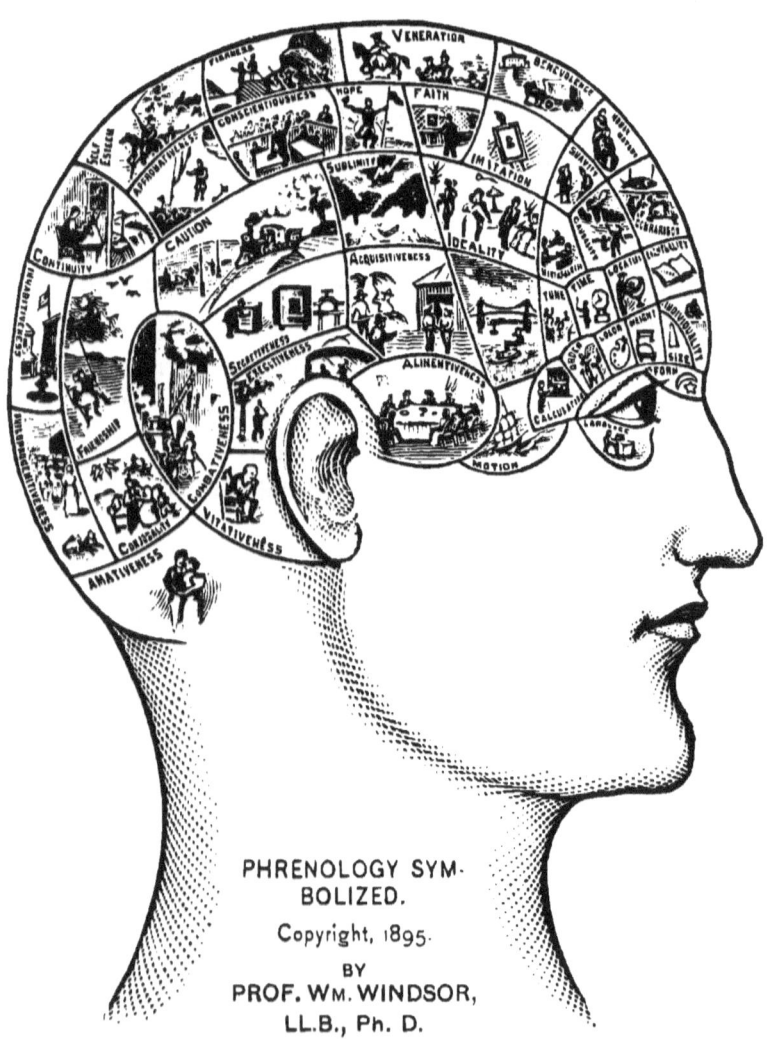

The Symbolical Phrenological Head, Showing the Location of the Organs of the Brain.

From the foregoing, we deduce the propositions that Love (Attraction), Hate (Repulsion), Enjoyment (Satisfaction), and Recollection (Memory) are each the product of the combined action of the powers of all the organs of the brain, and the force resulting from this combination which ultimately governs the action of the individual is called *Reason*.

Therefore, to constitute an individual perfectly Reasonable, he must have a complete cognition of his environment by the possession of a complete equipment of the organs of sense, and a complete brain, educated to the full use of every faculty. Every organ of the brain and every corresponding faculty is equally valuable, and none can be neglected in development or education without an equally serious loss. The ideal state of complete development and complete education is attainable and will be reached by the human race whenever this philosophy is accepted and enforced.

PHRENOLOGY.

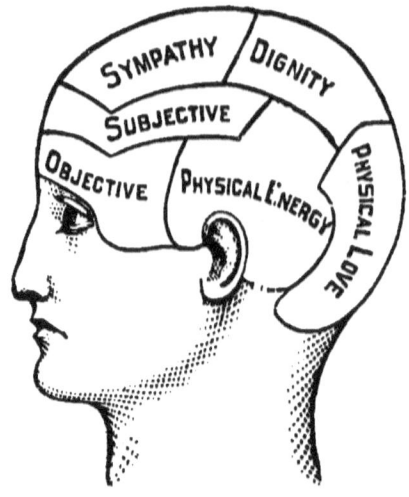

GROUPS OF ORGANS.

DEFINITIONS OF THE FACULTIES OF INTELLIGENCE.

PHYSICAL LOVE.

Amativeness—Reproductive love; love of the opposite sex, and desire to unite in sexual relations and enjoy its company.

Conjugality—Conjugal love, sexual friendship and fidelity.

Philoprogenitiveness—Parental love; love of offspring and pets.

Friendship—Adhesiveness; gregariousness; love of family; desire for companionship; attachment to friends.

Inhabitiveness—Love of home, place of abode; love of country and offensive and defensive patriotism.

Continuity—The faculty of connection. The ability to comprehend continuousness or interruption; to give undivided and continued attention to one subject, or to interrupt intelligently; application, connectedness.

PHYSICAL ENERGY.

Vitativeness—The love of life; desire to exist.

Combativeness—Defense; courage; defiance; force of character; energy and indignation.

Executiveness—Executive ability; extermination; thoroughness and severity.

Alimentiveness—Desire for food and drink; faculty of discriminating taste.

Acquisitiveness—Desire for property; industry; economy in acquiring property; realization of value.

Secretiveness—Reserve; concealment; policy; conservatism.

Caution—Prudence; solicitude; timidity; fear; apprehension of danger.

DIGNITY.

Approbativeness—Love of display; the desire to please; ambition to gain admiration and popularity.

Self-Esteem—Dignity; governing power; independence; self love.

Firmness—Stability; perseverance; decision; inflexibility of purpose.

Conscientiousness—Justice; self-examination; integrity; circumspection; scrupulousness in matters of duty.

SYMPATHY.

Hope—Belief in future joy; tendency to high expectations.

Faith—Trust and belief. Confidence.

Veneration—Reverence and worship; deference for superiors, and submission to superior power.

Benevolence—The desire to do good; sympathy; philanthropy.

Imitation—The copying faculty. The ability to conform to existing customs, conditions and facts by imitating them.

Human Nature—The power to discern motives, character and qualities in other persons by sympathetic action.

Suavity—Agreeableness; tendency to speak and act in a pleasant manner.

OBJECTIVE INTELLECT.

Individuality—Observation and desire to see things, to identify and separate objects.

Form—Observation of the shape of things. Sensitiveness to correctness or the lack of it in shapes.

Size—Power to measure distances, quantities and sizes.

Weight—Perception of the effect of gravity, and sense of the perpendicular.

Color—The discrimination of hues and colors.

Order—Faculty of arrangement; method; system; neatness.

Calculation—The power to count, enumerate, reckon, etc.; faculty of number.

Motion—Ability to comprehend movement. Love of motion, sailing, navigation, riding, dancing, etc.

Eventuality—The historic faculty; faculty of experience and occurrence.

Locality—Discernment of position, perception of place.

Time—Consciousness of duration; faculty of time; promptness.

Tune—Appreciation of sound; ability to distinguish musical tones.

Constructiveness—Dexterity and ingenuity; ability in construction; faculty of adjustment.

Language—Power of expression and ability to talk; verbal expression; vocabulary.

SUBJECTIVE INTELLECT.

Causality—The ability to comprehend principles, and to think abstractly; to understand the relation between cause and effect.

Comparison—The analyzing, illustrating and comparing faculty.

Ideality—Love of the beautiful; desire for perfection, refinement.

Sublimity—Love of grandeur and the stupendous; appreciation of the terrific.

Mirthfulness—Wit; humor; love of fun.

The Phrenological Examination.

The Phrenological Examination is designed to show in an accurate and scientific manner the size and development of *Brain* of the person measured, and to furnish a basis upon which an accurate and reliable knowledge of the character may be determined. The measurements can only be correctly made by an expert familiar with the principles of *Phrenology*. When these measurements are determined according to the system, the Phrenologist is enabled to make a Complete Delineation of the character, describing the amount and kind of sense possessed by the individual, his adaptation to a particular *Business, Trade or Profession*, where that kind and amount of Intelligence is required, the adaptation in *Matrimony or Business Partnership,* together with special directions as to faults and how to correct them, health and longevity and how to secure both. The expert must be able to judge the Physiological Condition, Temperament and Organic Quality of the individual with scientific accuracy, and these are important elements in a scientific delineation of character.

Phrenological Examinations are said to be given *orally* when no record is made of the conclusions of the examiner. A Phrenological Chart is a blank prepared for concise written statements, and the chart filled out is said to constitute a Delineation of Character.

PROF. WINDSOR'S ASSISTANTS MAKING A PHRENOMETRICAL SURVEY.

Phrenometrical Measurements are given by means of the *Phrenometer*, an instrument used for measuring the head, by which the exact form and size of sections of the head can be reproduced upon diagrams prepared for the purpose. This is the most valuable and reliable way of making an examination.

A Phrenograph is a written description of the character of an individual, giving all the minute points and shadings of character in the language of the examiner, and its value depends upon the perspicuity and literary expression of the writer not less than upon his skill as a phrenologist.

It must be evident from the foregoing that the value of the service rendered by the phrenologist varies, as in all other professions, according to his education and training, the instruments with which he works, the elaborateness of the product and the adaptation of the phrenologist to his own business.

The public should be warned against patronizing men who practice Phrenology in a way that would bring any business into ridicule. Men who are uneducated, who do not use the latest and best equipments, who have never had any professional training, who do not comprehend professional ethics or dignity, and who do not possess the elements of success in their own characters, are hardly the ones to whom an intelligent man would submit the most important questions concerning his own welfare with the hope of receiving competent advice. But Phrenology has been cursed with this class of quacks, perhaps even more than the profession of medicine. And it is largely due to the stupendous blunders of such pretenders that Phrenology is not recognized more generally by intelligent scientists. Considered in its beauty and simplicity, it certainly offers a more rational and practical system of mental philosophy than has ever been otherwise formulated.

EXAMPLES OF PHRENOMETRICAL MEASUREMENTS.

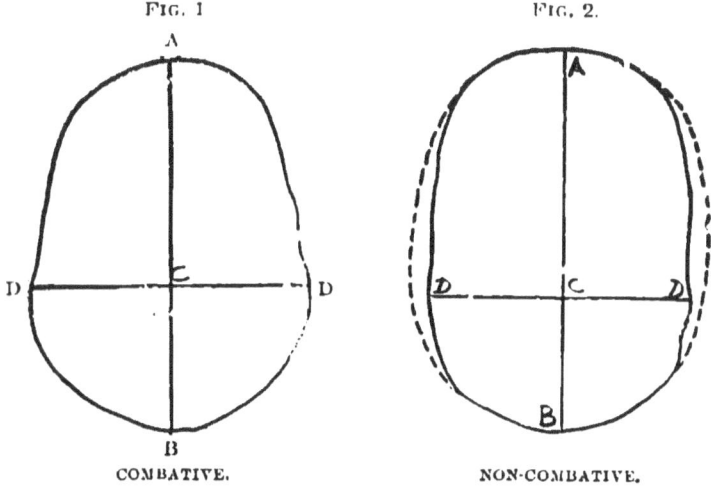

Sections of base of brain, showing development of physical energy. The dotted lines in Fig. 2 show the deficiency in alimentiveness, executiveness and combativeness.

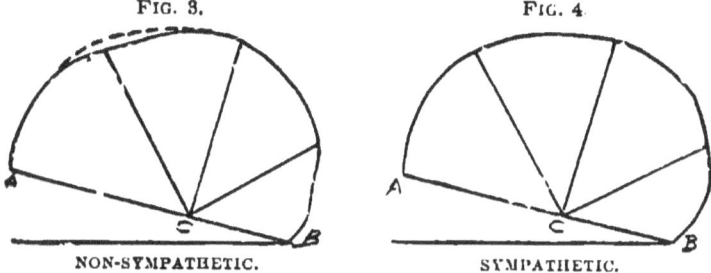

Profile sections showing development of sympathy and dignity. The dotted line in Fig. 3 shows deficiency in Human Nature and Benevolence.

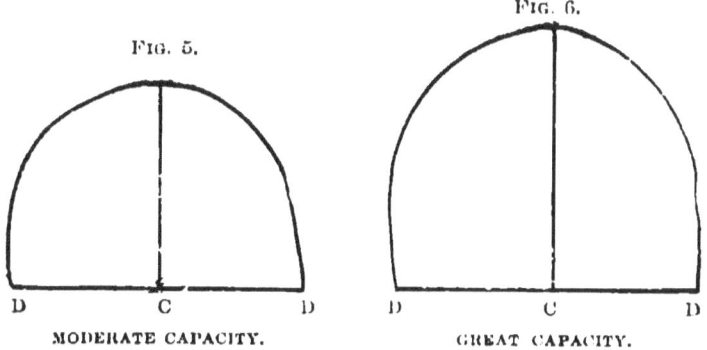

Two sections of the region of subjective intellect, showing different capacities of two individuals.

ADVERTISEMENTS.

THE WINDSOR & LEWIS PUBLISHING CO.,

406 MARIA AVE., ST. PAUL, MINN.,

Are the exclusive publishers of all of Professor Windsor's works on Phrenology and Social Science, and are the business managers of

THE INTERNATIONAL COLLEGE OF SCIENCE.

All correspondence in relation to books and publications, tuition and courses of study in the college, payments for books or tuition should be addressed to

THE WINDSOR & LEWIS PUBLISHING CO.,
406 Maria Ave., St. Paul, Minn.

Professor Windsor's personal correspondence, and letters containing photographs for examination or requests for scientific information, and all private correspondence of his patrons concerning matters of a confidential nature should be addressed as follows:

PROF. WILLIAM WINDSOR, LL. B., PH. D.,
Care The Windsor & Lewis Publishing Co.,
406 Maria Ave., St. Paul, Minn.

and marked "PERSONAL."

In sending remittances, please send postoffice or express money orders, payable at St. Paul, Minn., or New York drafts. Money may also be sent by express and by registered letter. Postage stamps in one or two-cent denominations will be accepted in sums less than one dollar at risk of sender. Checks on local banks must have ten cents added to the amount to cover cost of collection through our bank.

As Professor Windsor is generally traveling at some distance from St. Paul, patrons may expect a few days' delay in receiving answers to personal letters addressed to him.

It is our purpose to carry a full line of equipments for lecturers and agents, and we will be pleased to hear from all persons engaged in the dissemination of information among the people. Our books and publications are up to date, and we allow larger commissions to good agents than other houses in the same line. Write for terms.

Fraternally,
Address—THE WINDSOR & LEWIS PUBLISHING CO.

THE SCIENCE OF CREATION
—— AND ——
ART OF REPRODUCTION.

A beautiful volume of four hundred pages, devoted to the clear exposition of facts relating to the propagation and improvement of the race. The first edition of this fascinating book was sold at five dollars in cloth and six dollars in Russia binding.

☞ **$2.50.** Now Reduced to HALF PRICE. **$2.50.** ☜

The second edition has been revised and corrected, and will be issued in cloth binding only and sold at half the original price, viz., two dollars and fifty cents.

SUBJECTS DISCUSSED IN SEPARATE CHAPTERS.

Introduction. I.—General Anatomy and Physiology. II.—Sexual Anatomy and Physiology. III.—Manhood and Womanhood. IV.—Manhood not Lost. V.—Manhood Restored. VI.—The Education of the Sexual Instincts. VII.—Marriage. VIII.—Sexual Magnetism. IX.—Prostitution. X.—The Selection of the Consort. XI.—Copulation. XII.—Mistakes of Married Men. XIII.—Reproduction. XIV.—Maternity. XV.—Conclusion.

This book discusses the foregoing subjects in a fearless and candid manner, giving the information desired in a complete and clear way, instead of darkly hinting at the topics.

It is also true that Professor Windsor teaches the doctrine that the functions of the body in all of its departments should be *enjoyed* in a legitimate and pure manner, instead of being suppressed and paralyzed, as would be the case if the teachings of a majority of writers on this subject were followed. It is the aim of the book to teach what a legitimate and pure enjoyment is. Like all of his writings, it is radical, revolutionary and independent.

It is just the book which every young man and woman should read who is anxious to obtain the best use of all the powers of mind and body, and who wishes to enter the relationship of marriage well informed as to the duties, rights, privileges and enjoyments of a husband and wife.

It is the very book which every intelligent parent has been looking for, to have his children read in order that they may be instructed against the vices, and encouraged to secure the highest possible development.

It is time that men and women understood themselves and each other. Professor Windsor has had the courage and intelligence to write and utter what should have been said long ago. He believes in the dignity of manhood, the sacredness of womanhood, the protection of childhood.

LOMA,
A CITIZEN OF VENUS.

The Most Sensational Book Ever Published in the English Language.

A scathing criticism on the civilization of the nineteenth century, by a philosopher who understands Human Nature, its capabilities, its needs and its wrongs.

The plot of this remarkable book is as follows: Myrtle Burnham, a beautiful and talented young girl, living with a wealthy uncle in Chicago, meets with misfortunes by which she is disgraced in the eyes of her uncle and aunt and is by them turned upon the street. After three days and nights of privation and hardship, she attempts suicide in Lake Michigan. She is rescued by a remarkable personage, who appears in the water at the critical moment, and upon the pier she and her rescuer meet a physician, who is also a philanthropist, who mercifully takes her to his home and provides for her comfort, and who also entertains her rescuer in a very hospitable manner. The latter introduces himself as Loma, a citizen of Venus, who has been sent to the earth for the express purpose of impressing Myrtle, and through her, her offspring, with the germs of new thought, representing an advanced civilization which her son is destined to proclaim to the world. The physician enters heartily into the scheme, and the remaining chapters of the book tell how Loma accomplished his mission. The work is pathetic, romantic, revolutionary and startling, and there is a sensation in every chapter. The denouement is sublime.

Incidentally, Loma makes the following remarkable scientific disclosures: That the wearing of clothing is a mistake, and productive of disease. That physical astronomy as now taught is radically wrong in its principles and statements. That Sir Isaac Newton's theory of the law of gravitation is a mistake. That matter does not attract matter, and that the sun does not radiate light or heat.

Loma's views on the prevailing vices, inconsistencies and absurdities of modern civilization are expressed in Professor Windsor's masterful literary style, and the utterances are characterized by the same fearlessness and freedom of expression which are such marked peculiarities of his lectures, addresses and other published works.

This extraordinary book consists of about five hundred pages, handsomely printed and bound in silk cloth, with gold title.

Price, $1.50.

Do You Wish to Understand

Yourself and Everbody Else? How to Become Rich? How to Select a Wife? How to Become Comfortable, Happy and Prosperous? If you do you should purchase and read

Phrenology; Choice of Professions; Matrimony;

A handsome little volume of 200 pages, containing the full text of Professor Windsor's three most popular lectures as delivered by him to overwhelming audiences throughout the United States.

In addition to the three lectures the book contains a number of interviews in which Professor Windsor describes phrenologically the mental characteristics of many prominent statesmen, philanthropists and criminals, in which startling contrasts and sensational facts are developed. Elegantly illustrated, with portraits of noted characters. Professor Windsor is acknowledged to be the highest living authority on the subject of which he treats. The entire book is Scientific, Witty, Instructive and Absorbingly Interesting. Price, in cloth, $1.00. Price, in paper, 50 cents.

HEALTH, WEALTH, AND SUNSHINE,
— OR THE —
SECRET OF A GOOD DIGESTION.

This valuable little pamphlet is one of Professor Windsor's greatest contributions to the relief of suffering humanity. It contains full instructions in regard to the Philosophy of Digestion, the causes of Indigestion and Constipation, the correct bill of fare for Proper Diet for each Temperament, and instructions for the radical cure of Indigestion and Chronic Constipation, without medicine or expense, enabling anyone to regulate the bowels perfectly without the use of poisonous cathartics. PRICE, $1.00. Sold only as a confidential communication and upon promise by the purchaser that its instructions will be confined to the members of the purchaser's own family.

NERVOUSNESS.
Its Cause and Cure. How to Banish the Blues.

A valuable pamphlet by Professor Windsor, giving directions by which three-fourths of all cases of nervousness may be cured without medicine. The cure of Insomnia, with valuable instruction for inducing dreamless sleep. Also, suggestions for obtaining rest without sleep when time is limited. Invaluable for overworked business men and nervous women. Price, 50 cents.

Great Secrets of Happiness.

In 1888 Professor Windsor published the first edition of what was then called his GREAT SEXUAL SECRETS, consisting of four small pamphlets, the largest of which contained eight pages. They were sold as confidential communications from a teacher to his pupils and were never intended for general sale. The first was a treatise on Pregnancy, containing some valuable facts which every prospective wife and mother should know; the second was a brief instruction on the restoration of sexual vigor by hygienic treatment; the third gave valuable sanitary advice designed to prevent the spread of contagious venereal disease; and the fourth and largest of the series was a plain and chaste direction as to the proper method of performing the act of copulation.

The sale of these pamphlets was remarkably large, notwithstanding the fact that they were sold at ten dollars apiece for Nos. 3, 4 and 5, and fifteen dollars for No. 1. The entire series was sold for fifty dollars, including a phrenological chart, which was at that time issued for ten dollars.

A second and enlarged edition was published in 1891, which has just been exhausted. The great favor with which these works have been received results from their BREVITY and TRUTHFULNESS.

Most writers in treating such subjects would have buried the information beneath a mass of verbiage. There are hundreds of books upon the market treating of these subjects, but the reader turns from most of them with a sense of disgust because so much has been written and so little has been said.

Professor Windsor has had the good judgment and the courage to write *the truth*. He has realized that the average man wants *facts* and not arguments on propositions of questionable value. Hundreds of men have remarked, after hearing Professor Windsor lecture on these topics, that in some way he had come into possession of a vast amount of truth upon subjects upon which there is general and much to be deplored ignorance.

The third edition of these valuable pamphlets is now ready. In view of the fact that since the last edition was published, Professor Windsor has made extraordinary new and startling discoveries, it has been necessary to rewrite the whole series.

While all that was valuable in the old editions has been carefully preserved, yet the pamphlets as now issued are practically new works, entirely rewritten, up to date, and contain about four times as much information as the last edition. For this reason it has been thought best to give the new series a new and more attractive title. Professor Windsor's

GREAT SECRETS OF HAPPINESS.

are now absolutely indispensable to the happiness of every man and woman in the world. In fact it may be safely said that without the information contained in Nos. 1 and 4 it is impossible to be happy in the marriage relation. The information contained in Nos. 2 and 3 is vitally important to every young man contemplating matrimony, and it is hardly safe for any young woman to entertain the proposition of marriage without the same information, while No. 5 is indispensable to every sane man or woman who wishes to preserve the happiness of married life. This pamphlet is a new and valuable addition to the series.

The world is full of blasted homes, broken hearts, and wrecked constitutions caused by ignorance of the facts set forth in these pamphlets. The prisons are full of criminals and the insane asylums are crowded, because men and women do not understand the true laws of parentage. Idiots, paupers and cripples on every hand, tell the sad story of parental ignorance. Nor is this the worst side of the question. Thousands of good and true men and women are yearly infected with the most loathsome and contagious diseases because the truth is not known in respect to these unhappy subjects. There is a maudlin sentiment extant which deprecates any effort to impart information on these topics. These sickly moralists seem to think that it is a lofty work to protect a community from smallpox while it is a moral obliquity to suggest sanitary precautions against a much more terrible form of disease. Both diseases result from the same cause, uncleanliness, under but slightly varying conditions.

One of the most fearful evils in existence to-day is the presence in every large city and in many smaller ones, of unscrupulous quacks who pose as physicians and prey upon the morbid sensibilities of uninstructed young men. It is the business of these human vultures to *persuade young men that they are afflicted with disease* when no such condition exists. Nearly every newspaper in the country is filled with the artfully worded advertisements of these unconscionable scoundrels. Professor Windsor has learned by actual professional experience that nearly fifty per cent of the young men he addresses in lectures on these subjects are in some form the victims of this kind of quackery.

The crime of abortion is frightfully on the increase, and will continue to disgrace society and the practice of the medical profession until greater intelligence prevails.

Men will not restrain their passions while the government fosters conditions which inflame and brutalize them. As long as money rules the world, intemperance will abound and women will be sacrificed to prostitution. There is no hope for a better condition of affairs until intelligence concerning the proper use of the sexual powers is widely disseminated.

With the earnest hope of teaching some men and women the true road to happiness, these pamphlets were first issued, and the last edition is sent forth in the same spirit. Each one of the series is aimed at some great evil in society, and while it condemns the wrong it teaches the right way.

Just a word in regard to the price. Under existing conditions in society everything is measured in money values. These pamphlets are sold at ten dollars each because they are worth it. The law of supply and demand must regulate here as elsewhere. No. 1 contains information which can be turned to practical account by any stock raiser to the extent of hundreds of dollars per annum. No. 2 is a godsend to the young men of the country and saves thousands of dollars from the rapacious pockets of the quacks, besides giving peace of mind and happiness to hundreds of young men who have been tortured with self-created fears. No. 3 is invaluable to every married man and woman who believes in cleanliness and who wishes to preserve good health and to transmit it unimpaired to offspring. No. 4 is probably the most popular of the series, and gives instruction which has brought happiness into many an otherwise clouded home, prevented hundreds of divorces and cured, without medicines or expense, embarrassments which have baffled the best of physicians and which were regarded as the results of disease, until this invaluable information showed that they were simply the fruits of ignorance. No. 5 will teach you how to preserve your domestic happiness after you have obtained it.

If you wish to be happy become well informed. Learn the truth and *"the truth shall make you free."*

Great Secrets of Happiness.

No. 1.

PERFECT OFFSPRING.

HOW THEY MAY BE CREATED, AND THE REGULATION OF SEX.

A short treatise on pregnancy, showing the conditions which cause perfection or degeneracy in offspring. How greatness is transmitted, the law of inheritance from father and mother and the causes which produce idiots, paupers and criminals. The information is condensed into a few pages of short, terse rules which anyone can commit to memory, and when followed the results are sure to bring the greatest happiness to prospective parents.

This pamphlet teaches the enormity of the crime of abortion, and is designed to awaken the public conscience in a matter which is threatening the very life of the nation. It clearly shows that this crime, like all others, grows out of ignorance, and is all the more to be deplored because it is wholly unnecessary.

It also gives full instructions for regulating the sex of offspring, enabling parents to produce a son or daughter at will. The same principle can be applied to animals by stock raisers, and full and complete directions are given for the various classes of animals, together with valuable suggestions in the application of the doctrine of impressions to animals, enabling stock raisers to produce greater speed in horses, greater productiveness in cows, sheep, poultry, etc., etc.

Parents should place it in the hands of marriageable daughters at least one year before marriage. It makes the procreation of superb offspring a possibility, reducing the number of idiots, paupers, criminals and invalids caused by ignorance of the laws of Nature. It sheds a flood of light on all these questions of such vital importance to women in particular and the race at large.

PRICE, TEN DOLLARS.

Great Secrets of Happiness.

No. 2.

MANHOOD RESTORED

OR THE

CURE OF NERVOUS WEAKNESS WITHOUT MEDICINES OR EXPENSE.

The object of this pamphlet is to place in the hands of every young man who may be suffering from the effects of early indiscretions, or who may have been led to believe that he is diseased when he is not, a simple, clear exposition of *the truth*.

If weakness actually exists, the proper way to treat it is by the hygienic method and not by stimulants or nauseating drugs.

This pamphlet contains a clear exposition of the causes and conditions which destroy sexual vigor. It exposes a great many tricks of the quacks, by which they extort money from their victims. It explains the true nature and causes of nervous debility, loss of memory, involuntary losses, etc., and gives simple and plain directions for a cure without medicines or expense.

The efficacy of this treatment is attested by hundreds of grateful patients in all parts of the world. It is not only valuable to the afflicted, but will prove a priceless boon to all men and women of every age and condition. Young men and women suffering from Nervous Prostration, Impotency, Loss of Sleep, Loss of Memory, Depression of Spirits, Varicocele and all kindred difficulties, will find in this instruction the priceless information which will enable them to restore health and become useful members of society and fit candidates for the sacred obligation of matrimony.

PRICE, TEN DOLLARS.

Great Secrets of Happiness.

No. 3.

CONNUBIAL CLEANLINESS

OR THE

CAUSE AND CURE OF VENEREAL DISEASES.

The alarming prevalence of the worst forms of venereal diseases is a matter of the greatest concern to society. The awful effects of these diseases are not confined to the unhappy violators of the laws of nature, but extend "even unto the third and fourth generation" of innocent offspring. Innocent men and women are often contaminated because of ignorance of the conditions of contagion. Diseases of this nature are frequently originated by innocent men and women who are ignorant of the conditions which produce disease.

This pamphlet contains clear and simple directions for the production of the highest form of sanitary conditions in the sexual relations. It explains the origin and cause of contagious conditions and how to avoid them.

It also contains the best and most effective prescriptions for the cure of these forms of disease.

The most advanced physicians and scientists now recognize the fact that the most effective treatment for these unhappy conditions consists in strict attention to cleanliness and the renovation of the tissues of the body by hygienic treatment. Drugs and mineral poisons are worse than useless, and the evil effects of mercury, which is so often ignorantly and copiously administered, are worse than the original disease. The treatment recommended in this pamphlet contains the most valuable features of the methods employed at the famous Hot Springs of Arkansas, and may be successfully applied at home, without inconvenience or expense.

PRICE, TEN DOLLARS.

Great Secrets of Happiness.

No. 4.

HOW TO BE HAPPY.

A TREATISE ON THE EMBARRASSMENTS OF WEDLOCK AND THEIR REMOVAL.

This pamphlet is Professor Windsor's masterpiece, and has carried more happiness to more persons than any information which has ever flowed from his facile and courageous pen. In this instruction he has considered the act of copulation from a strictly scientific and utilitarian standpoint, and has shown that the reason why so many people are unhappy in the marriage relation is because they are ignorant and uninstructed in the performance of the highest of life's great functions.

If reproduction is the highest privilege of mankind, as it surely is, then certainly as much attention should be paid to the intelligent study of the act of reproduction as to any subject within the intellectual grasp of mankind. Yet, strange to say, this pamphlet is the only book ever written in which an attempt has been successfully made to explain the scientific conditions underlying the physical details.

The instruction herein given is based upon three cardinal propositions, to-wit:

1. That reproduction should only be performed by those who are capable of producing the best possible offspring.

2. That the perfection of offspring is always in exact proportion to the pleasure experienced by the parents in producing it.

3. That the act of copulation is designed not only for the reproduction of offspring, but also for the fortification and reproduction of the powers of the participants.

Following this line of argument, this pamphlet shows:

1. The conditions essential to perfect reproduction.
2. The conditions essential to the highest development of enjoyment.
3. The evils attendant upon excessive, unnatural and immoral uses of the sexual functions.
4. The benefits derived from the correct use of these powers in the perfection of offspring, the enjoyment of the sexual relations and the development of self-control.
5. The full explanation of Professor Windsor's extraordinary doctrine that by the proper employment of the sexual relations *every organ of the brain can be enlarged and strengthened and all forms of diseases can be cured.* This is the most startling and revolutionary of all his doctrines, but one which is demonstrably true.

This pamphlet, perhaps more than any of the series, contains *information of priceless value*—information absolutely necessary to all who would obtain happiness in the marriage relation, perfect health of husband and wife, mutual enjoyment and superb offspring. Every young man or woman contemplating matrimony, all married persons and parents who have the welfare of their children at heart *must* obtain this knowledge. Thousands of homes are blasted annually through sexual ignorance; thousands of idiots, paupers, criminals and deformities are born annually through violation of the laws of nature, expounded in this instruction. Debilitated wives and mothers endure the pains of martyrdom, through ignorance of simple facts now for the first time placed within reach. Whole armies of young men are driven to desperation and many to insanity and suicide through Sexual Diseases resulting from imprudence and ignorance of the consequences of violating Nature's Sexual Laws.

PRICE, TEN DOLLARS.

Great Secrets of Happiness.

No. 5.

THE PRINCIPLES OF HARMONY

APPLIED TO THE SELECTION OF SEXUAL CONSORTS.

This pamphlet contains a clear exposition of the laws of nature governing the selection of companions for life. It shows what temperaments are adapted to each other, and what are discordant, and the reason why. It explains the great laws of electro-magnetic affinity, the relation of the anatomical temperaments and the laws of chemical affinity as expressed in human organization. It also gives directions for the detection of organic sexual weakness in either sex and the signs of complete manhood and womanhood. It is the design of this pamphlet to instruct every young man and woman in the principles that underlie the conditions of happiness in the marriage relation, so that no mistake will be made in the selection of a companion for life. It shows:

1. How to judge what temperament is suitable to your own.
2. How to test the possibility of love and enjoyment of companionship.
3. How to avoid those who are unfitted for matrimony by disease or organic incompleteness.
4. How to conduct a magnetic courtship.
5. How to preserve the harmonies when they have been secured.
6. Causes and cure of jealousy.
7. The true philosophy of divorce, showing for what reasons and how a marriage should be terminated, and the behavior of the parties after divorce.

PRICE, TEN DOLLARS.

HOW TO OBTAIN PROFESSOR WINDSOR'S GREAT SECRETS OF HAPPINESS.

The confidential nature of the information imparted in these pamphlets, together with the fact that they represent the accumulated experience of a life devoted to the investigation of the subject, which has cost the author thousands of dollars as well as almost incredible labor and self-sacrifice, precludes the possibility of a general and indiscriminate sale. The information is of such a character that it will not be demanded except by those who are sufficiently advanced to recognize its importance, and the author does not care to place the information in the hands of those who will abuse it. Those who earnestly desire the advancement of the human race and themselves, will be willing to comply with the conditions of sale, which are as follows:

Carefully copy the following obligation of non-disclosure, sign it and forward, with the price of the pamphlet desired, to the Windsor & Lewis Publishing Co., 406 Maria avenue, St. Paul, Minn. Do not cut or mutilate this page.

....18...

In consideration of receiving Professor Windsor's Great Secrets of Happiness, I hereby promise not to reveal the same to any person, under any circumstances, except as hereinafter stated, but to keep the said pamphlets for my own personal use, free from the observation of others.

This pledge, however, permits a husband or wife to reveal the said information to the consort, and permits parents to instruct their children, in all cases, however, previously exacting a promise from the person so instructed to observe the same pledge. It does not extend to brothers, sisters or other relatives, or to business partners, or to any person not specifically allowed as above.

Signed,

....

On receipt of the above pledge, properly signed with your name and address, and the price of the pamphlets ordered they will be sent to you in a plain envelope, securely sealed from observation. Be sure you designate the pamphlets you desire, both by number and title, so there will be no mistake in filling your order.

THE INTERNATIONAL COLLEGE OF SCIENCE

(Incorporated 1897.)

BOARD OF DIRECTORS,

WILLIAM WINDSOR, LL. B., PH. D.; T. H LEWIS,
WM. H. GROSS.

FACULTY.

WILLIAM WINDSOR, LL. B., PH. D., President,
Professor of Phrenology, Anthropology, Hypnotism and Social Science.

T. H. LEWIS, Vice President,
Professor of Archæology, Ethnology and Natural History.

L. W. ROBERTS,
Professor of Astrology.

FRANK J. JUNGEN,
Professor of Phrenology, Hygiene and Dietetics.

ALFRED B. WESTRUP,
Professor of Political Economy.

M. M. BURNHAM, Secretary.

BUSINESS MANAGERS,
THE WINDSOR & LEWIS PUBLISHING CO.,
406 Maria Ave., St. Paul, Minn.

This college is incorporated under the laws of the State of Minnesota, for the purpose of conducting courses of instruction under competent teachers in all branches of science, by new and improved methods, especially by courses of lectures delivered at the college by the best talent obtainable, and also by special courses of lectures and instruction delivered in all parts of the United States by missionaries sent out by the college for the purpose. With this college as a center, it is proposed to inaugurate a complete system of instruction, which shall extend all over the world, by the organization of associations, classes and special courses of lectures, arranged to cover the most desirable forms of instruction upon topics of the greatest value.

Correspondence courses of instruction in such branches as admit of the method will be inaugurated, by means of which persons in any part of the world may obtain the instruction of masters of the various subjects at minimum cost.

Degrees, emoluments and certificates of merit are conferred in recognition of work actually accomplished by students.

For further particulars address the business managers,
THE WINDSOR & LEWIS PUBLISHING CO.,
406 Maria Ave., St. Paul, Minn.

Forms and Prices of Phrenological Examinations, Charts and Phrenographs Given by Professor Windsor.

I.

An Oral Examination consists of a careful measurement and estimate of the mental and physical powers of the applicant, by the examiner, who will explain:
 1. The Physical Condition and General State of Health.
 2. The Mental Development and Peculiarities of Character.
 3. Suggestions as to Faults and how to correct them, Talents and how to improve them.
 4. The Best Business, Profession or Vocation to which the applicant is adapted, also suggestions of desirable studies to be pursued.

In the case of children, this form also includes advice as to Culture (Physical and Mental), and the best methods to be pursued in government and discipline. This form is wholly verbal and does not include any written memoranda. Price, Two Dollars and Fifty Cents.

II.

A Business Chart is a written statement upon a form prepared for the purpose, giving all the above information in such form as can be preserved for future reference. It also contains an estimate of the Temperament and Organic Quality and such notes and explanations of technical terms as will enable the applicant to understand it thoroughly when properly studied. The Business Chart includes—
 1. A statement of the characteristics of the applicant, his Faults and Virtues.
 2. A memoranda of his Best Business, Profession or Vocation.
 3. A memoranda of Studies Recommended.
 4. Rules for the development of all the Phrenological Organs of the Brain and for the Preservation of Health, carefully marked with reference to the culture desirable for the person examined. Price, Five Dollars.

III.

THE COMPLETE PHRENOLOGICAL CHART AND WRITTEN DELINEATION OF CHARACTER, contains:

1. A careful estimate of the Physiological Condition, Temperament, Organic Quality and Phrenological Development of the applicant.
2. An analysis of his Business Capacity and Adaptability, with full directions for the choice of a Trade, Profession or Occupation.
3. A complete Physiological and Phrenological Description of the person adapted to the applicant for Matrimony or Business Partnership.
4. Memoranda of Desirable Studies and Branches of Education.
5. A complete Digest of Rules for the development of all the Phrenological Organs of the Brain, and Preservation of Health, carefully marked with reference to the Culture desirable for the applicant. Price, TEN DOLLARS.

This is a very desirable form of Examination and is designed to convey all the necessary information. This was the most complete chart given previous to the invention of the PHRENOMETER.

The foregoing forms are *estimative*. That is to say, the statements contained in each are the conclusions drawn from the estimates made by the skillful examiner, whose long practice enables him to tell with great accuracy, the essential elements of the character from the inspection of the head. A strictly scientific and mathematically exact result may be obtained, however, by the use of the PHRENOMETER, an instrument invented and patented by Professor Windsor. By the use of this instrument, the exact dimensions of the head are shown upon charts prepared for the purpose, in five sections. The results attained by this method are extremely satisfactory. The exact development of the head in all its parts is shown, enabling the examiner to perform his work with mathematical accuracy and revealing for the first time to the applicant the true form of his head. The strong and weak developments are shown with such fidelity to nature as to make a great impression upon the person examined. If the head is handsome in outline and well developed, it is one of the most powerful incentives to ambition and culture to see it, as displayed on the

Phrenometer charts. If there is any weakness or deformity the Phrenologist immediately suggests the remedy, and teaches how to overcome it. The measurements can be preserved and compared with those taken at later dates, showing exactly how much has been accomplished in the interval by way of culture, and in just what direction the character is developing.

IV.

A COMPLETE PHRENOLOGICAL CHART AND WRITTEN DELINEATION OF CHARACTER, WITH PHRENOMETER MEASUREMENTS, includes all the information given under the third form, with the addition of the Phrenometer measurements and full explanations in an attractive form to be preserved for future reference. Price, FIFTEEN DOLLARS.

V.

A PHRENOGRAPH is a written statement of special advice, written out at length by the examiner, or copied on the typewriter. A Phrenograph usually consists of about one thousand words, which may be extended to such length as the exigencies of the case require. The charges for Phrenographs are in all cases regulated by the nature of the case, the value of the information imparted and the number of words required to convey the meaning of the examiner. The usual charges range from FIVE to TEN DOLLARS.

It is desirable that everyone who can afford to do so should take A COMPLETE PHRENOLOGICAL CHART AND WRITTEN DELINEATION OF CHARACTER WITH PHRENOMETER MEASUREMENTS, and a PHRENOGRAPH relating at least to the subjects of Health, Character, Adaptation in Business and Matrimony, all of which usually cost TWENTY-FIVE DOLLARS. This enables the examiner to discuss every subject for the applicant which is of the highest importance. The examination and Phrenographs, however, can be indefinitely extended to the profit of the applicant, for it is practically impossible to exhaust the subject.

THE BEST TIME TO BE EXAMINED is *right now*. Every day that you postpone your examination you are losing the benefits which Phrenology confers. Mr. W. A. Harris of Fort Worth, Texas, examined by Professor Windsor in 1890, reported two hundred dollars profit in two days, and many similar cases could be mentioned.

THE BEST AGE AT WHICH TO BE EXAMINED is as early as possible. Parents, do not wait until your children develop before having them examined, but bring them to the Phrenologist and learn *how to develop* them.

The younger the child, the greater the benefits of an examination. Remember that the Phrenological Examination is *purely educational*, and the earlier its suggestions are applied the better

DISCOUNTS TO CLUBS.

The following table shows the discounts made to clubs of five or more persons. To obain these prices, in all cases the list of names must be made up and money paid in advance to the examiner. Members of clubs may then take their examinations at their convenience.

	Single Examination.	Club of Five.	Club of Ten.	Club of Twenty.
Oral Examination	$2.50	$2.00	$2.00	$1.50
Business Chart	5.00	4.00	3.50	3.00
Complete Phren. Chart and Written Delineation of Character	10.00	8.00	7.50	7.00
Complete Phren. Chart and Written Delineation of Character, with Phrenometer Measurements	15.00	12.50	11.00	10.00

☞All correspondence upon the subject of Phrenological Examinations should be addressed to

PROF. WM. WINDSOR, LL. B., Ph. D.,
Care Windsor & Lewis Publishing Co.,
406 Maria Ave, St. Paul, Minn.

Marked "Personal."

EXAMINATIONS FROM PHOTOGRAPHS.

Phrenological examinations can be made from photographs with accuracy, provided the photograph is a correct likeness, and some additional information can be supplied. Owing to obvious difficulties, absolute correctness cannot be guaranteed, but the results are sufficiently valuable to justify the expedient wherever it is impossible to submit the living head.

To obtain satisfactory results the photograph should be cabinet size, and should show the form of the head and face as plainly as possible. Very little can be told from a photograph when a hat is worn, or when the personality is covered with millinery, wigs, bangs, uniforms, etc. etc.

A plain photograph, showing a three-quarter view of the face, is best. Front views and profiles are valuable for some points and worthless for others. When it is possible, a three-quarter view, front and profile may all be submitted with good results.

The forms of examinations and charts from photographs and prices charged for the service are the same as for the living subject, except that the Phrenometer measurements cannot be given from a photograph, and an oral examination cannot be given by mail. Forms II and III and Phrenographs are entirely practicable and very valuabe.

Opinions on the Adapation in Business, Partnership or Matrimony are given at the following rates: Short opinion, two dollars; elaborate opinion, ten dollars. (This gives all minute points requiring usually one thousand words.) In all cases submit photos of both candidates.

Persons who have already been examined by me and who hold certificates for Forms II, III or IV, may have opinions on Business Partnership or Matrimony at one dollar for short opinion, and five dollars for the elaborate form.

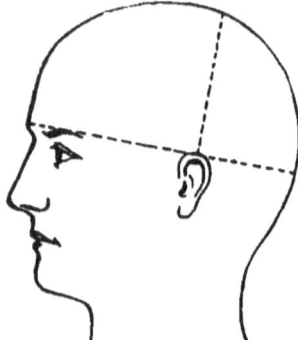

INFORMATION REQUIRED.

Take the following measurements of the head: Pass a tape measure around the circumference of the base of the brain, passing just above the eyebrows and just above the ears. This is called the *basilar circumference*. Also measure the distance from the bottom of the orifice of one ear to the corresponding point of the other, over the top of the head at the highest point. This is called the *trans-coronal* measurement. Then copy and fill out the following blank, and submit with the photograph:

☞Do not cut or mutilate this page.

Name of original of photo..................................
Address ....
Age ....Weight ....Height............
Sex ....Color of hair..........Color of eyes..........
Basilar circumference of head.....................inches.
Trans-coronal measurement ....inches.
Circumference of chest, lungs empty................inches.
Circumference of chest, lungs filled..................inches.
Condition of health......................................
....
Amount of education received............................
....'.................................
Present occupation ....
Information most especially desired.......................
....
Number of photographs enclosed..........................
To be returned to.......................................
(Write return address plainly.) ....
Form of examination requested..........................
Fee enclosed, $........   Stamps enclosed for return.......

When all the above points can be stated it is desirable that it should be done. When it is impossible to do so, the blanks may be filled out in part, and I will in all cases do the best that can be done with information at hand. Address all correspondence on this subject to

PROF. WILLIAM WINDSOR, LL. B., Ph. D.,
Care The Windsor & Lewis Publishing Co.,
406 Maria Ave., St. Paul, Minn.

Marked *"PERSONAL."*

www.ingramcontent.com/pod-product-compliance
Lightning Source LLC
Chambersburg PA
CBHW022116300426
44117CB00007B/735